"This engaging book is a must-read for anyone who cares about making the evaluation process more useful and inclusive. The Model for Collaborative Evaluations is a refreshing, new framework from two noted scholars that provides helpful tools to build relationships that strengthen the process and involve stakeholders at every stage."

—Caroline Altman Smith, Senior Program Officer, The Kresge Foundation

"To read this book is to enter into collaboration with recognized experts in this approach to evaluation. The reader gains access to the authors' wealth of experience in the field, as well as their enthusiasm for collaborative evaluation. This book inspires as well as it instructs."

—Michael Nokes, Michigan Department of Corrections

"*Collaborative Evaluations* is a map for the novice and seasoned alike. The landmarks in it are easily recognizable—from stakeholders to logic models and summative evaluation to standards. The guidelines are both creative and insightful. However, the authors' truly unique contribution is how they weave together these ingredients to help ensure full participation and collaboration."

—David M. Fetterman, President and CEO, Fetterman & Associates and Past President, American Evaluation Association and American Anthropological Association

"This book should be in the toolbox of every evaluator! Bringing the lessons from their experiences to the masses, the authors demonstrate how to use the Model for Collaborative Evaluations, providing a succinct set of guidelines for the process of evaluation. This book makes the MCE palatable for users with any level of evaluation expertise."

—LaShonda Coulbertson, President and CEO, Nia Research Consulting and Evaluation, LLC

"Collaborating during an evaluation can be a challenging experience, riddled with pitfalls and potholes. An evaluation will sink or swim based on the communication skills of the evaluator. *Collaborative Evaluations* presents a comprehensive framework for working with stakeholders who have a vested interest in the evaluation. This book provides bedrock principles for smooth and collaborative evaluation project management."

—Willis H. Thomas, Chief Learning Officer, lessonslearned.info and Past Vice President, Project Management Institute, Grand Rapids, Michigan Chapter

Collaborative
Evaluations

To SANDY:
An inspiring person
to many of us!
Rigo 2/25/14

Second Edition

Collaborative
Evaluations
Step-by-Step

Liliana Rodríguez-Campos
Rigoberto Rincones–Gómez

Stanford Business Books
An Imprint of Stanford University Press, Stanford, California

Stanford University Press
Stanford, California

Special discounts for bulk quantities of Stanford Business Books are available to corporations, professional associations, and other organizations. For details and discount information, contact the special sales department of Stanford University Press. Tel: (650) 736-1782, Fax: (650) 736-1784

Printed in the United States of America on acid-free, archival-quality paper

Library of Congress Cataloging-in-Publication Data

Rodríguez-Campos, Liliana, 1970– author.
 Collaborative evaluations : step-by-step / Liliana Rodríguez-Campos and Rigoberto Rincones-Gómez.—Second edition.
    pages cm
 Includes bibliographical references and index.
 ISBN 978-0-8047-7808-4 (alk. paper)—ISBN 978-0-8047-7809-1 (pbk. : alk. paper)
 1. Participatory monitoring and evaluation (Project management) I. Rincones-Gómez, Rigoberto, 1970– author. II. Title.
 HD69.P75R635 2012
 658.4'03—dc23   2012031154

Designed by Bruce Lundquist
Typeset by Classic Typography in 10/14 Minion

To Michelle, our most wonderful gift.

Contents

Foreword

I AM PLEASED to have this opportunity to comment on the second edition of *Collaborative Evaluations*. The first edition, published in 2005, was a timely contribution to the evaluation literature in that it addressed an important problem in the practice of evaluation. That problem is the difficulty evaluators often have in engaging stakeholders in planning, conducting, and using evaluations—in other words, getting them to take evaluation *seriously*. The first edition provided a step-by-step guide for evaluators, with notable attention to detail, on how to involve key individuals and groups in evaluation in a meaningful way.

This second edition extends the achievements of the first edition in three important ways: (1) conceptual clarity has been enhanced on the basis of the past seven years of experience in applying the content of the book, (2) references to contemporary thinking in evaluation theory and practice have been used to integrate collaborative evaluation into the mainstream of evaluation literature, and (3) actual evaluation questions and issues have been used to ground the presentation of the collaborative approach in terms that most evaluators should recognize.

Drs. Rodríguez-Campos and Rincones-Gómez have done an excellent job in preparing an easy-to-read, comprehensive guide to the collaborative evaluation approach and related literature. In developing the collaborative approach to evaluation, they have provided a roadmap for greater and more serious stakeholder engagement in the evaluation process. This engagement in turn should lead to a greater regard for, and use of, evaluation in the future by key stakeholders. This, in my judgment, constitutes a major step forward for the field of evaluation. The authors are to be congratulated on a job very well done.

James R. Sanders, Ph.D.
Past President, American Evaluation Association
Professor Emeritus, Western Michigan University

Collaborative
Evaluations

Introduction

WE HAVE CONTINUOUSLY sought ways to improve our evaluation practice, and our varied experiences have reaffirmed the importance of using collaboration in evaluation efforts. Collaborative evaluation is an approach that offers many advantages, including access to information, quality of information gathered, opportunities for creative problem solving, receptivity to findings, and use of evaluation results. From a broad perspective, collaborative evaluation belongs to the *use* branch of the evaluation theory tree described by Alkin in *Evaluation Roots* (2004), concerned with enhancing evaluation use through stakeholder involvement. We wrote this book to help you involve stakeholders collaboratively throughout the evaluation process.

Over the past decades, stakeholder involvement in various phases of evaluation has received increasing attention, and the literature has reflected this through a number of publications outlining the primary assumptions of the stakeholder approaches to evaluation, their historical chronology, their practical applications, their constraints, and their benefits (Rodríguez-Campos, 2012a). Stakeholder approaches to evaluation typically imply the incorporation of stakeholders in one or more components of the evaluation process (for example, in evaluation design or interpreting evaluation results) with the goal of increasing utilization, promoting development, or both. Examples of these approaches are responsive evaluation, democratic evaluation, utilization-focused evaluation, participatory evaluation, empowerment evaluation, and collaborative evaluation.

Theory and practice of evaluation are still evolving, and evaluators from a wide variety of backgrounds have been expanding current thinking about these stakeholder approaches and formalizing their components. This has provided opportunities for unique insights in a purposeful and systematic way. Also, this has brought together evaluators and stakeholders to exchange knowledge on how collaboration can be used as a strategic tool for fostering and strengthening evaluation practice.

National and international evaluation associations have contributed to the steady maturation of several stakeholder approaches. For example, in 1995 the American Evaluation Association (AEA) created the Collaborative, Participatory, and Empowerment Evaluation Topical Interest Group (CPE TIG). Since then, this TIG has provided a forum for evaluators to exchange experiences about the many ways in which these approaches can be used. In an attempt to reach consensus, a comparison of the essentials of collaborative, participatory, and empowerment evaluation (as a result of this TIG discussions) has helped in further clarifying their similarities and differences. For example, each approach is designed to enhance evaluation use and organizational learning capacity; however, they differ in the way they pursue these goals.

After a thorough examination of the CPE approaches, and taking into account the audience's feedback at several AEA meetings, proponents have cautiously developed definitions. Specifically, **collaborative evaluators** are in charge of the evaluation, but they create an ongoing engagement between evaluators and stakeholders, contributing to stronger evaluation designs, enhanced data collection and analysis, and results that stakeholders understand and use (Rodríguez-Campos & O'Sullivan, 2010); **participatory evaluators** view control of the evaluation as jointly shared by evaluators and program staff—participants are involved in defining the evaluation, developing instruments, collecting and analyzing data, and reporting and disseminating results (Shulha, 2010); and **empowerment evaluators** view stakeholder participants as in control of the evaluation—empowerment evaluators are critical friends providing advice and guidance to maintain rigor and keep the evaluation on target (Fetterman & Wandersman, 2010).

While the stakeholder approaches have influenced and shaped the evaluation field, they are not the answer for every evaluation. An evaluator who wishes to use these types of approaches should be flexible and tolerant of contextual difficulties and variations in stakeholders' willingness to participate (Garaway, 1995). To optimally use the stakeholders' approaches to evaluation, or any other approach, there needs to be clear expectations of their advantages and disadvantages based on the specific situation. In any case, the benefits gained by adopting a stakeholder approach to evaluation should outweigh the potential difficulties that may ensue.

Among other stakeholder approaches, the future of collaborative evaluation looks promising, as there are an increasing number of evaluators and clients interested in this type of approach. Our primary goal was to write a user-friendly book that included detailed explanations and illustrations of how to apply collaborative evaluation in daily practice; a book that could be used by anyone with a certain degree of familiarity with how to conduct evaluations. In other words, we want to make collaborative evaluations accessible to you.

This book is intended to help you gain a deeper understanding of how to build collaborative relationships within an evaluation while recognizing that the level of collaboration varies for each evaluation. We introduce the Model for Collaborative Evaluations (MCE) for transforming evaluations into a joint responsibility process between you (the evaluator) and specific collaboration members (CMs). When people are involved in a collaborative process and develop a nuanced appreciation for aspects beyond their tasks, they are more willing to assume responsibility for the entire effort. The MCE creates precisely this kind of commitment, and we share our experiences in a way that will enable you to apply the information in this book immediately.

As we have traveled around the world, attempting to speak in other languages, we have experienced that people initially make assumptions about our choice of words. It is only after they recognize our positive intentions that they invest the time and effort to thoroughly understand the meaning of the words we use. It is our hope that we can transmit the meaning of the MCE beyond just the words used to present it in Figures I.1 and I.2. Before we explain the characteristics of the model, let's review some important terms to establish a common understanding and a foundation for the chapters that follow.

Evaluation is a systematic study designed and implemented to determine the value (such as merit or worth) of an evaluand, providing a basis for guiding the decision-making process. **Evaluand** is anything evaluated, such as a system, organization, program, project, or personnel (also called evaluee). **Evaluator** is the individual (such as you) who accepts responsibility for the overall evaluation and its results, employing defensible criteria to judge the evaluand value.

Collaboration is a process in which two or more people actively work together in a mutually beneficial and well-defined relationship in order to achieve a vision not likely to occur in isolation. It is more than simply sharing information or coordinating efforts toward a mutually beneficial end. It brings together resources, strategies, and ways to address concerns or create something new (Wilson, 2000). **Collaborative evaluation** is an evaluation in which there is a substantial degree of collaboration between evaluators and stakeholders in the evaluation process, to the extent that they are willing and capable of being involved (see, for example, Cousins, Donohue, & Bloom, 1996; Rodríguez-Campos, 2005, 2012b).

Collaboration members (CMs) are specific stakeholders (possessing unique characteristics) who work jointly with the evaluator(s) to help with particular tasks in order to achieve the collaborative evaluation vision. Although the number of CMs may vary, the group size has to be manageable (for example, a limit of six CMs) to maximize the benefits of their contributions. For large or complex evaluations, several groups of CMs can be created to represent a greater range of expertise and to minimize delays in the evaluation.

Model is a term loosely used to refer to a conception or approach or even a method of doing evaluation (Scriven, 1991). It is "[a] thing or person to be imitated or patterned after; that which is taken as a pattern or an example" (*Webster's Dictionary & Thesaurus*, 2000, p. 629). In addition, a model "characterizes its author's view of the main concepts and structure of evaluation work . . . " (Stufflebeam, Madaus, & Kellaghan, 2000, p. 19).

The **Model for Collaborative Evaluations** (MCE) is a framework for guiding collaborative evaluations in a precise, realistic, and useful manner. This model revolves around a set of six interactive components specific to conducting a collaborative evaluation. It has a systematic structure that provides a basis for decision making through the development of collaborative evaluations. The MCE helps to establish priorities in order to achieve a supportive evaluation environment, with a special emphasis on those factors that facilitate collaboration.

The MCE core components have emerged from a wide range of collaborative efforts that we have conducted in the business, nonprofit, and education sectors. Figure I.1 provides the conceptual framework for viewing the MCE components interactively: (1) identify the situation, (2) clarify the expectations, (3) establish a collective commitment, (4) ensure open communication, (5) encourage effective practices, and (6) follow specific guidelines. The center of the MCE includes the phases or stages of the evaluation, with the arrows representing the interdependent flow in order to facilitate collaboration. (Note that Chapter 2 will help you understand how to clarify the evaluation process.)

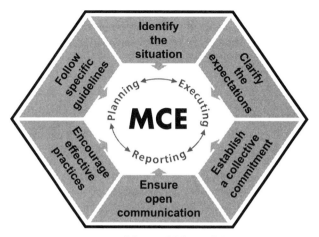

Figure I.1 Components of the Model for Collaborative Evaluations

The novelty of the MCE resides in the way in which each of its elements (components and subcomponents) influences the others and, as a consequence, the overall collaborative evaluation. Even though the MCE could create an expectation of a sequential process, it is a system that incorporates continuous feedback for redefinition and improvement in which changes in one element affect changes in other parts of the model. To accomplish a comprehensive collaborative evaluation, we recommend the interactive use of the MCE elements on a rotating and remixing basis. However, you may also gain new insights by using each of the model components individually to reap some of its benefits.

The MCE helps to perform a systematic, careful examination of where the evaluation stands in terms of the subcomponents, present within each MCE component (see Figure I.2). The model is a constant source of information because it provides a simple and innovative way of presenting the activities that have to be carried out, avoiding possible tensions among you and the CMs about when and whether to make decisions on potentially sensitive topics.

Each of the MCE subcomponents, shown as bullet points in the outer ring circle of the figure, includes a set of ten steps suggested to support the proper understanding and use of the model (for example, when and how the various MCE elements need to be used). The MCE also serves as an iterative checklist that provides consistent guidance for the collection of relevant evidence to determine the value of the evaluand (see the Appendix for a more traditional formulation of such a checklist). Checklists reduce the chance of forgetting to

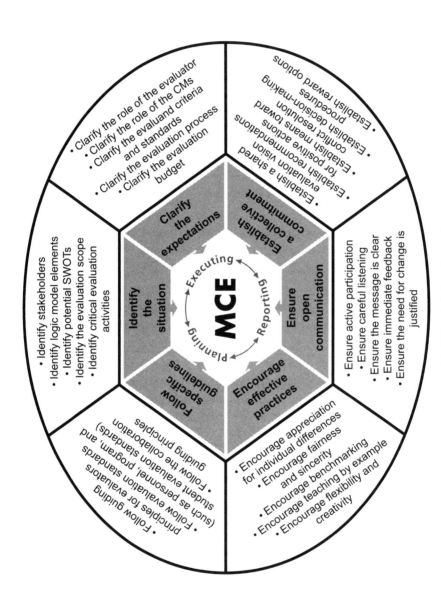

Figure I.2 Model for Collaborative Evaluations

check something important, are easier for the layperson to understand, and reduce the influence of the halo effect by forcing the evaluator to consider each relevant dimension of merit (Scriven, 2005).

The MCE has been developed in such a way that, while keeping its design intact, its feedback mechanisms help to foresee and manage the unintended events that can appear along the way. In other words, this model establishes a solid basis for auto-analysis, because each component of the MCE and its sub-components can be continually revised as necessary. In collaboration, people keep coming back to the beginning in order to build on and improve what they have been doing (Winer & Ray, 2002).

In our experience, the implementation of the MCE has been very effective, because it is possible to make adjustments during execution as well as to immediately recover from unexpected problems; for example, the extent and various levels of collaboration required throughout the evaluation. The versatility of this model can help you to handle "surprises" that may arise and also ensure that possible flaws or deviations with regard to the evaluation plan can be controlled through the use of feedback mechanisms. Furthermore, the MCE facilitates training, reducing the costs for professional development and selection of new CMs.

The MCE has a wide potential applicability for conducting collaborative evaluations because different aspects of it will have greater relevance in certain cases depending on specific contextual factors. For instance, each program evaluated will have its own unique group of people, interests, and disagreements. Thus the subcomponent "Establish Means Toward Conflict Resolution" could be more relevant in one evaluation than in another. To reinforce interconnectivity among the MCE elements, we have included some reminders throughout the book to illustrate the relationships among them. For example, when we explain "Clarify the Evaluation Budget" in Chapter 2, we connect it with "Encourage Benchmarking" in Chapter 5 by writing, "See Chapter 5 on how to encourage benchmarking."

In this book, we blend theoretical grounding of the MCE with practical tips for "real life" applications. The aim is to increase the quality of your evaluation, because you can establish a more open and shared evaluation culture while attending to the intended and unintended effects of the collaborative relationships. Specifically, the book consists of six chapters; each chapter contains a description of one of the components of the model with its corresponding subcomponents and activities laid out in a step-by-step fashion. Each of the chapters can be visited individually as needed because they are easy to follow and allow for quick guidance. However, we recommend reading all the chapters in the book first to clearly understand the MCE before using it.

To further illustrate the application of the MCE in particular situations, we invite you to explore the MCE through recurring vignettes about several fictional evaluators (Eliot, Ernest, and Evelyn) and their evaluation clients who decide to use a collaborative evaluation approach. These short, simple, and re-alistic stories appear in each chapter, bringing the MCE to life in a practical way while showing how it emphasizes a systematic stakeholder engagement throughout the evaluation process. They are composites based on lived experi-ences, and represent an attempt to capture the essence of the MCE from vari-ous perspectives in order to produce a valuable understanding of the different stances that often arise in this type of evaluation and to provide a useful basis for decision making.

This book is presented in a way that allows you to clearly understand how to conduct collaborative evaluations in your own work. It is not intended to address all extant alternatives for collaborative evaluation. Rather, the intention is to deepen and share new knowledge, contributing to and benefiting the col-laborative effort with the use of the MCE. The aim of this model is for you to achieve a holistic learning environment by understanding and creating collab-orative evaluation opportunities. In such an environment, everyone involved will better understand the evaluation process and therefore be more likely to use its findings. We wish you a superior quality of work in your collaborative evaluations!

Chapter 1

Identify
the Situation

The **situation** is a combination of formal and informal circumstances deter-mined by the relationships that surround and sustain the collaborative evalu-ation. This component is very important because the success of the evaluation will depend, to a large degree, on how well the situation is understood. Al-though you and the collaboration members (CMs) may be able to influence the environment in some way, keep in mind that you do not have total control over it. Understanding the situation is the foundation for all the evaluation decisions and prepares you to anticipate opportunities and threats throughout the collaborative process.

The way you perceive the situation will determine the approach you will take to achieve the desired results. Those evaluation results will be based on specific situational characteristics, such as resources (for instance, people or time) and a particular setting (for example, physical, social, political, economic, geographical, or demographic). Rather than simply accepting the perception that the client has of the situation, you should gain a broad sense of the situ-ation on your own. In addition, instead of just stopping with what the client wants, pursue what the client needs, because the difference between "want" and "need" is your value added (Weiss, 2009).

An early indication of the situation with regard to the potential constraints and benefits needed to support the collaborative evaluation (such as funds, staff, materials, scope, and context) helps you better manage it and be prepared to overcome barriers. It also helps to determine strategies to deal with any con-cerns raised and to develop a beneficial evaluation plan. To gain a better un-derstanding about the situation surrounding the evaluation you may conduct observations of the evaluand and stakeholders in their day-to-day activities. Always have multiple inside and outside sources for gathering helpful informa-tion, in order to understand the evaluand culture (for example, interview key stakeholders or review documents and reports).

The situation sets the foundation for everything that follows in the collaborative evaluation. Among other resources, the time needed to identify the situation varies depending on the complexity of each evaluation, which also leads to the amount of effort invested in it (for example, the number of meetings needed). Because people are going to collaborate within the evaluation, it is also necessary to determine what level of collaboration will be required depending on the situation. The better you understand the situation and the more fully you analyze it, the easier your collaborative evaluation will be (and the application of the remaining components of the Model for Collaborative Evaluations [MCE]).

This chapter provides you with step-by-step suggestions on how to identify information in order to understand the current nature of the evaluand, its surroundings, and the scope for the collaborative evaluation. In other words, we show you how to carefully identify the situation. In addition, we present information on how to prioritize the activities toward which you need to focus your resources in order to accomplish clear evaluation results. Thus the MCE component presented in this chapter is divided into the following subcomponents: (a) identify stakeholders, (b) identify logic model elements, (c) identify potential SWOTs, (d) identify the evaluation scope, and (e) identify critical evaluation activities (see Figure I.2).

IDENTIFY STAKEHOLDERS

A **stakeholder** is a person who is interested in the collaborative evaluation because he or she may be directly or indirectly affected by its results (see Figure 1.1). Identify early the individuals who have at least some interest or stake in the evaluation and how their roles can help to accomplish the overall goal. The **audience** is a person, or group of persons, who receives the evaluation results (for example, a written or an oral evaluation report).

There are five types of stakeholders who are associated with almost any evaluand: (a) policymakers, such as governing board members; (b) administrators or managers, those who direct and administer the evaluand; (c) practitioners, those who operate the evaluand; (d) primary consumers, those who use the evaluation results, such as evaluation clients; and (e) secondary consumers, those who are affected by what happens to primary consumers, such as community groups (Fitzpatrick, Sanders, & Worthen, 2011). After you have a comprehensive knowledge of the stakeholders, then you are ready to identify the CMs.

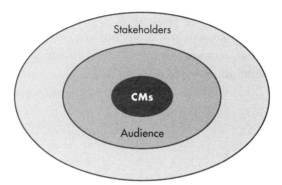

Figure 1.1 From Stakeholders to CMs

Identifying the stakeholders is critical for the collaborative evaluation because their specific needs must be understood in order for them to be addressed in a useful way. Therefore, make a favorable first impression to develop strong relationships from the very beginning. From your first meeting, make direct eye contact, display excellent manners, and use appropriate body language in order to develop effective rapport.

Your goal is to understand who the stakeholders are, what they want and need, and how the evaluand is being affected by them. As a result, you can identify and select specific stakeholders to become CMs who will be involved in depth in the collaborative effort (see Figure 1.1). Of course, always consider the views of the broader range of stakeholders who also collaborate in a less active way.

Identify General Stakeholders

As we mentioned in the Introduction, the MCE is a systematic approach with feedback mechanisms that allow you to come back to this subcomponent and increase (or decrease) the number of identified stakeholders as needed. You may have to seek new CMs, in response to changing needs (for example, a negative climate due to an inappropriate cross-section of members). We suggest the following steps to identify general stakeholders:

1. Be clear that your responsibility is to meet, or even better, exceed your client's expectations while ensuring that particular interests of all relevant stakeholders are considered throughout a balanced collaborative evaluation.

2. Learn as much as you can about your evaluation client, and later about other potential stakeholders, in order to establish a beneficial relationship. For example, read from the evaluand's or client's website and other sources of information.

3. Think carefully and write down all the questions you need the client, and later other potential stakeholders, to answer (for instance, who needs to be informed, who is to receive the evaluation results, and whose collaboration is crucial).

4. Seek clarification (with a courteous attitude) to your questions when meeting with the client, and later with other potential stakeholders, as feasible. For example, if doubts arise after a meeting, then seek to clarify all those doubts.

5. Listen rather than just making statements or educating about the evaluation process (avoid interrupting). For example, wait silently and patiently during pauses, because generally the most important information follows them.

6. Identify diverse points of view (such as the strongest supporters and opponents) in order to diffuse any resistance toward the collaborative evaluation and ensure that everyone's contributions will be adequately considered.

7. Make a preliminary list with the client's assistance (and others as applicable) of the key stakeholders affected by the evaluation. For example, distinguish who would gain or lose the most from the evaluation under different scenarios.

8. Invite your client to review and add or delete names from the preliminary stakeholder list. By doing this, you can have a better idea of who the key stakeholders really are and their possible contributions to the evaluation as future CMs.

9. Gather feedback on a regular basis using a previously agreed-upon system (including meetings, emails, and surveys as feasible). This will help in monitoring the stakeholders' identification process and making updates as needed.

10. Provide the client and other stakeholders as appropriate with a summary report of this experience (for example, an updated list of the stakeholders) as a baseline for identifying the situation of the collaborative evaluation.

Identify Collaboration Members

Now that you have a list of the stakeholders, identify the CMs who will work jointly with you to help with particular evaluation tasks in order to achieve the evaluation vision (see Chapter 3 on how to establish a shared evaluation vision). The CMs should want to be members, be able to fulfill specific evaluation requirements, and work well together. Also, the client must agree with the selected CMs and allow, as applicable, time from their regular duties for them to participate.

This step is critical for the collaborative evaluation process because the CMs can help ensure their own (and other people's) involvement and consequent use of the evaluation results. In other words, the use of the evaluation results will be improved by involving stakeholders in the evaluation process. Specifically, their buy-in proves to be very helpful when evaluation recommendations are being implemented. We suggest the following steps to identify the CMs:

1. Make a preliminary list of essential characteristics that are desirable in the CMs. With this goal in mind, you will be able to later match specific stakeholders to this list while being prepared to be flexible in the selection process.

2. Agree with your client, and other key stakeholders as feasible, which stakeholders from the list can have the most active involvement in the collaborative evaluation, becoming potential CMs (including the client or not, as appropriate).

3. Create, with the potential CMs' help, a calendar that shows their availability during the different evaluation stages and how they see themselves fitting into the collaboration. For example, determine who will be available and when.

4. Learn about each potential CM in terms of their individual characteristics (such as strengths and weaknesses) before making a decision on which individuals you are going to officially invite to become CMs of the evaluation.

5. Identify which of the potential CMs may require special training to enhance their evaluation skills. Sometimes you may not find enough qualified CMs, so they will need appropriate training to build specific evaluation skills.

6. Agree on the final CMs with the client, once you have met with all the key stakeholders, as feasible. Be sure that major stakeholders are represented (that is, specific characteristics) across the main areas affected by the evaluation.

7. Ensure that you and the client are making a fair decision on the CMs' selection (for example, that you have all the relevant facts to make a decision) and on how to match their skills and abilities to the expectations of the collaborative evaluation.

8. Determine if the selected CMs agree to formally collaborate as such in the evaluation, and get started with those who are willing to do it. In other words, find who is genuinely interested to collaborate in the evaluation efforts.

9. Consider the morale of the non-selected stakeholders, who may feel disappointed with the selection. For example, ensure open communication with them, because they can provide important feedback for the collaborative evaluation.

10. Gather feedback on a regular basis using a previously agreed-upon system, such as meetings, and summarize it in a written format (including an updated list of the CMs) so it is available to each CM and other stakeholders as appropriate.

Carefully select CMs with varied characteristics to facilitate involvement within the collaborative evaluation and achievement of its vision. Through the years, we have noticed that differences in education, authority, or other personal characteristics can result in lack of involvement by those who are at the end of the scale (typically the lower end) in regard to those characteristics. Hence, keep in mind that the same evaluation may have a different set of CMs for each of its main needs.

For large, more complex evaluations you may need to create several groups of CMs, so that greater diversity of expertise can be represented. Avoid creating groups larger than six members, because then people tend to feel less individual responsibility for the evaluation results. Be aware that sometimes there may be some poor fits among the CMs selected even though you have been very careful with the identification process. Learn from this experience and continuously monitor the CMs' commitment, performance,

Identify Stakeholders

Eliot: I am currently working on an external evaluation in a private company and have already met with several stakeholders. However, I just talked with Mr. Smith, who has worked for over twenty years for the program I am evaluating. He says he doesn't consider himself a "stakeholder" and therefore he is not planning to go to any of the meetings. Given his time with the program, I think his involvement is really important. Do you have any suggestions for how I can engage him?

Evelyn: I know that can be frustrating! One way to approach the situation might be to gather additional information about him. As you meet with other stakeholders, ask them about Mr. Smith and how *they* see his impact in the program. You may learn about some positive contributions he has made and maybe some that he hasn't even thought about himself or that nobody has ever shared with him. Once you have gathered feedback from others, schedule a follow-up meeting with Mr. Smith and share that feedback. Help him see how his colleagues value his involvement and explain how you believe his contributions would enhance the evaluation. For example, explain that the evaluation will seek, among other things, to serve stakeholders' information needs, so it is essential to identify ways to strengthen the collaborative efforts. Perhaps he knows about existing data within the company and effective uses of the evaluation findings. After learning these benefits, he may be more likely to change his mind and come to the meetings.

and satisfaction by obtaining accurate information (see Chapter 4 on how to ensure immediate feedback).

IDENTIFY LOGIC MODEL ELEMENTS

A **logic model** is a tool that visually shows, through a graphic illustration or picture, how a particular initiative (such as an evaluand or evaluation) is intended or perceived to occur through logical relationships. It is the logic model elements and their connections (how the elements are linked to each other) that provide a complete picture of the initiative.

A logic model can be used to identify the basic theoretical framework of an initiative and to clarify what should be measured and when. For example, how is the evaluand supposed to work? Is the evaluand working as depicted in the logic model? A logic model is like a roadmap that clearly shows the connection of interdependent elements in order to achieve specific outcomes (Rincones-Gómez, 2009). In general, a logic model consists of the following elements: input, activity, output, and outcome (see Figure 1.2).

- **Input.** This includes all the resources invested and used by an initiative in order to achieve its activities, outputs, and outcomes. In general, resources are the facilities, equipment, materials, staff, information, and money. For example, inputs are items provided internally (such as volunteers) and by an external source (such as grant funding).

- **Activity.** This is what an initiative offers or does with the inputs in order to lead to specific outputs. For example, activities may include delivering services and developing products. At this stage, you and the CMs do not know yet if the activity has made a difference to the specific stakeholders, but the activity needs to be executed in order for outputs and outcomes to occur as intended.

- **Output.** This is the direct result of the activities, and it is related to the number of products or services delivered by an initiative in measurable terms. For example, output may be the number of computers sold or the number of participants who attended a particular professional development workshop. Thus the outputs refer to what has been done by an initiative. Outputs lead to outcomes in which you and the CMs will know whether the output has made a difference to the specific stakeholders.

- **Outcome.** This is the effect or change that an initiative makes on stakeholders (individuals, groups, or communities) as a consequence of its outputs. In particular, you and the CMs want to know what intended or unintended difference has been made for stakeholders. Outcomes can be short term, medium term or long term (also called impact or final value). For example, outcomes can be specific changes on stakeholders' attitudes, skills, knowledge, awareness, status, motivation, and behavior.

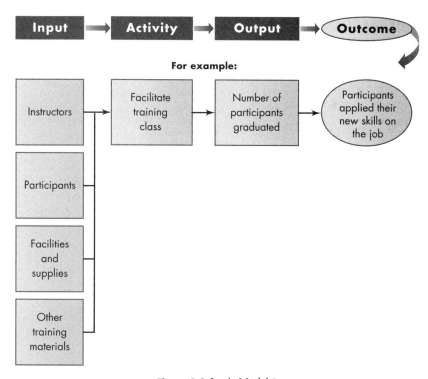

Figure 1.2 Logic Model 1

Next time you (or the CMs) need to diagram a simple logic model you may follow the example provided in Figure 1.2. However, when you need to diagram a more complex logic model, the presence of many arrows can become extremely confusing. For this reason, we created the logic model structure shown in Figure 1.3, which includes a label or identifier for each box to show the relationship. In this type of logic model representation, you write at the left-hand side of each box the label belonging to the previous connection that is helping generate the box you are currently considering. For example, *I.1* represents the input 1 or "Instructors," *A.1* represents the activity 1 or "Facilitate training class," and *O.1* represents the output 1 or "Number of participants graduated."

As shown in Figure 1.3, if *I.1* is used to generate *A.1*, then you write *I.1* at the left-hand side of that particular *A.1* activity box. Also, if *A.1* is used to generate *O.1* or "Number of participants graduated," then you write *A.1* at the left-hand side of that particular *O.1* output box. Moreover, if *O.1* is used to generate the outcome "Participants applied their new skills on the job," then you write *O.1* at

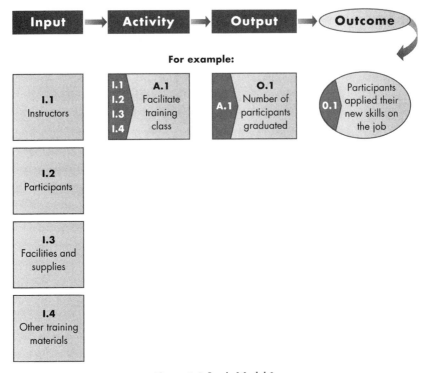

Figure 1.3 Logic Model 2

the left-hand side of that particular outcome box. In addition, for logic models in which you have to specify different outcomes levels, you can divide those labels as follows: short-term outcomes or *Os* (for example, *Os.1*), medium-term outcomes or *Om* (for exatmple, *Om.1*), and long-term outcomes or *Ol* (for example, *Ol.1*).

Reading from left to right, a logic model illustrates an "if-then" relationship among its elements. It helps you and the CMs understand how one element is perceived to affect another one. Figures 1.2 and 1.3 show a feedback arrow at the top right of the logic model. Basically, it attempts to illustrate that a logic model element (such as an outcome) links back to make a difference on another element (for example, an input). In other words, it may connect the end of the logic model to its beginning, because environments are dynamic (their situations continuously change) and the logic model needs to capture these environmental changes.

Sometimes your client does not have a written logic model or has never heard of this concept, but he or she is clear on its content and with your

Identify Logic Model Elements

Eliot: One of my clients asked me whether a logic model is a good tool to help her and her group identify intended results. I told her that logic models are one of my preferred tools and that I could facilitate a series of working sessions in order to help them develop a logic model. The only caveat to her request is that she wants this done in *one* session; she suggested we take a full day and work with all the key stakeholders to get it done. In my few years as an evaluator, I have never been asked this type of request. What do you think about that? Is it feasible?

Evelyn: Well, although not ideal, having the opportunity to have all the key stakeholders in one room for a full day is a good start. However, your client needs to understand that building a logic model will require several iterations of revision, feedback, and redrafting. You might explain it in this way: logic models are a *perceived snapshot in time*. They only represent a *perception* of the program and what it is supposed to accomplish during a *specific* period. Explain to your client that if time is a limitation, you would recommend two shorter sessions instead of a long one. For example, you could schedule the first session for an afternoon, and the second session the following morning. That way, participants will be able to reflect on the information shared during the first session and come fresh with new ideas the next morning. Keep in mind that ongoing communication throughout those meetings is key to their success. Try this idea and let me know how it goes!

assistance is willing to draft it for you. Although no specific rules exist on how to elaborate a logic model (for example, horizontal, vertical, or circular relationships), it must be clearly understood by intended users. In other words, your goal should be to identify a logic model that visually explains how an initiative supposedly works in terms of its inputs, activities, outputs, and outcomes. Thus we suggest the following steps to identify logic model elements:

1. Make sure that you and the participants (CMs and other key stakeholders) have a clear understanding of the initiative's characteristics and the organization or institution as a whole (including the vision and mission).

2. Share with participants a summary comparison of similar initiatives and their logic models (this is done for obtaining new ideas). For example, refer to information from the literature, Internet sites, and other experts in the area.

3. Establish a clear logic model scope that is based on the informational requirements of the initiative and the agreement of participants. For instance, are the logic model elements going to represent the entire initiative or just a part of it?

4. Agree with all the participants on the most convenient arrangement of the logic model elements. For example, use a priority order or an alphabetical order arrangement for each of the inputs, activities, outputs, and outcomes.

5. Assist participants in identifying the logic model elements following this order: (a) most essential outcomes, (b) outputs needed to generate outcomes, (c) activities needed to generate outputs, and (d) inputs needed to generate activities.

6. Solicit participants to outline the logic model connections (perhaps using arrows or labels) in order to show the relationships between its elements. For instance, how do the outputs link with the outcomes? How do the activities link with the outputs?

7. Delete all those elements and connections that are duplicates, seem unreasonable, or irrelevant. For example, check with participants that each of the boxes is connected with other(s) and make sure the connections are logical.

8. Write a brief description that clearly reflects the meaning of each of the boxes in the logic model. Otherwise, only the people who have collaborated in the development of the logic model will have a complete understanding of it.

9. Agree with all the participants and other stakeholders as appropriate (for example, board members) on a definitive logic model. This final version of the logic model should be clearly aligned with the initiative's vision and mission.

10. Gather feedback on a regular basis using a previously agreed-upon system, such as meetings, and summarize it in a written format (including an updated logic model) so it is available to each participant and other stakeholders as appropriate.

The resulting logic model should be depicted in a single picture, bringing detail and understanding to the intended goals. It should establish clear directions on how to carry out particular tasks or responsibilities. However, the logic model can be modified as needed because it incorporates continuous feedback for improvement.

With a logic model you and the CMs can clarify assumptions regarding the initiative's inputs, activities, outputs, and outcomes. Moreover, everyone can observe its intended connections and identify underlying issues of an initiative. Therefore, the logic model is both a management tool and an evaluation tool that helps verify the perceived reality of how an initiative works.

IDENTIFY POTENTIAL SWOTS

SWOTs are the evaluand Strengths, Weaknesses, Opportunities, and Threats that affect the collaborative evaluation process. The SWOTs show the current characteristics of the evaluand and the future tendencies within its context that are implicitly connected to the evaluation (see Figure 1.4). The identification of potential SWOTs provides an opportunity to be proactive in planning the evaluation. For example, placing focus on threats to the critical evaluation activities could lead to taking preventative measures that could save money.

With the SWOTs, you and the CMs can identify when positive or controversial issues may surface within the evaluand and plan on how to approach those issues (as a dynamic process for decision making) in the collaborative evaluation. Also, with the SWOTs everyone involved can assess the evaluation in a more realistic way because there are often many good reasons why the evaluation is not carried out as planned or why objectives are not achieved. Hence, you and the CMs have to be engaged in identifying what internal and external forces may work for or against the evaluand as the

Evaluand (Current)	Context (Future)
Strengths (blue)	Opportunities (green)
Weaknesses (yellow)	Threats (red)

Figure 1.4 Example of a SWOTs Matrix

basis for decision making (see Chapter 3 on how to establish procedures for decision making).

- **Strengths.** These are current characteristics of the evaluand that contribute to the achievement of its vision. For example, a strength may be the current availability of resources, including specific data, equipment, and materials.

- **Weaknesses.** These are current characteristics of the evaluand that constitute an obstacle for the achievement of its vision. For example, a weakness may be the current lack of resources, including specific data, equipment, and materials.

- **Opportunities.** These are ideal outcomes within the evaluand context that are uncontrollable and could be observed in the future. Their occurrence would facilitate the achievement of the evaluand vision. For example, an opportunity may be helpful conditions external to the evaluand such as a future growing economy.

- **Threats.** These are negative outcomes within the evaluand context that are uncontrollable and could be observed in the future. They are obstacles that would impede (or interfere with) the achievement of the evaluand vision. For example, a threat may be harmful conditions external to the evaluand such as competitive initiatives developed.

The SWOTs allow you and the CMs to formulate and implement managerial strategies in order to develop the evaluation plan (see Chapter 2 on how to clarify the evaluation process). We suggest the following steps to identify potential SWOTs:

1. Create a SWOT matrix on a flipchart (poster or other similar option) and have available a variety of color-coded, self-adhesive cards (such as blue for strengths, yellow for weaknesses, green for opportunities, and red for threats).

2. Review relevant data (for example, historical information on this and other evaluands) to have some examples that could be identified as SWOTs, such as technology and information availability, assigned budget, and time considerations.

3. Divide the participants (including CMs and other stakeholders as needed) into four teams representing strengths, weaknesses, opportunities, and threats. Then provide each team the color adhesives identifying their particular SWOT.

4. Instruct each team to write one specific idea per adhesive, under their specific team SWOT, until they run out of ideas. Then the team leader will read to their members each of the ideas and, with their feedback, eliminate any overlap.

5. Place the color adhesives on the flipchart, under the specific team SWOT, so the rest of the teams can read them. In the case of the opportunities and threats, only leave those that have at least a 50 percent chance of occurrence.

6. Solicit participants to each make note of their own new ideas about the SWOTs (to make sure all the most important ideas are addressed) and share each of those ideas while adding them to the SWOTs matrix as appropriate.

7. Ask for ideas or feedback from other stakeholders who may help identify additional realistic SWOTS (such as unintended results or areas that may have been overlooked). Question every alternative before adding it to the SWOTs matrix.

8. Agree with all the participants and other specific stakeholders, as feasible, on a definitive SWOTs matrix. This final version of the SWOTs matrix should be clearly aligned with the evaluand vision and mission to understand which issues deserve attention.

9. Design with the participants emergency procedures (for example, risk analysis, predefined action steps, or contingency plans) and plan for timely feedback throughout the evaluation to provide early warning signs of specific problems.

10. Gather feedback on a regular basis using a previously agreed-upon system, such as meetings, and summarize it in a written format (including an updated version of the SWOTs report) so it is available to each CM and other stakeholders as appropriate.

The SWOTs matrix represents an important point of reference to make informed evaluation decisions. Also, it fosters ownership of the evaluation decisions made, making you and the CMs more determined to overcome any obstacles. In addition, it gives insight into how and why everyone needs to respond to situations in a defined way, depending on their probability of occurrence or implications for the evaluation. However, this identification process, as does any self-awareness process, requires a high level of introspection and the ability to internalize feedback from others (George, 2004).

Threats Versus Risks in the Evaluation

A **risk** is a measure of uncertainty that involves the probability of attaining (or not) a specific evaluation achievement. Also, it is the possibility that something (such as political instability) could interfere with the completion of the evaluation. Threats and risks are more or less synonymous, so we can lump them together in the same analysis (Lewis, 2010).

There is not a single rule on how to avoid risk; however, the more precautions you take in the evaluation, the more safeguards it will have against risks. As we mentioned before, the SWOTs provide the basis you and the CMs need to capitalize on strengths and opportunities and minimize the impact of weaknesses and threats (see Chapter 4 on how to ensure the need for change is justified).

Risk should be taken very seriously yet accepted as a condition for growth and improvement. People are typically optimistic at the beginning of the evaluation and fail to take risks seriously (for example, lack of information on potential hazards and probability of their occurrence) and later make decisions based on their perception and tolerance for such risks. Thus you and the CMs need to anticipate and prepare for potential evaluation crises to minimize their occurrence and be able to manage the consequences if they occur. In a crisis, the worst decision is no decision and the second worst decision is a late one (Sawle, 1991).

Descriptions of potential risk events should generally include estimates of (a) the probability that the risk event will occur, (b) alternative possible outcomes, (c) expected timing of the event, and (d) anticipated frequency in case it happens more than once (PMI Standards Committee, 2008). In addition, several authors (for example, PMI Standards Committee, 2008; Heldman, 2009; Pinto & Trailer, 1999) described some tools used to help manage risks that have a potential of causing unwanted change:

- **Risk Analysis.** This provides early recognition or warning signs of potential risks (what can go wrong and what is most probable). You and the CMs may draw a decision tree that is based on how you understand the interactions among decisions and outcomes (see Figure 1.5). The decision tree is useful when there are actions or possible outcomes that are uncertain. Then, priorities can be determined by combining an event's probability of occurrence and the severity of its consequences.

- **Contingency Plan.** This represents predefined action steps you and the CMs should take if a risk occurs. It helps to prepare for a potential crisis and to do what is necessary to fix it (such as know whom to notify).

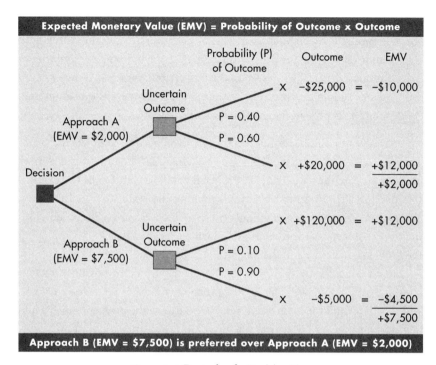

Figure 1.5 Example of a Decision Tree

Hence, if you and the CMs have previously done a risk analysis, then you can develop plans to prepare for the broadest range of emergencies.

- **Flowchart.** This is a diagram that provides the specific steps, critical procedures, or actions to follow in a crisis (for example, emergency response operations) through a logic structure (see Figure 1.6). The flowchart helps you and the CMs better understand the causes and effects of risks and prepare for them, because when a crisis occurs people cannot necessarily think clearly, so they need procedures to follow.

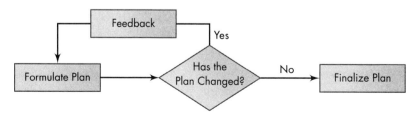

Figure 1.6 Example of a Flowchart

- **Tabletop exercise.** This is used to discuss, rehearse, and solidify the response to a potential crisis. The tabletop exercise uses the risk analysis information and involves simulating or acting out possible scenarios as a consequence of a foreseen evaluation crisis. It is usually done in a conference room as a practice, because few people will sit to read instructions if they are in the middle of a crisis.

Your client may indicate, for example, that you need to complete the evaluation in six months, but the CMs and you agree that nine months is a more accurate and appropriate estimate of when it could be completed. To be proactive, develop a contingency plan at this point of the evaluation. However, you also may choose to not do anything until a problem occurs (without developing any contingencies) and then lose valuable time due to lack of planning on the problem occurring and the magnitude of its impact.

Always remember to minimize risks by describing all the possible effects as a result of any action, and identify the probability of each negative event. This will allow you and the CMs to address the source of the problem quickly and appropriately. Avoid taking risks if the rewards are small, because whenever you take an action within the collaborative evaluation, other issues may arise (and you must respond to those unintended consequences, too).

Several authors (for example, Heldman, 2009; Kerzner, 2009a, 2009b; Lewis, 1999) provided options for reducing risk or responding to it. These options have some commonalities with the means toward conflict resolution that we explain in Chapter 3.

- **Avoidance.** It is when you (and the CMs) do not accept the risk option because of the potentially unfavorable results. Hence, you try to eliminate a specific risk event by eliminating its cause.

- **Mitigation.** It is when you (and the CMs) take preventive measures or make contingency plans to reduce the risk cause or its impact (that is, reducing its probability of occurrence, its monetary value, or both).

- **Acceptance.** It is when you (and the CMs) know the risk exists and prefer to accept its consequences if it occurs. If necessary, you may do the minimum planning to overcome it.

- **Transfer.** It is when you (and the CMs) deflect the risk, share it with others, or even transfer the entire risk to them (for example, through insurance). Thus you try to convert the risk into an opportunity.

Identify Potential SWOTs

Ernest: I have a client who asks a lot of interesting questions! As we were leaving the elevator yesterday, looking at possible places and times to meet, my client suddenly changed the topic of our conversation to SWOT analysis. He asked if a particular strength can also be a weakness. I guess he had some reservations about the analysis we had just finished. My immediate answer was that I will get back to him! I just felt I shouldn't answer the question without carefully thinking about my answer. At first, I decided that a strength could not also be a weakness. However, as I think more about it, it seems there may be cases where yes, a strength can easily be a weakness. How off am I on this assumption?

Evelyn: I don't think you are that far off. I have experienced that same thing with one of my clients. Imagine a room with people fully engaged in the process of identifying potential SWOTs. We were talking about the possibility of implementing a new technology program at this organization. All key elements were in place, including one of the identified strengths: *a fully tested and robust information technology (IT) infrastructure.* However, everything changed as soon as the only IT person in the room said, "Well, that is one of our greatest weaknesses, too. Most of our computers are at least five years old and this new software will simply not work." The energy in the room plunged. However, everything came back to normal once the president clarified that the current project had provided a large amount of resources for a major upgrade on hardware. So this is one example where a strength could also be perceived as a weakness if complete information has not been properly shared with all members of the team.

Be aware that many decisions contain uncertainty, so you and the CMs need to use your own judgment in order to understand which potential risks deserve attention (see Chapter 3 on how to establish procedures for decision making). Also, be especially careful with those risks that may have an impact on critical evaluation activities in order to develop sound contingency plans. Obviously, you cannot identify every potential risk, but by identifying those risks with a high probability of occurrence, you avoid spending excessive time on contingency planning for low-probability risks.

Use the SWOTs matrix as a tool to determine the underlying assumptions in your evaluation. In addition, keep in mind that this matrix needs to be reviewed and updated regularly to be effective. The unexpected can occur because circumstances tend to change, so it is vital to work closely with each key stakeholder to anticipate and preempt potential changes. The MCE allows you to adapt quickly to those changes, since it contemplates the handling of unexpected events.

IDENTIFY THE EVALUATION SCOPE

The **evaluation scope** is the area covered by the collaborative evaluation itself or the range of work to be accomplished. It provides clear information about what the evaluation will and will not focus on, depending on the boundaries set. By having a realistic scope, you and the CMs can establish an achievable set of needs, expectations, and deliverables. This is essential in order to avoid wasting time and energy on activities that are not needed in the evaluation.

The evaluation scope establishes the evaluation boundaries as the basis for a clear planning and responsibility assignment. In addition, it leads to the establishment of criteria used in the collaborative evaluation (see Chapter 2 on how to clarify the evaluand criteria and standards). Obviously, a well-defined scope gives a client confidence on the evaluation because there is a clear understanding on what the evaluation is to accomplish.

Clarifying the boundaries early on in the collaborative evaluation helps you and the CMs make sound decisions among choices to be considered throughout this process. It also improves the evaluation effectiveness by concentrating on the issues important for the long-term results. Therefore, gather specific information to later establish priorities for enhancing the understanding of the evaluand value.

Some of the main evaluation scope questions that we usually ask the appropriate stakeholders are (a) Why was this evaluation solicited? (b) When should the evaluation start and finish? (c) What do you expect the evaluation will achieve (or what are the evaluation questions)? (d) What happens if results differ from your expectations? (e) How are you planning to use the information provided by this evaluation? and (f) Do other main stakeholders agree with you on how to use the evaluation results?

Basic Distinctions

There are two basic evaluation distinctions that can help you better understand the evaluation scope (see Figure 1.7). The first distinction differentiates the evaluation depending on its role or purpose (formative versus summative evaluation). The second distinction differentiates the evaluation depending on the characteristics of its evaluator (internal versus external evaluation).

A **formative evaluation** is conducted when the evaluand is in its developmental stages in order to make decisions for improving and strengthening it during those stages. Thus formative evaluations are not used to prove whether the evaluand is worth the funding received; they serve more to guide and direct it (Royse, 2010).

A **summative evaluation** is conducted once an evaluand is stabilized in order to judge its final value (such as merit or worth) or aid in a decision about its future; for example, prolonging, expanding, or terminating the evaluand. A summative evaluation is conducted after completion of the activity (or after stabilization) and for the benefit of some external audience or decision maker (Scriven, 1991).

An **internal evaluation** is an evaluation conducted by evaluators who are employees of the organization where the evaluation is done. These evaluators are likely to (a) be more familiar with the evaluand history, (b) know the decision-making style of the organization, (c) be present to remind others of

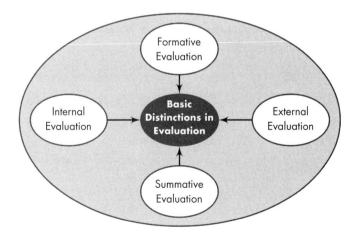

Figure 1.7 Basic Distinctions in Evaluation

results now and in the future, and (d) be able to communicate technical results more frequently and clearly (Fitzpatrick, Sanders, & Worthen, 2011).

An **external evaluation** is an evaluation conducted by independent evaluators who are not employees of the organization where the evaluation is done. In other words, you are neither directly responsible nor involved with the activities being evaluated. External evaluators are likely to (a) bring greater perceived objectivity and credibility to outside audiences, (b) bring with them a fresh or outside perspective, and (c) have knowledge of how other similar evaluands work (Fitzpatrick, Sanders, & Worthen, 2011).

Although the external evaluator is the perfect candidate for a summative evaluation, sometimes the collaboration of internal evaluators is allowed if there is not a problem with credibility issues. Whenever possible, it is beneficial to combine external and internal evaluators within formative and summative evaluation efforts.

The combination of internal and external evaluators can compensate for several disadvantages. For example, an external evaluator may be unfamiliar with the evaluand, and an internal evaluator can help to compensate for this weakness. Furthermore, the external evaluator can help provide specialized knowledge, objectivity, and credibility to the evaluation.

Evaluation Questions

An **evaluation question** is an inquiry that provides focus for the collaborative evaluation, because it establishes what specific answers the evaluation is expected to provide. It is the basis for defining the tasks and outcomes for the evaluation depending on the client's needs and expectations. Obviously, the evaluation questions determine what will be included in the evaluation and what falls outside of its scope.

Prior to soliciting your client, and other key stakeholders as appropriate, to officially identify the evaluation questions, you and the CMs (which generally will include the client) could gather ideas from other sources about potential evaluation questions. For example, you could find similar evaluands and evaluations in the literature, ask the views of expert consultants in the area, and trust your own professional judgment. Then, through brainstorming with your client,* you and

---

*Brainstorming is an idea-generation technique that promotes the spontaneous sharing of collaborative evaluation ideas through nonjudgmental discussion between you and the CMs (or other stakeholders).

the CMs can help identify the evaluation questions. If this technique of brainstorming is not feasible, then questionnaires and interviews can also be used to obtain pertinent data.

We suggest the following steps to identify the questions that the collaborative evaluation will answer:

1. Ask the client (the CMs and other key stakeholders as appropriate) about the history of the evaluand and, specifically, if it has previously been evaluated. If so, ask what evaluation questions were used at that time and what results were found.

2. Identify the amount of resources (such as time, people, materials, and funds) available for the evaluation. This will determine the feasibility of increasing or reducing the number of evaluation questions that can be manageable.

3. Ask the client directly for an initial draft of evaluation questions (if the client is able to give you a direct answer). For example, what are the main questions he or she wants the evaluation to answer? Are those questions consistent with specific needs?

4. Ask the client indirectly for an initial draft of evaluation questions (if the client is not able to give you a direct answer). For example, what should be accomplished as a result of this evaluation? What problem should the evaluation address?

5. Listen rather than make comments about any of the evaluation questions at this point (avoid interrupting). For example, wait silently and patiently during pauses, because generally the most important information follows them.

6. Recognize and address any type of insistence on including potentially biased or unanswerable questions. For instance, find out who would be affected by a particular question (and why), especially if the answer is different than expected.

7. Assist the client (with the CMs' or other stakeholders' feedback as appropriate) in narrowing down the original list to a manageable number of preliminary questions (for example, those that are realistic depending on budget, time, and feasibility).

8. Invite the client to select, as a result of a previous thorough analysis, all the final evaluation questions that will be addressed throughout the

collaborative evaluation (with the CMs' or other stakeholders' feedback as appropriate).

9. Agree with the client (in writing) on the final evaluation questions that will be answered by the collaborative evaluation. This is only done after solving any possible concerns on the feasibility of those evaluation questions.

10. Provide the client, each CM, and other stakeholders as appropriate with a summary report of this experience (including a list of the evaluation questions) as lessons learned for developing questions in similar collaborative evaluations.

If the evaluation questions need to be narrowed down, you and the CMs may help your client to rank order them using these criteria: (a) it is of interest to key audiences; (b) it reduces present uncertainty; (c) it yields important information; (d) it is of continuing interest; (e) it is critical to the evaluation's scope; (f) it has an impact on the course of events; and (g) it is answerable given available financial and human resources, time, methods, and technology (Cronbach, 1982). Remember that a feeling of shared ownership increases the chances that the stakeholders will use the evaluation results. If you cannot have consensus on the evaluation questions, then you should delay the collaborative evaluation until consensus is reached.

Once you get a set of agreed-upon evaluation questions, identify (with the help of the CMs and other key stakeholders) all the potential activities that should be carried out in order to find the answers to those questions. For example, how are you going to collect data to answer a specific question, including methods, sources of information, who will collect the data and when, and what instruments will be used? All this information will be included in the evaluation plan. In this way, you may be able to easily establish the activities needed to answer those evaluation questions using the work breakdown structure.

Work Breakdown Structure

A **work breakdown structure** (WBS) is a method of dividing the major work components in the collaborative evaluation (such as the evaluation questions) into smaller, more manageable units in order to improve the accuracy of the evaluation plan. Each descending level of the WBS shows an increasingly in-depth description of the evaluation elements, with the items at the lowest level referred to as activities.

The WBS provides a common understanding of the evaluation scope, because work not included in the WBS will be considered as being outside of the scope. Keep in mind that the WBS does not show the sequence of the evaluation, because this is going to be done when you determine the schedule of this effort.

After identifying the evaluation questions, identify what actions should be taken to answer those questions. By identifying the evaluation activities (actions with a clearly observable beginning and end), you are providing the starting point to analyze when they will be completed and who will complete them. We suggest the following steps to identify the WBS:

1. Identify the long- and short-term evaluation goals in order to put into context what needs to be achieved and the option(s) to make it happen within the collaborative effort. For example, determine what should happen in the evaluation.

2. Provide a summary or example with a definition of the WBS to the CMs, and other relevant stakeholders if appropriate, and discuss it with them in order to make sure there is a clear understanding (or make clarifications as needed).

3. Divide each of the evaluation questions (or any other main evaluation components) into groups, with the help of the CMs, and give each evaluation question a unique identification number for record-keeping purposes.

4. Break down each of the evaluation questions into smaller, concrete activities (and sub-activities if required) to show an increasingly in-depth description. Thus an element in a higher level is equal to the sum of all its sub-elements in the next lower level.

5. Stop when the WBS reaches a level, such as an activity, that is conveniently measurable and manageable (for example, when the responsibility of an activity and authority over it can be assigned to a particular, skillful CM).

6. Determine a logical order for each activity (within each group) and assign an identification number to each. This makes it easy to understand later how one activity may affect the timing of other activities and the evaluation as a whole.

7. Check with the CMs that all the required activities per group have been considered (without any gaps). In other words, check with the CMs that there is a logical subdivision of the evaluation work against the reporting requirements.

8. Write a brief description that clearly reflects the meaning of each of the boxes (work components) in the WBS. Otherwise, only the people who created the WBS (for example, you and the CMs) will have a complete understanding of it.

9. Gather feedback on a regular basis using a previously agreed-upon system (such as meetings, emails, and surveys as feasible). This will help you and the CMs monitor the suitability of the WBS and make updates as needed.

10. Provide each CM and other stakeholders as appropriate with a summary report of this experience (including the WBS with each of its descending levels) as lessons learned for future similar situations within collaborative evaluations.

The expectation should be to form levels, where in the superior level you write the main evaluation components (for example, evaluation questions). Then you subdivide each evaluation component in packages of work until the final level is reached (see Figure 1.8). A work package is the lowest level in the WBS. At this level is where the activities can be scheduled, cost and duration

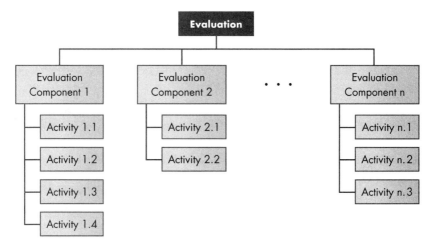

Figure 1.8 Example of a Work Breakdown Structure

of activities can be estimated, and monitoring and control of activities can be conducted. There is no "right" way to build a WBS (Heldman, 2009). As an example, a main evaluation component could be "1. Conduct stakeholders' interviews." Then you might subdivide this component into the following subsequent activities: "Activity 1.1. Interview stakeholders," "Activity 1.2. Analyze data," "Activity 1.3. Summarize findings into a report," and "Activity 1.4. Present report to stakeholders."

The WBS can help to define or limit the scope of the evaluation presenting the specific activities or work packages approved for the evaluation. One of the typical mistakes is to begin implementation of the evaluation before having developed a comprehensive plan. For this reason, the WBS is a very important tool that you and the CMs may consider using in order to list the activities that must be completed in the collaborative evaluation. Obviously, if a complex evaluation is broken down into small activities, you can make an easier-to-follow evaluation plan.

When you and the CMs develop the WBS, you may find information that leads you to make the decision that it is unfeasible or inappropriate to conduct the evaluation at this time. Some conditions under which evaluations are inappropriate are when (a) the evaluation would produce trivial information; (b) the evaluation results will not be used; (c) the evaluation cannot yield useful, valid information; (d) the evaluation is premature for the stage of the evaluand; and (e) the propriety of the evaluation is doubtful (for example, it will strain or violate professional principles) (Fitzpatrick, Sanders, & Worthen, 2011).

Determining when to use a collaborative evaluation most likely depends on the answers to a number of questions. For example, what experience does the client have with collaborative evaluations? How committed is the client to promote learning from collaborative practices? Is the client willing to involve a number of stakeholders in the evaluation? There are additional related tools, such as the responsibility assignment matrix, that help to identify the resources within the collaborative evaluation.

The **responsibility assignment matrix** (RAM) identifies which resources (such as people or materials) are going to be available for each of the evaluation activities (see Figure 1.9). A RAM is a tool you can use when you need to assign roles and responsibilities for specific evaluation activities to the CMs or other key stakeholders. It clearly delineates who is accountable for each task. This is necessary for schedule development and consequently determining the critical activities in the evaluation.

Work Breakdown Structure			Person				
			A	B	C	D	...
Evaluation	Evaluation Component 1	Activity 1.1	C	A	E		
		Activity 1.2		A	E		C
		Activity 1.3		A			C
		Activity 1.4	C	S	C		
	Evaluation Component 2	Activity 2.1		S	E	A	
		Activity 2.2		A		A	
	⋮	⋮	⋮	⋮	⋮	⋮	⋮
	Evaluation Component n	Activity n.1	R	A		A	P
		Activity n.2		S			U
		Activity n.3		S			

A = Approves   C = Collaborates   R = Reports   U = Uses
E = Executes   P = Provides Input   S = Supervises

Figure 1.9 Example of a Responsibility Assignment Matrix

Who does what (roles) and who decides what (responsibilities) should be closely linked to the scope definition, and these may vary over time (PMI Standards Committee, 2008). To facilitate the selection of CMs from the rest of the stakeholders, potential CMs provide information to build the RAM shown in Figure 1.9. This type of matrix can be easily adjusted to other types of resource allocation (such as materials) also needed in the collaborative evaluation.

The RAM helps to avoid overlaps among resources. It aids in the analysis of how a decision will affect the collaborative evaluation, because everyone's roles and responsibilities are clearly defined. As a result, you and the CMs know, for example, who should supervise or who should report a particular activity. Still, conduct regular meetings to keep the CMs informed of the evaluation progress (see Chapter 4 on how to ensure open communication). This helps you check if there are any unanticipated role conflicts (see Chapter 3 on how to encourage conflict resolution).

Once you have identified the availability of the CMs, draw in the RAM chart their suitability for each evaluation activity. Remember that an accurate

Identify the Evaluation Scope

Ernest: Mr. Carter, this is Evelyn, one of my most respected colleagues. Evelyn has been my mentor in the evaluation field; we have known each other for at least twenty years. Evelyn, this is Mr. Carter, a newly appointed senior program director at XYZ Foundation. Mr. Carter has invited me to write a proposal to evaluate one of the foundation's programs. We were discussing what would be the most appropriate approach to selecting the final questions for this evaluation. He mentioned that the program's executive director has already proposed a comprehensive list of potential evaluation questions. However, I suggested that we might use a work breakdown structure, or WBS, to help refine the list of evaluation questions. Would you agree with that suggestion?

Evelyn: Absolutely! A WBS helps frame the evaluation because it communicates its scope and guides it toward more meaningful and sound decisions. In fact, I would suggest bringing together the CMs and complete what I call *a full run of the WBS*. That is, assuming all ideal conditions are in place, you will discuss the WBS and its major work components. For example, ask CMs about the viability of each particular component, common understandings, and competing assumptions. Once everyone involved has agreed on the overall WBS, then you all can identify if a particular or several evaluation questions need to be modified in order to improve the quality of the overall evaluation.

resource allocation is very important in the collaborative evaluation, because this helps to determine how you and the CMs will complete a specific activity on schedule. Keep in mind that it may not actually be true that a more experienced person can do the job faster than a less experienced person.

After identifying the RAM, establish a clear evaluation schedule. For instance, once you have initially matched individuals to particular activities (for example, according to their interests and skills), learn about their availability and then formally agree on their responsibilities in the collaborative evaluation. Obviously, some of the potential CMs may be uninterested (perhaps due to conflict with other CMs) in the collaborative evaluation at that time. In this case, determine the cause of the problem, and if necessary, consider their replacement.

IDENTIFY CRITICAL EVALUATION ACTIVITIES

The **critical evaluation activities** are high-priority actions that directly determine the completion of the collaborative evaluation on time, so they must be carefully managed. You and the CMs have to agree on evaluation priorities or essential components that must be completed within schedule so that the entire collaborative evaluation can also be completed within schedule.

The critical evaluation activities vary during the evaluation (and from evaluation to evaluation) depending on their particular characteristics. In other words, they are not of equal and stable importance over the life of the evaluation, becoming critical or not at different stages. Throughout the evaluation, work with the CMs to carefully identify each critical evaluation activity and its implications, such as how it relates to the adequate use of time (for example, by using appropriate scheduling techniques).

We suggest the following steps to identify the critical evaluation activities:

1. Determine with the client when the evaluation should begin and end in terms of calendar or real dates (taking into consideration breaks for nonworking days and unrelated meetings, among others) to avoid different perceptions later.

2. Identify with the CMs all major activities from the WBS and their possible duration. For example, use historical information on similar activities, or estimate how many hours (or dates by which) each activity needs to be completed.

3. Use the best scheduling technique available (such as a network diagram) to draft the collaborative evaluation schedule on the basis of its deadline(s), the number of resources available, and backup strategies in case problems occur.

4. Identify the critical evaluation activities (those without slack time) and verify that each of them is manageable and realistic (for instance, in terms of time and effort). These overall critical activities must be completed within the scheduled time.

5. Divide every critical evaluation activity into categories (for example, you or the CMs control it; you or the CMs indirectly control it; you or the CMs do not control it), and try to move the not-controlled activities to, at least, being indirectly controlled.

6. Choose the high-priority critical evaluation activities over which you or the CMs do not have control and allocate special time and other resources so that those critical evaluation activities do not consume more time than scheduled.

7. Reserve sufficient slack time to handle unforeseen problems or constraints throughout the evaluation. For example, when there is no logical sequence among activities, they may be completed at the same time (if resources are available).

8. Agree with the CMs on the specific dates set for each of the evaluation activities and the overall evaluation, to make sure again that all the resources (such as people or materials) will be available at the time they are needed.

9. Gather feedback on a regular basis using a previously agreed-upon system (for example, meetings, emails, and surveys as feasible). This will help you and the CMs monitor the critical activities and make updates as needed.

10. Provide each CM and other stakeholders as appropriate with a summary report of this experience (including a report with the schedule of each critical evaluation activity) as lessons learned for future similar situations within collaborative evaluations.

The more you and the CMs focus energy and resources in a clear evaluation scope, the more effective you will all be to the success of the collaborative evaluation. A split in focus can cause conflict and have a negative effect on the critical evaluation activities. Also, consider that no one is available to work on the evaluation 100 percent of the time, and the maximum is usually around 80 percent (Lewis, 1999), because of unrelated distractions and so on. As circumstances change there may be areas that no longer require so many resources or as much time.

The critical evaluation activities help to identify some potential problems that should be acknowledged and solved through the formulation of a specific evaluation plan (again, see Chapter 2 on how to clarify the evaluation process). The critical evaluation activities are the prime means for coordinating, scheduling, and planning of activities, thereby developing a basis for better decision making. Well-specified critical evaluation activities are essential to monitor collaborative evaluations adequately.

Techniques for Scheduling Critical Evaluation Activities

The duration of activities (number of work periods to complete an activity from start to finish) is often difficult to estimate because of the different factors that can influence those activities (including resource availability and resource productivity). Keep in mind that all the evaluation activities will vary in duration, depending on who does them and when they are done.

A **schedule** is the planned dates and times for performing the evaluation activities. A schedule helps you and the CMs to develop a timeframe of when you are planning to start and finish each evaluation activity, and what their total duration will be (depending on surrounding conditions or constraints). Obviously, this schedule is preliminary until resources have been confirmed in the evaluation plan. A schedule provides a visual picture of how to track and measure the evaluation efforts. Developing the schedule of the evaluation activities is one of the most important tasks within the collaborative evaluation, because there is a need to determine when (and subsequently how) the evaluation resources are going to be integrated to the activities in a systematic way. It has to be clear that unanticipated events may occur (for example, you may need to collect additional information), so updates may be needed.

There are several techniques that can help you and the CMs estimate your evaluation schedule. Each can help to determine which activities occur simultaneously among other evaluation constraints. Clearly, the schedule needs to be realistic if you and the CMs want to complete the evaluation on time. Some of the most common scheduling techniques are (a) a chart, (b) a network diagram (such as arrow diagram methods or precedence diagram methods), and (c) a management map.

Chart

A **chart** is an outline that shows evaluation information in the form of a graph, diagram, or map. A chart is a great help to easily highlight deadlines to be met throughout the evaluation. Following are some of the most common charts in collaborative evaluations.

Gantt Chart

A **Gantt chart** is a bar chart that visually indicates how long an evaluation activity will take to be completed. It includes a time scale on the horizontal axis and the evaluation activities on the vertical axis. A Gantt chart is a very easy way to visually present the evaluation plan because it shows the activities' expected durations as horizontal bars, including the start and end dates (see Figure 1.10).

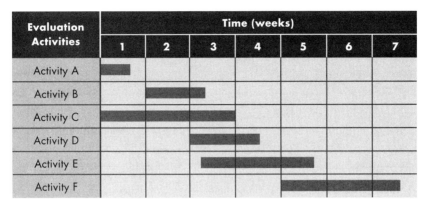

Figure 1.10 Example of a Gantt Chart

This type of chart is commonly used for showing the progress of specific work required to accomplish an objective (Kerzner, 2009a). A simple Gantt chart does not show interdependencies or logical relationships among activities (some can show a minimum of dependencies and interrelationships between activities). It is a very simple-to-understand technique for evaluation analysis, and it is very easy to expand if necessary. Also, it shows which activities overlap, so you and the CMs can check the RAM to determine if there is an overlap of the same resources at a particular time.

A Gantt chart is useful only in simple collaborative evaluations, or in the early stages of schedule planning for complex evaluations, for showing individual activity timelines with a minimum of interdependencies among them. Keep in mind that when you or the CMs have overlapping commitments on different activities, assigning some of those activities to other people can reduce the overlap.

Milestone Chart

A **milestone** is a special achievement (such as a particular deliverable or evaluation report), an important activity, or an event (for example, an activity start or finish date) that marks a major progress in the evaluation. A **milestone chart** is a scheduling tool that divides the evaluation into logical, measurable milestones allowing you and CMs to verify if it is on track (see Figure 1.11).

A milestone chart provides a way to clarify what you and the CMs are going to deliver at a particular stage in the evaluation. Make sure that the CMs' perceptions of the milestones to be completed are the same as yours throughout the collaborative evaluation (see Chapter 2 on how to clarify the expectations). Milestone

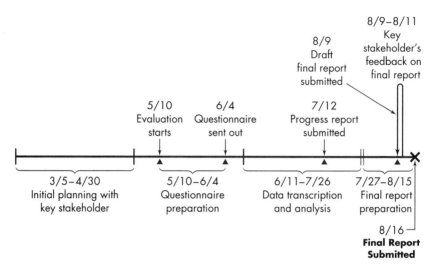

Figure 1.11 Example of a Milestone Chart

charts help to monitor progress, because you generally will schedule evaluation reviews when you reach a milestone, such as the completion of an activity.

Depending on who is responsible for a particular milestone and the length of a particular activity, you will draw more or fewer milestones on the chart. Milestones can also be interim steps within an evaluation activity drawn so you and the CMs can measure the evaluation activity progress. A major disadvantage with milestone charts is the inability to show the interdependencies between events and activities (Kerzner, 2009a). Hence, when you need to specify interdependencies you may consider constructing a network diagram.

Network Diagram

A **network diagram** is a step-by-step display of the activities and their relationships used to determine how much time is needed to complete the collaborative evaluation. The resulting dates (for example, start and end) from the network diagram indicate the dates or time periods within which each evaluation activity should be scheduled (taking into consideration any potential resource constraints).

This type of scheduling technique provides you and the CMs with the necessary facts for contingency planning and decision making (for example, including potential uncertainties such as time delays and slacks). It also increases everyone's ability to relate to the total evaluation and provides a sense of belonging from the early stages of the evaluation.

It is important to note that the network diagram is often incorrectly called a PERT chart (for Program Evaluation and Review Technique). A **PERT chart** is a specific type of project network diagram that is seldom used today (PMI Standards Committee, 2008).

To design a network diagram, first identify each activity previously developed in the WBS and the expected dates or times that each will last. Next, it is essential to identify the activities that immediately precede and follow the current activity. As a result, the diagram is constructed displaying both the logical relationships and interdependencies within the general evaluation activities and the critical path activities. Sometimes, you and the CMs may be able to complete different activities simultaneously through several paths in the network.

A **critical path** is the longest road or evaluation duration in the network. Hence, it shows the shortest possible time when the overall collaborative evaluation can finish. A **slack** or **float** is the amount of available time an activity has without delaying the final evaluation deadline. It is the difference between the latest possible date to finish an evaluation activity and its earliest expected date. It is the amount of time that an activity can be postponed from its early start without delaying the early start of any immediately following activities or the final finish date.

A critical path shows the critical evaluation activities, because its activities do not have slack time, and delays in any of those activities would mean not meeting the final evaluation deadline. The critical path helps you and the CMs to reschedule other activities that do have slack time in order to balance the use of resources to their full extent. For example, after identifying which activities lack flexibility within the schedule, you may reduce evaluation costs by using resources (such as people and equipment) in those activities while they wait to start in their initially scheduled activity. Also, you and the CMs could shorten the evaluation schedule by reallocating or increasing resources available for activities in the critical path.

Several authors (for example, Kerzner, 2009a, 2009b; PMI Standards Committee, 2008) have explained that there are important values that need to be identified in a network diagram. Those values may change as the collaborative evaluation progresses and adjustments are made to its plan (see Chapter 4 on how to ensure the need for change is justified).

- **Earliest Start Time (EST).** This is the earliest time when each evaluation activity can start, based on the network logic and any schedule constraints.

- **Earliest Finish Time (EFT).** This is the earliest time when each evaluation activity can finish, based on the network logic and any schedule constraints.

- **Latest Start Time (LST).** This is the latest time when each evaluation activity can start, based on the network logic and any schedule constraints. In the critical path method, it is the latest possible point in time that an activity may begin without delaying a specified deadline (for example, the evaluation finish date).

- **Latest Finish Time (LFT).** This is the latest time when each evaluation activity can finish, based on the network logic and any schedule constraints. In the critical path method, it is the latest possible point in time that an evaluation activity may be completed without delaying a specified deadline (such as the evaluation finish date).

Although there are several acceptable approaches to drawing a network diagram, for the purposes of this book we are going to briefly describe two of the most common and useful approaches: the arrow diagram method (ADM) and the precedence diagram method (PDM). Figure 1.12 shows a typical identification for these two diagramming methods.

Arrow Diagram Method

The **arrow diagram method** (ADM) is a method of constructing a network diagram using arrows to represent the activities and connecting them at nodes (for example, circles) to show the dependencies (PMI Standards Committee, 2008). For instance, in Figure 1.13, the arrows represent activities, which are connected at circles called nodes. The tail of each arrow represents the start and the head represents the finish of the activity (ADM only represents finish-to-

A) Typical ADM Identification   **B) Typical PDM Identification**

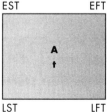

Figure 1.12 Typical Network Diagram Identification

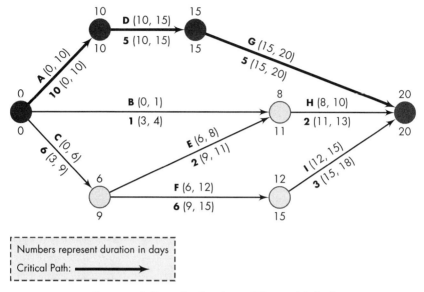

Figure 1.13 Example of an Arrow Diagram Method

start dependencies among activities). The length of the arrow displayed in the diagram does not represent the expected duration of each activity.

Precedence Diagram Method

The **precedence diagram method** (PDM) is a method of constructing a network diagram using nodes (for example, boxes) to represent the activities and connecting them with arrows in order to show the dependencies (PMI Standards Committee, 2008). There are four possible types of logical or precedence relationships in which Activity A is the "from" activity and Activity B is the "to" activity:

- **Start-to-Start (STS).** Activity A must start before Activity B can start. Figure 1.14 shows that Activity B can start two days after Activity A starts.

- **Start-to-Finish (STF).** Activity A must start before Activity B can finish. Figure 1.14 shows that one day after Activity A starts, Activity B will need three days in order to finish.

- **Finish-to-Start (FTS).** Activity A must finish before Activity B can start. Figure 1.14 shows that Activity B can start as soon as Activity A finishes.

- **Finish-to-Finish (FTF).** Activity A must finish before Activity B can finish. Figure 1.14 shows that once Activity A finishes, Activity B needs four days in order to finish.

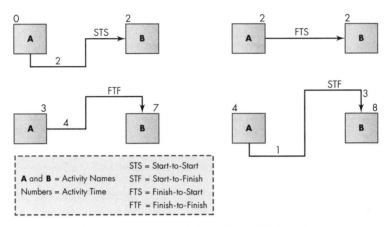

Figure 1.14 Example of a Precedence Relationship

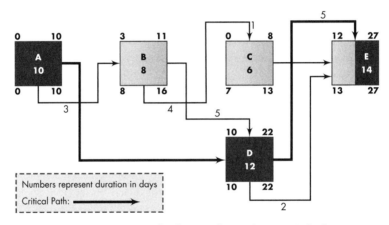

Figure 1.15 Example of a Precedence Diagram Method

As mentioned earlier, each activity in PDM is linked to others by several precedence relationships to show the dependency or activity sequence. For this reason, PDM is a method widely used by project management software packages. Figure 1.15 shows an example of a network diagram drawn using PDM, where each box (or node) represents a particular activity.

Management Map

A **management map** is a picture that combines in only one graphic several tools (for example, a WBS, a Gantt chart, and network diagrams), including important information needed for developing the evaluation plan. As shown in Figure 1.16,

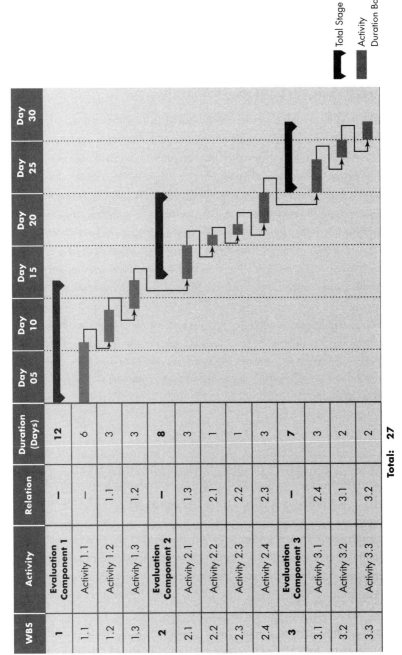

WBS	Activity	Relation	Duration (Days)	Day 05	Day 10	Day 15	Day 20	Day 25	Day 30
1	**Evaluation Component 1**	–	**12**						
1.1	Activity 1.1	–	6						
1.2	Activity 1.2	1.1	3						
1.3	Activity 1.3	1.2	3						
2	**Evaluation Component 2**	–	**8**						
2.1	Activity 2.1	1.3	3						
2.2	Activity 2.2	2.1	1						
2.3	Activity 2.3	2.2	1						
2.4	Activity 2.4	2.3	3						
3	**Evaluation Component 3**	–	**7**						
3.1	Activity 3.1	2.4	3						
3.2	Activity 3.2	3.1	2						
3.3	Activity 3.3	3.2	2						

Total: 27

Total Stage

Activity
Duration Bar

Figure 1.16 Example of a Management Map

Identify Critical Evaluation Activities

Evelyn: So you're still working with ABC Unlimited? I've worked with them before, and I find their staff and organizational culture fascinating. But sometimes their tendency to focus on minutia interfered with getting things done on time. Have you faced any of those challenges?

Ernest: As a matter of fact, yes, and very recently! This week we worked on identifying the critical evaluation activities for our collaborative evaluation. What really surprised me was how hard it is for them to make a decision and move on to the next steps of the evaluation process. While trying to determine the critical evaluation activities for a particular component, we ended up with a list of fifteen activities they all considered to be critical. I explained to them that *critical* referred to those few activities that do not have slack time so delays would mean not finishing the evaluation on time. I decided to use a diagram to help them prioritize. I listed each of the fifteen activities and worked with everyone to rank-order each activity from the most critical to the least critical. Then, together we identified the five most critical ones. They unanimously agreed to those five activities on the basis of their own ranking. Afterward, they said the diagram really helped them see the "big picture" and to understand how and why the team considered other activities to be important. I am glad to tell you that we did finally move on to our next task in that evaluation!

a management map provides an in-depth description of how the evaluation schedule needs to be followed. A management map may be formal or informal, highly detailed or broadly framed depending on the needs of the collaborative evaluation.

A management map is a supplemental element of the overall evaluation plan. This is because it is a tool to oversee the total collaborative evaluation, and it is needed to structure and control resources (such as people, money, or equipment). However, as in any evaluation effort, it must be open to adjustment in response to changing circumstances.

A good management map must specify at least the activities to be performed and the timeline for each evaluation component (for example, evaluation questions). Subsequently, you and the CMs can develop the evaluation plan in which you consider the resources needed to complete each activity. This plan becomes the basis to effectively manage not only the evaluation activities but also the resources to carry them out.

The time required to complete an activity depends on the resources assigned to it; if those resources are not available, then the evaluation cannot be completed as planned. Make sure that the fixed resources are going to be available when everyone needs them. Also, make sure that the schedule is realistic, achievable, and that everyone involved agrees on the same evaluation expectations.

There are several authors, among many others, who provide extensive information on project management. For more information, see Avison & Torkzadeh, 2009; Bell, 2010; Berkun, 2008; Crowe, 2006; Englund & Bucero, 2006; Fabac, 2006; Heldman, 2009; Kendrick, 2004; Kerzner, 2009a, 2009b; Kerzner & Saladis, 2009; Ladika, 2008; Lewis, 2010; MacMaster, 2000; Meredith & Mantel, 2011; Schmidt, 2009; Stackpole, 2009; Thomas, 2012; and Wysocki, 2011.

In this chapter, we emphasized the importance of identifying the situation that surrounds and sustains a collaborative evaluation. We focused on stakeholders early in the process in order to address their evaluation needs in a useful way. We also discussed how logic model elements and potential SWOTs help to formulate and implement evaluation strategies. In addition, we presented various aspects of the evaluation scope that included the evaluation questions and work breakdown structure. Furthermore, we provided guidance on how to identify critical evaluation activities and specific techniques for scheduling them. Finally, as in other chapters, we incorporated examples to reinforce interdependence among the MCE elements, such as clarifying the expectations throughout the collaborative evaluation, the topic discussed in Chapter 2.

Clarify
the Expectations

An **expectation** is the anticipation that good (or bad) may come out of the collaborative evaluation. It is the assumption, belief, or idea we have about the evaluation and the people involved. A clear expectation is very important because it influences all the decisions made during the evaluation. Perceiving the evaluation as a necessary effort has a strong impact on its likelihood to be used in the future.

Learn what the full range of responsibilities is and what cannot be delegated to other people so that the evaluation can maintain its appropriate direction, achieving what is proposed as part of the planned steps. To create a mutual understanding, you and the CMs need to clearly recognize who you are and what the implications are of the work you do. Also, clearly understand each other's responsibilities, rights, and distribution of power so that evaluation results can realistically be attained.

By clarifying the expectations, everyone understands which issues must be addressed and what the best ways are to achieve desired results. In other words, by clarifying the expectations there is less conflict within the evaluation (see Chapter 3 on how to establish means toward conflict resolution). Everyone operates efficiently at different levels of responsibility. In addition, there is higher productivity, greater satisfaction, and trust in the collaborative process because everyone knows what to anticipate.

To ensure collaboration, for example, you and the CMs need to make it a rule at the beginning of every meeting (or main evaluation task) to state and discuss its overall purpose, so it can be clearly understood by everyone. This is because the best way to improve meetings is to start by clarifying expectations. Also, apply effective techniques such as briefly listing the major topics of the meeting in order to be able to go back to those major points if the discussion goes in an unrelated direction. Explain the reasoning for those topics and ask if changes to the agenda are needed to make sure all relevant topics are covered.

This ensures that everyone knows what to expect from the meeting and how it connects to the evaluation vision.

Clarifying the expectations involves some level of negotiation or conferring with others to reach an agreement regarding the evaluation and its responsibilities. Obviously, this is ongoing because it occurs at many times and levels during the evaluation. In every stage, know exactly what the evaluation is about and how others can benefit from it. Everyone involved should understand what needs to be done and feel motivated toward its achievement. However, refuse to give away evaluation tasks that are best left to you while guiding the collaborative evaluation through an open communication (see Chapter 4 on how to ensure open communication).

A collaborative evaluation process will make sense if it is clear, timely, accurate, and relevant to everyone involved. As a result of clarifying the expectations, you and the CMs can fully understand the constraints and benefits of each evaluation choice made. Also, a control process can be followed to show whether evaluation activities are being carried out as planned. For this reason, the MCE component presented in this chapter is divided into the following subcomponents: (a) clarify the role of the evaluator, (b) clarify the role of the CMs, (c) clarify the evaluand criteria and standards, (d) clarify the evaluation process, and (e) clarify the evaluation budget (see Figure I.2).

CLARIFY THE ROLE OF THE EVALUATOR

The **evaluator** is the individual (such as you) who accepts responsibility for the overall evaluation and its results, employing defensible criteria to judge the evaluand value. The **role of the evaluator** is a description of the set of actions expected from the evaluator in terms of what needs to be done in the collaborative evaluation (for example, what you are there to do or what potential effects you have on the collaborative evaluation).

Prior to clarifying your role to the CMs and other key stakeholders, determine which type of role is best suited to the particular collaborative evaluation (Rodríguez-Campos & Rincones-Gómez, 2001, 2003). Obviously you should have good managerial and leadership skills in order to tailor the evaluation to its unique requirements. Different individuals have different perceptions regarding your specific role, and this affects performance. Clarify your role early in the collaborative evaluation because the CMs' differences in perception may potentially result in conflict (see Chapter 3 on how to establish means toward conflict resolution).

An evaluator is expected to possess various competencies (including technical, administrative, and interpersonal) that are important for the evaluation. Specifically, some of the competencies needed by evaluators would include the ability and sensitivity to work with a variety of stakeholders; research, planning, and management skills to carry out the evaluation in a timely, cost-effective fashion; ethical standards; and communication skills to convey results (Fitzpatrick, Sanders, & Worthen, 2011). Decide your best role as the evaluator through a multidisciplinary knowledge of the evaluation needs.

Recognize that the CMs form their personal opinions and expectations of your (and their own) role from the very beginning of the collaborative evaluation. After people decide what they think of another person, this conclusion is resistant to change, and they will bend new information to maintain their initial assumptions. Therefore, interact with others using a positive outlook and confidence (such as straight posture, direct eye-contact, and warm smile). People who are driven to achieve tend to be optimistic, even in the face of failure or setbacks (Goleman, 2004).

It is not necessary that the CMs like you, but it is essential that they respect you and the role you play within the collaborative evaluation. For instance, some research indicates that only 7 percent of the meaning in any conversation is contained in the words and the majority of information is communicated by a complicated mixture of appearance, gesture, gaze, and expression (Lewis, 1995).

An excellent way of making a good impression is being a good listener instead of being a gifted speaker and genuinely making others feel appreciated. Before clarifying your role to the CMs and other key stakeholders, understand the particular evaluation situation. For example, what actions on your part should be expected in the current evaluation situation to achieve specific evaluation goals? For this reason, we suggest the following steps to clarify your role as the evaluator:

1. Ask general questions to the CMs about their expectations of your role. For example, "I am interested in learning about your perceptions of what my role should be within the collaborative evaluation" produces abundant responses.

2. Listen to the expectations the CMs have of your role (for example, how they expect you to behave and their specific concerns). Always allow room for the CMs to provide their answers at their own pace without being judgmental.

3. List what you believe are the CMs' expectations of your role as the evaluator. This is a very important step that helps you prepare in advance a thorough and appealing message of what your role will be in the collaborative evaluation.

4. Present a summary of your qualifications (such as a biographical sketch) and how you can be a valuable asset to the collaborative evaluation. For example, explain your background, your ethical values, and how they link with the evaluation goals.

5. Inquire about the CMs' emotions (for example, their motivation regarding the evaluation) or how they feel about you and the collaborative evaluation. In this way, you can later address their concerns when you clarify your role as the evaluator.

6. Present your specific role as the evaluator, mentioning how it relates to the CMs' expectations and the evaluation scope. For example, clarify what you are there to do (and not to do) in order to ensure an effective working relationship.

7. Request feedback and distinguish real requests or concerns from personally beneficial opportunities. Remember that you are continuously tested for any vulnerable areas throughout the evaluation, so be confident of what you are doing.

8. Help the CMs look beyond their particular perspectives in order to reach an understanding of your role and its relationship to the evaluation. You might use a responsibility assignment matrix (RAM) to visually document your role and responsibilities.

9. Gather feedback on a regular basis using a previously agreed-upon system (for example, meetings, emails, and surveys as feasible). This will help you and the CMs monitor the suitability of your role as the evaluator and make updates as needed.

10. Provide each CM and other stakeholders as appropriate with a summary report of this experience (including a formal description of your evaluation role) as lessons learned for future similar situations within collaborative evaluations.

Your general role as the evaluator should be to attend to how things should get done and what each decision or task means to the collaborative evaluation and the CMs. By clarifying your role as the evaluator, you are also explaining what type of leader (and manager) you will be within the collaborative effort. Leadership couples emotional intelligence with the courage to raise the tough questions, challenge people's assumptions, and risk losing their goodwill (Heifetz, 2004).

Your role is multifaceted, and you are required to have strong conceptual, technical, communication, and interpersonal skills. Evaluators are trained to be skeptics, to raise insightful questions that otherwise may never have been considered (Fitzpatrick, Sanders, & Worthen, 2011). In addition, you should be the person responsible for fostering evaluation use. Always remember that evaluation is a good tool only if you have a good evaluator behind that tool.

Evaluator as a Leader Versus as a Manager

A **leader** is an individual (such as you) with the ability to encourage and influence a particular behavior in others to voluntarily attain a mutual goal. For instance, the best leaders are attuned to themselves and their relationships with others; they understand who they are as leaders and how they affect followers (Kelley, 1992).

The most favorable situation for leaders is when they have good leader-member relations, when they have a powerful position within the organization, and when they are directing a highly structured job (Fiedler, 1967; Rincones-Gómez & Rodríguez-Campos, 2003). In addition, evaluators are engaged because of the expertise they bring, and leadership for the evaluation resides with that expertise (O'Sullivan & D'Agostino, 2002). As an evaluation leader you need to positively influence the collaborative actions by establishing mutual objectives that will determine the direction of the evaluation.

A **manager** is an individual (such as you) in charge of establishing strategies; balancing demands; and making decisions through the planning, control, and direction of resources. Managers tend to adopt impersonal attitudes toward goals, help the process along by planning when controversial issues should surface, and reduce tensions (Zaleznik, 2004). Obviously, as a manager you are driven by a particular evaluation need instead of an individual aspiration.

A manager is responsible for ensuring that tasks are completed at a specific performance level, time, budget, and scope. The major responsibilities of a manager include the production of the end item with the available resources and within the potential constraints of time, cost, and performance (Kerzner,

2009a). As an evaluation manager you should be able to apply knowledge, tools, and skills for a sound evaluation.

To compare leaders with managers, leaders are active instead of reactive, shaping ideas instead of responding to those ideas (Zaleznik, 2004). While managers often involve other people in different ways when making decisions, leaders go beyond that and are able to create and communicate a vision that inspires followers (Owens & Valesky, 2010).

As the evaluator, perform the role of leader and manager in order to meet or, even better, exceed the evaluation expectations. As a leader, you have to help develop a shared vision while enabling everyone involved to overcome obstacles and satisfy their needs. Furthermore, as a manager, you are directly responsible for all the inner workings that must be attended to in order to produce the results expected by the evaluation.

Power of the Evaluator

As the evaluator, keep in mind that people can be lifted into their better selves, and this is the secret of transforming leadership (Burns, 2010). Hence, as both a leader and a manager you may use different types of power to foster an atmosphere in which everyone involved feels committed to a collaborative effort (looking beyond their own interests).

Power is the force or capacity you and the CMs have to affect others' behavior in the way in which you want and would otherwise not get. The power of leaders is voluntarily granted by followers because they are convinced that the leader can represent them well (Owens & Valesky, 2010). In addition, **authority** is a specific form of power that is officially recognized by others as the legitimate or formal way to exercise control (such as holding a specific position or administrative power).

According to several authors (for example, Gibson, Ivancevich, & Donnelly, 2008; Owens & Valesky, 2010), there are five interpersonal power bases:

- **Legitimate Power.** Also called formal power, this is the ability to gain support because of an individual's position. It is the authority conferred by holding a position in an organization recognized as having a legitimate right to obedience.

- **Reward Power.** This is the ability of an individual to control others' rewards, inducing others to comply with this individual's wishes (for example, regarding salary, promotion, bonuses, future work assignments, and other privileges).

- **Coercive Power.** Also called penalty power, this is the ability to (directly or indirectly) punish noncompliance, or control potentially punishing resources that will induce others to avoid them.

- **Expert Power.** This is the ability of an individual to gain support on the basis of special expertise or knowledge. Others want that expertise so much for themselves that they will be induced to comply in order to benefit from it.

- **Charismatic Power.** This is the ability of an individual to gain support because of personality or style of behavior (that is, personal charisma). This individual has ideas and beliefs so admired that others want to become more like him or her.

These five bases can be divided into two major categories: organizational and personal. Legitimate, reward, and coercive power are primarily prescribed by an organization, while expert and charismatic power are based on individual qualities (Gibson, Ivancevich, & Donnelly, 2008). Remember that although some of the CMs may not have legitimate power, they may exert power within the evaluation through other means (such as expertise, control of information, or persuasion).

The image of your role as the evaluator must be appropriate to both the situation and your desired goal for the evaluation. Make a cordial yet confident impression from the very beginning and take into consideration that people with little genuine status but an exaggerated sense of their own importance typically attempt to dominate others to bolster their egos (Lewis, 1995). If you fail to recognize this, you can expect your authority to be undermined early on in the collaborative evaluation.

You might perform multiple roles within the same collaborative evaluation, which may increase the complexity of your behavior. Also, be aware that your role may change from evaluation to evaluation depending on its particular needs. For this reason, try to understand the perceptions of the CMs in order to clarify those perceptions regarding your role. Once your evaluation role is clearly defined, the CMs will understand not only the scope of the evaluation but the evaluator as well.

The goals of a collaborative evaluation can be achieved when everyone feels motivated to work collectively. A successful evaluator is both a manager and a leader, and to get the best from others it is essential to set credible and positive examples yourself (see Chapter 5 on how to encourage teaching by example). Finally, because followers tend to model themselves after their leaders, the straightforward leader is less likely to have manipulative followers (Offermann, 2004).

Clarify the Role of the Evaluator

Eliot: Last time we talked, you mentioned you had a great story about clarifying the role of the evaluator. I think you said there was one CM blaming you for not having up-to-date notes from each meeting you have had. This was after an administrative assistant that had been helping with this task was dismissed from her job and so they ended up not having notes from several meetings. What happened?

Evelyn: It is so important to clarify the expectations from the very beginning, even in writing as feasible. Now, I always remind everyone what my role is from time to time as the evaluation continues. From the beginning, I always stated that I would facilitate most meetings, taking notes on flipcharts as needed, but that I must have some additional help from one of the staff members for capturing the details. They all agreed to that and made the administrative assistant the official scribe. But that person was recently dismissed from her job—and not taking notes was one of the many reasons she was let go. The last three weeks have been very intense; we have met at least three times per week. The former administrative assistant was supposed to send me her notes within forty-eight hours after each meeting, but that didn't happen, so we thought we had lost the details from all of those meetings. The good news is that this story has at least one happy ending. After every single meeting I facilitate, I always take pictures of every flipchart page I used. Thus I was able to go back to those pictures and reproduce the notes needed to document our progress and inform the next steps of the evaluation. Of course, this required some additional time and work on my part, but I am glad I was able to recapture all our work while the client continues searching for a new and reliable administrative assistant!

CLARIFY THE ROLE OF THE CMS

The **collaboration members**, or CMs, are specific stakeholders (possessing unique characteristics) who work jointly with the evaluator(s) to help with particular tasks in order to achieve the collaborative evaluation vision. The **role of the CMs** is a description of the set of actions expected from each of the CMs in terms of what needs to be done in the collaborative evaluation (for example, what each CM is there to do or what potential effects they have on the collaborative effort).

Everyone's roles should be clearly defined, without being overly restrictive, to avoid overlap with your role or other CMs' roles (see Figure 1.9). If CMs are unclear about their expected roles, there is a risk of having different perceptions of what those roles should be within the collaborative evaluation. The perceived role is the set of actions that a person believes he or she should enact, and the enacted role in contrast is the action that a person actually carries out (Gibson, Ivancevich, & Donnelly, 2008).

Each CM has a unique personality and style that needs to be acknowledged (see Chapter 5 on how to encourage appreciation for individual differences). Therefore, take time to study each individual and understand what they need from you—for example, the level of guidance they need throughout the collaborative effort. You may have to use a different leadership style to suit each of the CMs' needs.

From the CMs' perspectives, the collaborative evaluation may be something new and mysterious. CMs want to understand clearly how their contribution is going to be made, and even more important, how they can benefit from the collaboration. Those individual expectations should be built into the evaluation goals and remain visible throughout the effort so everyone feels motivated to do their best. An understanding of how the CMs' contributions affect the collaborative evaluation has a highly positive influence on performance.

Collaborative evaluations present many advantages, including access to information, quality of information gathered, creative problem solving, and receptivity of findings. However, keep in mind that the CMs (and you) bring their own experiences and views, which may affect the evaluation, and some could potentially bias findings in order to secure positive (or negative) evaluation results. To protect the credibility of the evaluation, care must be taken when determining what role everyone will play in the effort. However, CMs should use their own initiative without inappropriate or unnecessary interferences.

Prior to clarifying the role of each CM, define the activities involved in the collaborative evaluation and who would be willing (and accountable) to perform them. After carefully considering the qualities of all CMs, you and the CMs are then ready to formally establish specific evaluation roles, bearing in mind specific strengths and weaknesses. For example, what actions should be expected from each CM in the current situation to achieve the evaluation goals? As a result, we suggest the following steps to clarify the role of the CMs:

1. Ask each CM about their qualifications and expectations of the potential evaluation role they would play. For example, ask general questions so CMs are able to feel free to choose answers that reflect their priorities or major concerns.

2. Write down in detail what each of the CMs expects to do within the evaluation, before discussing any particular task. This is not the time to be judgmental; instead, this is the time to generate all the information possible about their expectations.

3. Identify each CM's needs within the collaborative evaluation to develop a methodical and logical view of how to meet each of them. This needs identification should use unbiased methods and strategies to provide accurate information.

4. Inquire about how you can address each CM's evaluation needs (carefully distinguish their real requests or concerns from personally motivated inquiries), and assist each CM to provide ideas for making improvements if feasible.

5. Discuss with each individual CM their qualifications (such as skills, background, or technical knowledge in a particular area) and why you believe they can be a valuable asset to the collaborative evaluation by performing a specific role.

6. Help each of the CMs look beyond individual expectations to reach an understanding of their role (including what needs to be done) and its relationship to the evaluation. For example, use a RAM for visual documentation.

7. Agree with each of the CMs on the role that best fits both their expectations and the evaluation goals, and make sure that they feel good about it. For example, allow the CMs to naturally settle into their roles without feeling pushed into them.

8. Sign with each CM (if needed) a document with the previously agreed-upon information to ensure a commitment to the collaborative evaluation. Among other things, the document may contain the CMs' roles, resources, and reporting responsibilities.

9. Gather feedback on a regular basis using a previously agreed-upon system (for example, meetings, emails, and surveys as feasible). This will help you and the CMs monitor the suitability of the role of each CM and make updates as needed.

10. Provide each CM and other stakeholders as appropriate with a summary report of each of their roles, and ensure they understand how each part relates to the evaluation and other CMs' roles (to avoid any confusion in the future).

Suit the evaluation tasks to each CM's interests, skills, and availability. Also, keep in mind that the CMs' roles should be clearly defined without being overly restrictive. Obviously, having a clear role increases the CMs' involvement because they are confident about what they are expected to do, and they are willing to commit to it. As a result, the quality of the collaborative evaluation is automatically increased.

Development of the CMs

The CMs have varied backgrounds and assimilate things through their respective views, which may lead to better ways of thinking than if individuals alone made decisions. They bring complementary characteristics to the collaborative evaluation. For example, the CMs have specific skills (perhaps technical or interpersonal) that combined with your own increase the productivity and evaluation value. Also, because they may know more about the evaluand than you do (such as the history of the evaluand, the background of other stakeholders, and where to find specific information), they can easily identify problems, opportunities, and decision alternatives.

The CMs should be made up of members who possess a blend of unique characteristics to perform the collaborative evaluation at hand and lead it forward. For this reason, it is critical that you choose the CMs on the basis of their potential for the evaluation and not only on personality. Also, you may provide training opportunities so the CMs can successfully perform their evaluation roles and responsibilities.

It is often challenging to match some CMs to the evaluation tasks suited for their particular skills. For this reason, you must carefully examine task content (for example, task description, objectives, and schedule), and preferred actions for the task. Many times the potential CMs want so much to be part of the evaluation that they may provide misleading information (for instance, regarding their level of expertise) in an attempt to please you.

Once you have defined the CMs' job responsibilities and scope, the CMs need to get started with the job in the way they know how and without unnecessary control. By intervening heavily, you may create resistance from the CMs, restricting their opportunity to gain experience or demonstrate their value. You may monitor the evaluation progress with a previously agreed-upon system of written reports or milestones and by observing performance (see Chapter 3 on how to establish decision-making procedures).

The CMs need to feel motivated to do their jobs the best way they can. They need to know at all times that your coaching is available when they want your feedback regarding particular issues. Also, they can make mistakes and discuss lessons learned with you in an open way instead of limiting access to this information. In general, groups proceed through four stages (Gibson, Ivancevich, & Donnelly, 2008):

- **Mutual Acceptance.** Members are reluctant to communicate with each other and are not willing to express opinions, attitudes, and beliefs. There tends to be little interaction until members accept and trust each other.

- **Communication and Decision Making.** Members begin to communicate openly with one another, resulting in increased confidence and even more interaction within the group (such as through problem-solving tasks or alternative strategies).

- **Motivation and Productivity.** Members expend effort to accomplish the group's goals working cooperatively rather than as an inter-competitive unit. As experience in working together increases, so does the effectiveness of the group's actions.

- **Control and Organization.** Members value group affiliation, and members are regulated by group norms, because group goals take precedence over individual goals. The ultimate sanction is isolation for not complying with the group goals.

The CMs are not equally committed at the beginning of the collaborative evaluation. As the evaluator, your goal is to move the CMs as quickly as feasible to the productivity stage, in which they can actively and collaboratively work on the evaluation. Keep in mind that relationships change over time, and the CMs need to feel comfortable with each other in order to work well together. You may also face the need to bring in outside individuals to refuel the evaluation and to ensure a diversity of viewpoints.

Sometimes evaluations may last a long time, and the CMs may stop looking for new challenges or improved ways of doing things. Encourage innovation through everyone's sense of ownership in their evaluation tasks and methods of operation. The CMs have to be involved in evaluation decisions related to their tasks. Failure to involve them can drastically reduce the potential for the CMs to use the information yielded by the collaborative evaluation.

Individuals must be permitted to know that their role is subject to development, which is limited only by their contributions (Prentice, 2004). This leads to a high level of involvement, which is the key to the collaborative evaluation because it recognizes that no one person has the full range of knowledge needed for the evaluation. Always remember that when the CMs feel their work and contributions are valuable, their commitment to the evaluation increases.

Contribution of the CMs

When you collaborate with and delegate specific evaluation tasks to the CMs, you then have time to successfully complete other tasks that you are not able to delegate and must do yourself. Be sure that the CMs are going to contribute to their assigned roles voluntarily because they consider them important and pleasant. They need to feel empowered in order to commit toward a successful collaborative evaluation (see Chapter 6 on how to follow the collaboration guiding principles).

People feel empowered when they (a) believe they have the ability to exert control over forces that affect their lives; (b) have the knowledge, skills, and resources to do so; and (c) are actually involved in making decisions and taking actions (Zimmerman, 1995). By feeling empowered, the CMs gain control over the evaluation efforts and feel ownership over its results and subsequent recommendations for evaluand improvement.

Although empowerment continues to be an attractive way to operate, there are a number of reasons why it is not universally embraced: (a) managers fear the loss of power, control, and authority; (b) employees are not able to make responsible decisions; (c) empowering employees was attempted before and it failed; and (d) sharing proprietary information means leaking ideas, plans, and knowledge to competitors (Ivancevich, Konopaske, & Matteson, 2010).

Throughout the collaborative evaluation, consider that working in one-to-one relationships takes a great deal of tolerance for emotional interchange (Zaleznik, 2004). For this reason, it is your responsibility to delegate evaluation tasks (and authority over them) to the right CMs and to foster a collaborative environment in which everyone can contribute appropriately. In other words, ensure that the CMs feel empowered to exceed the evaluation expectations.

When you delegate the responsibility of an evaluation task you are also delegating the CMs' right to decide on that task and be accountable for its results. Openly encourage the CMs to provide ideas and use their own initiative at various stages of the collaborative evaluation (as needed), as an important

Clarify the Role of the CMs

Eliot: I am so glad we have a chance to talk about your evaluation report. I am intrigued by the Task Based Role (TBR) concept you use with the CMs and I wonder if it isn't too prescriptive for a collaborative evaluation. I have two questions: Why did you suggest this approach? and Has it been effective?

Ernest: Interestingly enough, this particular group of CMs indicated early on that they would appreciate as much clarity as possible, and even a great degree of prescriptiveness, for their roles. They have all been working together for many years, and this approach has proven to be highly effective for them. Most of the CMs have an engineering background, so they like things to be as specific as possible! That way they can focus their energy on individual and group responsibilities. We developed a matrix together that lists the type of activities each person needed to complete and our expectations for that activity. This group is indeed very different than previous ones, but this methodology has been very effective. I am happy with the results; the execution of this evaluation has always been on time and is showing quality results. Another benefit is that CMs have developed a sense of ownership of the evaluation and responsibility for its success.

motivational boost. For example, foster a collaboration spirit so that the CMs can think of answers to particular problems and openly share them with you, instead of just bringing the problem.

Keep in mind that evaluation performance feedback is very important. It enhances clarity in the evaluation, allows learning opportunities through a proactive interchange of ideas, and provides assurance that the evaluation can be accomplished because ambiguity is avoided. Hence, you actively seek the input of those involved in the evaluation and constantly remind them of the importance of their collaboration.

With the CMs' commitment you will be able to collaboratively achieve the evaluation objectives. The consequences of lack of involvement are low commitment to the job, incorrect work estimates (time, cost, and other factors), omissions of work, and other errors (Lewis, 1999). Treat the collaborative evaluation as a partnership in which the CMs continuously have sufficient information to study the implications of their contributions and act on them.

Your own expectations, as well as the expectations of the CMs, are a major influence on the success or failure of the collaborative evaluation. Understand the perceptions, hopes, and fears of everyone involved in the collaborative effort and how those contribute to its success. Also, make sure that those expectations are realistic and that they are in balance between the individual and evaluation needs.

CLARIFY THE EVALUAND CRITERIA AND STANDARDS

Criteria are points of reference used for judging the value (such as merit or worth) of the evaluand. They need to be measurable, useful, and easily understood by the intended audience. Criteria provide an objective way to determine if your intervention is working (Weiss, 2009). Criteria are used to delineate the characteristics of an implementation (for example, an evaluand) and are sometimes implicit in the evaluation questions (Fitzpatrick, Sanders, & Worthen, 2011). Their associated cost should be adequate in relation to the type of information to be obtained within the collaborative evaluation. Examples of criteria that could be personalized for your evaluation include the following:

- **Effectiveness.** This is a relationship of impact. This measurement is marked by the capacity of exerting positive influence on what an individual perceives regarding the evaluand, such as satisfaction with the evaluand or loyalty to a particular unit. For example, the individual resultant perception (real impact) is contrasted with the expectations (programmed impact) established at the beginning of the process.

- **Efficacy.** This is a relationship of achievement or capacity of producing an intended result (such as meeting a target). You can say that the evaluand has a high efficacy when it achieves what is proposed, such as products, outcomes, or policies. For example, the resultant achievement (real goal) is contrasted with the expectations (programmed goal) established at the beginning of the process.

- **Efficiency.** This is a relationship of costs. In other words, it is the capacity to accomplish a job with a minimum expenditure of assigned resources (including money, time, and materials). For example, the resultant cost (real cost) is contrasted with the expectations (programmed cost) established at the beginning of the process.

Standards are commonly agreed-upon guidelines that provide information to distinguish how well the evaluand is doing or performing on specific criteria. For example, a specific level of performance (say, 90 percent minimum) that the evaluand is expected to achieve on the criteria to be considered a success. Standards establish how the evaluation results are going to be interpreted within the collaborative evaluation.

These evaluand standards may be absolute (for example, numbers or proportions) or they may be relative (better or worse than) to a comparison evaluand. A cutting score defines a standard, but standards can also be given in qualitative contexts, such as requiring a B average in graduate school or providing exemplars, as in global grading of compositions (Scriven, 1991).

As an example, Table 2.1 shows that for a specific criterion (such as effectiveness), the acceptable response would be when results fall at least within the "medium level" (at the 20 percent scale and above). In other words, the key stakeholders, including the CMs if appropriate, agreed at the beginning of the evaluation that the results should be at least 20 percent in order to say that a specific criterion for judging the evaluand indicated that expectations are being met. Obviously, the content of the table will vary for each collaborative evaluation (for example, its scale) to conform to the evaluand's particular needs.

Table 2.1 Example of Standards for Judging the Evaluand

Performance Level	Description	Scale
Very High Level	The criterion (e.g., effectiveness) for judging the evaluand indicates that expectations are being highly exceeded.	Values: 75% and up
High Level	The criterion (e.g., effectiveness) for judging the evaluand indicates that expectations are being exceeded.	Values: 50% to 74%
Medium Level	The criterion (e.g., effectiveness) for judging the evaluand indicates that expectations are being met.	Values: 20% to 49%
Low Level	The criterion (e.g., effectiveness) for judging the evaluand indicates that some improvement is needed.	Values: 6% to 19%
Very Low Level	The criterion (e.g., effectiveness) for judging the evaluand indicates that immediate improvement is needed.	Values: 0% to 5%

The criteria and standards used within the collaborative evaluation have to be agreed upon during meetings and be specific to each evaluation question. Experts can assist evaluators in setting standards and in confirming the significance of the findings (Fink, 2005). Prior to the collection and analysis of evaluation information, we suggest the following steps to clarify the evaluand criteria and standards:

1. Provide copies of the evaluation questions to the CMs and other stakeholders at the beginning of the meeting. This keeps the focus on the evaluation questions and allows new relevant ideas to be associated with them.

2. Present the proposed evaluand criteria for each of the evaluation questions and ask for feedback. For example, criteria may be implicit in the evaluation question wording or they may need to be elicited from participants.

3. Present the proposed evaluand standards and ensure they are clearly understood (they have the same meaning for everyone) and fit particular evaluand requirements. This is done to avoid misunderstandings when later reporting the evaluation results.

4. Receive feedback about each proposed criterion and consequent standards. For example, is each criterion relevant? Which results for a specific criterion would be acceptable in this collaborative evaluation? Is there prior information?

5. Look for areas of potential conflict (for example, disagreements on specific levels of performance) that could jeopardize the success of the meeting in order to immediately solve them and maximize the benefit of the collaborative evaluation.

6. Agree on specific changes of the evaluand criteria and standards (before evaluation data are collected) to reflect the evaluation vision. For example, what changes will be considered as positive (or not) within this evaluation effort?

7. Ensure that all the needed criteria and standards have been included (by taking a holistic view), and that they are unbiased. Otherwise, a dishonest stakeholder could later wrongfully claim that the evaluation results are exactly as expected.

8. Present the evaluand standards to be used for each criterion based on the prior feedback received. For example, standards may be absolute (numbers or scales), or they may be relative (better or worse than) to a comparison evaluand.

9. Gather feedback on a regular basis using a previously agreed-upon system (for example, meetings, emails, and surveys as feasible). This will help you and the CMs monitor the evaluand criteria and standards and make updates as needed.

10. Provide each CM and other stakeholders as appropriate with a summary report of this experience (including an updated version of the evaluand criteria and standards report) as lessons learned for future similar situations within collaborative evaluations.

Almost all judgments about failure are subjective, because they are based on personal perception, circumstances, and expectations (Lewis, 1999). Thus agreed-upon criteria and standards for judging the evaluand are even more difficult to establish when multiple stakeholders are involved in the collaborative evaluation. If you and the CMs clarify these expectations (for instance, clarify what will constitute success or failure) early in the process, then the evaluation results will be easily understood (for example, without implying that a negative evaluation result should be considered as a positive one or vice versa). The function of evaluation is to be able to distinguish between failure and success (Alkin, 2004).

You and the CMs have to carefully attend to the perceptions (including hopes, fears, and questions) of the key stakeholders toward the criteria and standards needed in the collaborative evaluation. Many times stakeholders have preconceived notions of the evaluation results. By documenting the criteria and standards as part of the collaborative evaluation process, you and the CMs feel encouraged to think very specifically about how you will interpret and demonstrate to others the evaluation results.

If a stakeholder, for example, demands excessive control over the selection of particular evaluand criteria or standards, then it must be determined whether this individual is being biased toward particular evaluation results (see Chapter 6 on how to follow specific guidelines). Also, request multiple opinions to avoid having advocates set standards too low or opponents set them too high (for instance, to guarantee evaluand success or failure).

Clarify the Evaluand Criteria and Standards

Eliot: As I begin working on this new collaborative evaluation, and with my limited experience, I am a bit concerned about clarifying the importance of setting realistic evaluand standards. Obviously, the key stakeholders want to show that the program is successful, but at the same time, the evaluand standards need to be carefully set. For example, we could take into account other similar program standards. Some stakeholders have suggested that if we set stringent standards and meet them, the program could be showcased nationally as exemplar. I am a bit worried about the possibility of not establishing realistic standards and then failing on our endeavor. Do you have any advice?

Ernest: You have touched on one issue I always advise my clients to review; that is, looking for comparative data to set realistic program standards. Something else you should keep in mind is the evaluand criteria you will be using during the evaluation. Another point to consider is that these standards should help to determine how well the program is performing on specific criteria. In addition, you should start thinking about different levels of performance, perhaps four or five. Consider previous program results and an ideal one that will show a noticeable level of performance. In any case, it is also important to explain that information and practical experience from everyone involved will help inform the overall decision about the specific evaluand standards.

CLARIFY THE EVALUATION PROCESS

The **evaluation process** is a structured set of activities (with a clear beginning and end) designed to generate an evaluation product, such as an evaluation report for a specific client. It implies a strong emphasis on how the evaluation is done within a unique situation. The evaluation process can be deconstructed into several subprocesses or phases including planning, executing, and reporting.

Clarify the Evaluation Planning

Evaluation planning is the phase when an evaluation plan is developed in order to establish standard procedures for achieving a shared vision. Planning may be described as generating a predetermined course of action within a forecasted environment (Kerzner, 2009b). Planning involves identifying, documenting, and assigning roles, responsibilities, and reporting relationships (PMI Standards Committee, 2008).

An **evaluation plan** is an arrangement of the flow of work that shows in advance what will happen throughout the implementation of the collaborative evaluation. An evaluation plan helps to monitor progress and provide ongoing feedback throughout the evaluation in order to review and update strategies as needed. However, keep in mind that a change in one part of the plan may generate (usually unintended) changes in the evaluation scope.

An evaluation plan should serve as a cookbook for clarifying several questions regarding the evaluation steps that need to be accomplished (what, who, when, where, and how). A detailed, step-by-step plan is essential for an effective collaborative evaluation. There are several reasons for planning: (a) to eliminate or reduce uncertainty, (b) to improve efficiency of the operation, (c) to obtain a better understanding of the objectives, and (d) to provide a basis for monitoring and controlling work (Kerzner, 2009b).

An evaluation plan helps to facilitate a common understanding and agreement of what is going to be accomplished in the collaborative evaluation. Any modification to the original plan should be immediately communicated to all the appropriate parties. The following is an example of sections identified in an evaluation plan. You and the CMs can modify them to fit specific needs.

1. Introduction (for example, evaluation context and audiences).

2. Evaluation procedures (for example, evaluation questions, evaluation approaches, and data collection methods).

3. Timeline (for example, schedule of evaluation activities).

4. Deliverables (for example, description of the final report content and dissemination).

5. Appendix (for example, evaluators' biographical sketches).

A plan can help establish a level of control because it shows what milestones the evaluation is supposed to achieve at a particular time. You and the CMs need to approach an evaluation plan without preconceived notions of the shape the evaluation should take. As appropriate, use multiple and complementary options to address a given evaluation question. Also, keep in mind that an evaluation plan can only be developed after the situation surrounding the evaluation has been identified, so it can be clear and applicable to all those involved.

Clarify the Evaluation Execution

Evaluation execution is the phase when the activities of an evaluation plan are implemented. It results in the completion of an evaluation that will meet the specific deliverable requirements of the client. Once the evaluation moves into this phase, all necessary resources should be in place and ready to perform the evaluation activities.

There needs to be an appropriate methodology implemented for each of the evaluation questions. This helps you to understand how the evaluation is compatible with the needs of the evaluand. If changes are made at the beginning of this phase, rather than later on in the collaborative evaluation, you and the CMs can easily adjust the schedule for each of the evaluation activities (see Chapter 4 on how to ensure the need for change is justified).

You and the CMs have to clarify, among others, how you are implementing the collection and analysis of the evaluation data. **Data collection and analysis** is the systematic compilation and examination of information from which evaluation conclusions may be drawn. One of the greatest challenges for the evaluation is the correct application of quantitative or qualitative methods of data collection and analysis.

According to several authors (for example, Creswell, 2009; McMillan, 2012; Yin, 2011), **qualitative methods** use rich descriptions, inductive logic, and flexible designs to collect and analyze information with minimal concern for quantities. **Quantitative methods** emphasize numbers, measurements, deductive logic, and control to collect and analyze information with a focus on establishing quantities.

The data-collection and analysis strategies implemented are fundamental to the evaluation, because if the client does not find them to be credible, the usefulness of the evaluation is jeopardized. For example, for each of the evaluation questions you may want to implement specific procedures for collecting and analyzing information (including qualitative, quantitative, or mixed-method design) following with specific dates in the plan.

You and the CMs implement the data collection and analysis once you have identified the data sources that will meet the evaluation requirements. For example, you and the CMs may use **triangulation**, which is the corroboration of data by comparing the results collected from different methods or sources. Besides seeking confirmation and consistency with other sources of information, consider any potential restrictions (for example, confidentiality versus anonymity) and approvals prior to data collection.

The right person (such as you) should collect and analyze the data at the right time and with the right conditions. Sufficient information should be collected whether it already exists or if additional data are needed. You and the CMs may ask key stakeholders to suggest where specific information can be best obtained. This is a way to further enhance the shared ownership that stakeholders have on the collaborative evaluation.

There are several authors who provide extensive information on quantitative, qualitative, and mixed methods. For more information, see for example Best & Kahn, 2005; Boeije, 2010; Creswell & Plano Clark, 2011; Denzin & Lincoln, 2005; Guba & Lincoln, 1992; King, Rosopa, & Minium, 2011; Krueger & Casey, 2008; McMillan, 2012; Morgan, Reichert, & Harrison, 2002; Patton, 2008; Shadish, 1995; Stake, 1980; Tashakkori & Teddlie, 2010; Thomas, 2003.

Clarify the Evaluation Reporting

Evaluation reporting is the phase when data are extracted from one or more sources and converted into an evaluation report format. An **evaluation report** is a document or presentation that provides useful evaluation information in a formal and specialized way. A report can be written, oral, or both and presented to a small or large audience with the specific intention of relaying evaluation information. In general, the findings of the evaluation are presented as aggregates, so that individuals may feel free to share sensitive information.

Depending on the evaluation needs, you and the CMs may plan to provide periodic reports or just one final report. For example, for each of the evaluation questions you may want to determine who will be the audience for the report (people who will receive the results of the evaluation); the format (for instance, written report or oral presentation); and the specific dates for it.

We always try to use a combination of oral and written reports because they have led to a greater understanding and appreciation of the evaluation. Obviously, this increases the balance, credibility, and usefulness of the evaluation findings. The following is an example of sections identified in a final evaluation report. You and the CMs can modify them to fit specific needs.

1. Executive summary (for example, brief information about the evaluation report)

2. Introduction (for example, evaluation purpose and audiences)

3. Overview of the evaluation procedures (for example, evaluation questions and evaluation approaches)

4. Evaluation results (for example, summary and interpretation of findings)

5. Conclusions (for example, evaluand value judgment based on specific criteria)

6. Recommendations (future steps as applicable)

7. Minority reports or rejoinders (if any)

8. Appendices (for example, instruments and transcripts)

Written Report

Results presented in the evaluation report should be clear to your particular audience (in terms of language, level of sophistication, and grammar). Also, results should follow the previously agreed-upon evaluand criteria and standards. Thus when it is time to read the results, the audience already knows the meaning and implications of the results presented in the evaluation report. Different types of perspectives or interpretations need to be considered in the evaluation report in order to avoid bias.

It has been our experience that audiences who received evaluation information only in a written report are less likely to agree with the evaluation results and recommendations than those who also received the information in another form (such as a multimedia presentation). The evaluation has to report accurate information that provides a basis for decision making and other purposes (such as accountability). Hence, you and the CMs should be clear and avoid trying to impress readers with a complex report that only you can fully understand.

The appearance of the evaluation report is of extreme importance. Provide the best possible type of report in terms of print quality and appealing colors for the graphics and cover. In other words, convince the readers that the information contained in the report is worth reading. For this reason, involve the key stakeholders throughout the evaluation (for instance, provide drafts), so you can understand their true needs and decide how to address them.

Oral Report

An oral presentation of the evaluation report allows you and the CMs to address varying interpretations of the findings. People interpret information in different ways, regardless of how the information is presented, due to their individual differences. By sharing the evaluation results with the audience, you can ask for their interpretations and clarify the meaning of those results (see Chapter 5 on how to encourage appreciation for individual differences).

Through the years, many people have asked us for some key pointers on how to be relaxed during the presentation. In general, we tell them that we like to know our specific audience's background and needs in order to prepare the most appropriate presentation for them. We also think of possible hard questions that a difficult audience might ask, and plan how we would answer those questions ahead of time. Moreover, we prepare for potentially embarrassing or time-wasting situations, such as equipment failures, and generate a backup plan. Furthermore, we build our confidence by practicing and timing our presentation to be sure that it is done within the specified timeframe.

Probably the most important thing we do to relax is to visualize the success of the presentation and its end result. Instead of focusing on what others may think of you, focus on the information you want to present (for example, how interesting it is and how the audience is going to benefit from it). Finally, make your presentations as powerful and as persuasive as possible, no matter who your audience is, what type of presentation you make, and where you make it (Weissman, 2009).

In this section, we focused on clarifying the different phases of the evaluation process including the evaluation planning, executing, and reporting. Accordingly, we suggest the following steps to clarify the overall evaluation process:

1. Provide copies of the preliminary evaluation plan (what needs to be done) to each of the CMs prior to the meeting. In this way, everyone can read it in advance and suggest new ideas to be shared later with other relevant stakeholders.

2. Hang posters on the wall with information about the evaluation scope, and the criteria and standards for judging the evaluand. By doing this, you and the CMs can refer back and avoid short-term goals taking over the collaborative evaluation.

3. Review the overall evaluation plan step-by-step and how each important portion was chosen. This includes the evaluation questions, resources (such as people or equipment), activities (for example, data collection), and schedule.

4. Describe in detail the communication needs of everyone involved (including who has to provide what information and when they should complete each task) and how they are linked to their overall evaluation roles and responsibilities.

5. Discuss which specific SWOTs are most likely to influence the evaluation process and how they are going to be monitored. This can provide a means for early identification and clarification throughout the collaborative evaluation effort.

6. Request feedback to adjust the evaluation as necessary (for instance, if a CM finds a particular inconsistency), while ensuring that each of the suggestions provided are specific, relevant, and achievable within time and budget constraints.

7. Elicit other key stakeholders' feedback on the viability of the overall evaluation process in order to make adjustments in light of the feedback received. This step is fundamental for stakeholders to later use the collaborative evaluation results.

8. Address concerns and comments to everyone's satisfaction before the end of this clarification period (such as when a particular resource will be available). Remember that unresolved issues will have a negative effect on the evaluation sooner or later.

9. Ensure that the CMs and key stakeholders have accepted the evaluation (for example, by having them sign a contract or formal agreement) with the understanding that it may be updated in the future if an important or unforeseen need arises.

10. Gather feedback on a regular basis using a previously agreed-upon system, such as meetings, and summarize it in a written format (including actions implemented and the reasons for them) so it is available to each CM and the other stakeholders as appropriate.

There are several reasons why an evaluation fails, such as (a) goals lack clarity so people work under different assumptions, (b) plans are based on insufficient data, and (c) execution is not conducted by the planning group. Every step in the evaluation has to be clear and consistent so you and the CMs can achieve what was intended to be accomplished. Obviously, it is your responsibility to involve the CMs so they can feel part of the collaborative evaluation. In addition, make sure it is clearly understood that the evaluation process is rarely sequential, because changes may occur throughout the collaborative effort.

Clarify the Evaluation Process

Evelyn: I need to tell you about my new evaluation; this is the first time someone has evaluated their program, and they are showing clear symptoms of what I call the Santa's messenger syndrome. Let me explain. As I met for the first time with my client and the CMs for this evaluation, there was obviously a high level of commitment, excitement, and collaboration among the group. But once I started facilitating the session about clarifying the methods of data collection, there were three CMs, including the client, with a list of data-collection "wishes" they wanted this evaluation to address. I felt like being one of Santa's messengers! One person even joked about these being Christmas wishes, interestingly enough. Have you faced a similar issue before?

Ernest: Yes, I have, and it is not that unusual. Perhaps they have a different name for it, but most people have their own ideas and expectations about what the evaluation should and shouldn't accomplish. However, I am sure you have also experienced that things will radically change once you show them the kind of activities and resources (particularly money) that will be needed should they decide to move forward with their proposed methods of data collection. Going over all those wish lists could be a great exercise to educate everyone involved about the level of complexity in evaluation work. Please let me know how it goes; there is always something new to learn from each collaborative evaluation project.

CLARIFY THE EVALUATION BUDGET

The **evaluation budget** is an estimate of expenditures for the collaborative evaluation over a given period of time. It is a statement of financial or monetary plans for the evaluation activities. A budget must be reasonable, attainable, and based on contractually negotiated costs and the statement of work (Kerzner, 2009b).

An evaluation depends on the necessary monetary provision, as it has a cost (for example, during data collection). The evaluation client should actively collaborate in the generation of the evaluation budget, as feasible, instead of just setting the budgetary limits or receiving your proposal. In this way, the client feels a greater ownership on the evaluation because you have worked together negotiating a budget in which the resultant fee structure is the product of your joint efforts.

Although the evaluation budget is often considered private information, show the CMs at least those figures that reflect the performance of their part of the evaluation. In this way, the CMs can understand the financial implications of their actions. Also, you may need to clarify other partial pieces of the budget with key CMs so they know the amount of resources available for related tasks and how they are going to be distributed throughout the evaluation. This will allow a mutual understanding of the critical budget areas or constraints and facilitate creative solutions within the collaborative effort.

Value-based billing (not a per diem or per head fee) is the best method for your client's investment and return (Weiss, 2009); hence you may work on a value-based fee, if it is demonstrated that this arrangement is in the client's best interest. Also, when the amount of money available is not clear, you can propose evaluation alternatives that differ in scope and cost so the client can select the appropriate ones after considering the consequences of each alternative. This is because the budgetary process is a mechanism for integrating several interests into the regularities of the political process (see, for example, Bastoe, 1999; Gray, Jenkins, & Segsworth, 2001).

The evaluation client may like the best evaluation option you can offer, but may consider that the proposed budget is too high. Hence, there are some cost-saving measures you might consider: (a) use available volunteers and local specialists; (b) reduce the scope of the evaluation, perhaps deferring some parts for later; (c) use existing instruments, data, or reports; (d) use inexpensive data collection when precision can be sacrificed without severe consequences; and (e) use public media to disseminate results (Fitzpatrick, Sanders, & Worthen, 2011).

It is a difficult task to clarify the evaluation budget. To generate a basic evaluation budget, understand in quantitative terms the cost of each of the resources needed to complete the collaborative evaluation. In this way, you can produce a more accurate budget that provides the basis for better decisions. For example, you may allocate the overall cost estimates to individual evaluation items as a base for better calculating the overall evaluation cost later. In general, it is useful to break down costs into the following categories:

- **Direct Cost.** The direct cost is equivalent to the evaluation expenses and may include the sum of resources such as (a) the evaluators, the CMs, and other staff salaries (for privacy purposes you may choose to share this information only with your client and key parties); (b) travel expenses (including airfare, ground transportation, and car mileage); (c) facilities and equipment (including property assets, environment requirements, and computers); (d) communications (including mail, telephone, and an Internet monthly bill); (e) services (including computer data entry, data analysis, printing, and copying); and (f) others (including lodging, meals, and training support).

- **Indirect Cost.** The indirect cost is sometimes known as shared cost, overhead, or general and administrative cost. It is generally a prescribed percentage of the direct cost. For example: Indirect Cost = Direct Cost $\times$ 25 percent.

- **Total Cost.** The total or actual cost is the sum of the direct cost and the indirect cost. In other words: Total Cost = Total Direct Cost + Total Indirect Cost.

The evaluation budget may differ radically among collaborative evaluations depending on the amount of information desired and the allocated resources. Specifically, budgets can be very complicated because they depend on particular evaluation circumstances (for example, personnel expertise, travel cost, and long-distance communication) and on the evaluation scope. Also, unexpected additional evaluation work can modify the evaluation budget. You and the CMs have to carefully identify the contingencies that potentially may occur during the collaborative evaluation, causing unplanned expenditures.

Be aware of several estimating pitfalls, including (a) misinterpretation of the plan, (b) improperly defined scope and schedule, (c) application of improper skill levels to tasks, (d) failure to account for risks (such as lack of qualified resources or lack of management support), (e) failure to account for cost escalation and inflation, and (f) failure to use the correct estimating technique (Kerzner, 2009b). You and the CMs, as feasible, can develop a reasonable and attainable budget statement by revising the timelines and other tools presented in the previous chapter.

Several authors (for example, Heldman, 2009; PMI Standards Committee, 2008) identified specific tools and techniques of cost estimating, such as the following:

- **Analogous Estimating.** This is a form of expert judgment (top-down estimating technique) that uses the actual cost of a previous, similar project as the basis for current estimation. It is frequently used when there is limited information about the project (such as in the early phases) and is generally less accurate than other cost estimations.

- **Parametric Modeling.** This involves using project characteristics (parameters) in a mathematical model to predict project costs. These estimates are most likely to be reliable when (a) the historical information is accurate, (b) the parameters are readily quantifiable, and (c) the model is scalable.

- **Bottom-Up Estimating.** This involves estimating the cost of individual items, then summarizing or rolling-up the individual estimates to get a project total. The cost and accuracy of bottom-up estimating is driven by the item size (smaller items increase both cost and accuracy).

- **Computerized Tools.** This includes tools such as project management software and spreadsheets that are widely used to assist with cost estimating. These computerized tools can simplify and thereby facilitate rapid consideration of many costing alternatives.

Budgets are essential for the planning and control of the evaluation, because they provide benchmarks to monitor performance against the plan (see Chapter 5 on how to encourage benchmarking). You and the CMs can coordinate the activities of the various parts of the evaluation to ensure that they are consistent with monetary resources allocated and make adjustments if needed. The more realistic the evaluation budget, the fewer problems you will have in the evaluation. We suggest the following steps to clarify the evaluation budget:

1. Provide a general (or specific, as appropriate) copy of the preliminary evaluation budget to key stakeholders (for example, client, CMs, board members, and funders) that accurately reflects the needs of the collaborative evaluation.

2. Explain each general item within the evaluation budget to avoid major revisions later. For instance, include the information used to develop the budget (such as bottom-up estimating) and the provisions made to mitigate risks (such as inflation).

3. Justify the specific figures within the evaluation budget to individual parties (for example, the client, each of the CMs, and other relevant

stakeholders) depending on how those figures are associated with their contribution to the collaborative evaluation.

4. Test the validity of each of the budget figures by requesting individualized feedback (make sure decimal points and commas are accurate, among other things), while ensuring that all the comments are clearly documented and reflect the evaluation scope.

5. Request feedback on the feasibility (including future costs that may occur) of the evaluation budget in terms of offering a realistic amount (neither too high nor too low) that is based on the resources available during the collaborative effort.

6. Agree on amendments to the budget, as appropriate, to make sure that all the figures are accurate. For example, ask colleagues with relevant expertise in the area to prioritize which specific changes in the evaluation budget are necessary.

7. Provide a general (or specific, as appropriate) copy of the updated evaluation budget for approval. In this way, the client, and others as needed, will revise and approve the final budget after clarifying any foreseeable problems.

8. Allow sufficient time for proper revisions of the evaluation budget to make new updates as required. For example, updates in the budget may need to serve constantly changing or unexpected evaluation needs (such as budget cuts).

9. Gather feedback on a regular basis using a previously agreed-upon system (for example, evaluation performance versus budget feasibility). This will help you and the CMs monitor the evaluation budget and make any changes as needed.

10. Provide each CM and other stakeholders as appropriate with a summary report of this evaluation budget experience (including actions implemented and the reasons for them) as lessons learned for future similar situations within collaborative evaluations.

Budgets provide a logical framework of the financial evaluation responsibilities that enhances effective communication. There are no rules about how to design the best possible budget layout, because each of them is suited for specific needs. You and the CMs should establish early on how the evaluation budget layout is going to look. For example, in order to satisfy the evaluation client's needs you may ask about their standard way of doing budgets and try to follow it, or learn from others who have done budgets for this client in the past.

Budgets require careful attention because they are a key part of the collaborative evaluation. Involve all the key stakeholders (at different levels of depth as needed) in the budgeting process to ensure an accurate expenditure forecast and reduce the risk of you and the CMs needing extra funds later in the evaluation. For example, consult with every appropriate stakeholder about the amount of resources needed and when they are needed.

Clarify the Evaluation Budget

Eliot: I have always admired you as a professional and am very impressed with your successful evaluation career. One of the many things I continue to see is that, I always learn something new with every evaluation. It reminds me of a comment you made about how you almost lost one very significant and important evaluation opportunity. How did that turn out?

Evelyn: Ah, yes. I remember that one well. Since my very first meeting with my client, we had agreed on a budget figure for the requested collaborative evaluation. I had produced a detailed budget based on the amount we originally agreed on. At the same time, my client was having conversations with her board of directors about potential budget cuts, but assured me that nothing would happen with the amount she had secured for the evaluation. However, the board approved a significant budget reduction for the overall operation of the organization, including the evaluation budget. In the meantime, I had been approached by a different client and was invited to submit a proposal for a major evaluation. I told this potential client that I was flattered by his invitation, but I was already committed full-time for the next ten months to another evaluation. So, I declined the invitation. At this point, I wasn't even aware of the budget cuts that had happened at the organization. She had forgotten to share that news with me! When she finally talked with me, I just couldn't believe it. As soon as I finished that conversation, I called the other potential client and let him know that I was indeed available and interested in his offer. The good news is that I was able to submit a proposal, which was accepted, and he is one of my current evaluation clients.

The budget is designed to fit an individualized evaluation need, and it has to be realistic; otherwise the CMs will lose motivation in the evaluation. You and the CMs may face some budget discrepancies during the collaborative evaluation that require careful management to be corrected. By clarifying the evaluation budget, everyone can understand how to collaboratively approach productive adjustments to reduce the chances of budget problems occurring in the future.

In this chapter, we emphasized the importance of clarifying the evaluation expectations to facilitate a deeper understanding of the constraints and benefits of each choice made. We focused on the role of the evaluator and the CMs through a comprehensive knowledge of specific needs. We also discussed the evaluand criteria and standards in terms of their relevance for the evaluation. In addition, we presented various aspects of the evaluation process, such as planning, executing, and reporting. Furthermore, we provided guidance on how to clarify a realistic evaluation budget. Finally, as in other chapters, we incorporated examples in order to reinforce interdependence among the MCE elements, such as establishing a collective commitment throughout the collaborative evaluation, the topic discussed in Chapter 3.

Establish
a Collective Commitment

A **collective commitment** is a compromise to jointly meet the evaluation obligations without continuous external authority or supervision. In a collaborative evaluation there is a need for a collective commitment in order to promote a desire to take responsibility and accountability for it. However, this can only be achieved when all the CMs are involved (from the very beginning and as appropriate) in the evaluation decisions.

Through a collective commitment, you and the CMs gain a sense of ownership of the effects of this process and its continuous improvement. This increases awareness of your own interactions and the willingness to make adjustments to enhance the quality of the collaborative evaluation.

A collective commitment involves your evaluation client as well, even if he or she is not a CM. This has to be clearly stated from the beginning of the collaborative evaluation (for example, in any type of written document). Keep in mind that others can think that you are not doing a good job when in reality the client did not support the project as agreed or did not supply resources in a timely manner (Weiss, 2009). Obviously, everyone's responsibilities will depend on, and should be specific to, the nature of each collaborative evaluation.

To work together successfully, everyone has to be awarded specific responsibility and authority for achieving the evaluation goals. In this way, the CMs can feel committed to fulfilling their evaluation tasks to the best of their abilities. It is important to delegate appropriate tasks to each specific individual and how to monitor their performance, as well as that of the group as a whole.

You and the CMs need to feel motivated to improve your performance in order to optimize your contribution to the collaborative evaluation. Hence, the MCE component presented in this chapter is divided into the following subcomponents: (a) establish a shared evaluation vision, (b) establish recommendations for positive actions, (c) establish means toward conflict resolution,

(d) establish decision-making procedures, and (e) establish reward options (see Figure I.2). Revisit this MCE component regularly to ensure that all the CMs support the evaluation and feel ownership of it.

ESTABLISH A SHARED EVALUATION VISION

A **vision** is the ability to anticipate in a credible and realistic way the ideal state or big picture to be reached or accomplished at the end of the collaborative evaluation. It is the representation of what people believe the evaluation should be in terms of results (without including activities or resources).

The vision should be specific, relevant, measurable, and challenging, yet achievable, because it identifies results that are possible to attain (so it does not produce frustration). A shared evaluation vision is, nonetheless, an ideal state because it is the representation of what the future should be as a consequence of the collaborative effort. It provides an inspirational picture of the direction toward which you and the CMs should move (serving as a clear guide for choosing courses of action), leading to a greater focused performance.

In a collaborative evaluation, you and the CMs should develop a shared evaluation vision and an understanding of how specific guidelines should be used to direct it. For example, a program vision could be, "To become number one in the field we serve," and an evaluation vision could be, "To deliver a sound evaluation that provides our client a basis for guiding their decision-making procedures to reach their vision."

To unify the evaluation vision, everyone involved needs to have an accurate and clear perception of that meaningful vision and how it is aligned with the evaluand vision and mission. Even when people think they have clear goals, these goals can be distorted on the basis of, among other things, individual perceptions, attitudes, and personality (see Chapter 5 on how to encourage appreciation for individual differences).

The vision helps you and the CMs to move in the direction everyone desires to go regarding the collaborative evaluation. Therefore, get the CMs' attention and interest in the evaluation vision in order to gain their support. Gaining their support may require actions ranging from simply clarifying the connection of the vision to the daily evaluation activities, to explicating its impact on the strategic choices to be made.

Make sure to establish a clear and mutual picture of the evaluation vision because this generates trust in the collaborative process and aligns everyone with the evaluation's day-to-day activities. We suggest the following steps to establish a shared evaluation vision:

1. Agree with the client, and other key stakeholders as appropriate, on the preliminary evaluation vision. This agreement is achieved as soon as the client approves the evaluation (for example, by signing a contract or formal agreement).

2. Present to CMs the preliminary evaluation vision statement approved by the client (one or two short sentences). The vision should be an ideal yet realistic statement of what will be reached at the end of the collaborative evaluation.

3. Make sure that CMs really understand the meaning of the vision (with a clear message tailored to them), because this will help relate the present to the desired collaborative evaluation, working back from the future to the present.

4. Encourage CMs, through an open discussion, to question every aspect of the vision (for example, check that it is truly achievable). This will allow you and the CMs to familiarize yourselves with any concerns and solve them to ensure commitment.

5. Use the technique of brainwriting* to help each CM prepare an improved, easy-to-remember statement of the evaluation vision. Make sure everyone thinks about how the vision may affect the group and not just their individual tasks.

6. Present the updated vision statement (discussing anything you or the CMs disagree with or potential obstacles observed to achieving it), and make sure to include the client, and key stakeholders as needed, for final agreement.

7. Write on a poster the attainable evaluation vision and keep it in focus throughout the collaborative evaluation. At the beginning of each meeting, spend the first minutes discussing the agenda and how it can be linked to the vision.

8. Prepare each of the CMs to achieve the vision while understanding and acting on their evaluation needs (such as communication or training), as feasible. For example, act on the CMs' evaluation needs that affect the vision the most.

---

*Brainwriting is an idea-generation technique that promotes the spontaneous sharing of evaluation ideas in writing, when little verbal communication is allowed.

9. Gather feedback on a regular basis using a previously agreed-upon system (for example, meetings, emails, and surveys as feasible). This will help you and the CMs monitor the evaluation vision and make updates as needed.

10. Provide each CM and other stakeholders as appropriate with a summary report of the shared evaluation vision experience (including actions implemented and the reasons for them) as lessons learned for future similar situations within collaborative evaluations.

Although the evaluation vision can be adapted, its core ideas are always present as a motivating force for the collaborative evaluation. In fact, CMs with a clear vision seize opportunities unimagined by others in order to strengthen the evaluation.

Vision and Formal Agreement

A **formal agreement** is a negotiated arrangement, typically a written document, that is accepted by all parties involved and contains important evaluation information (for example, evaluation plan and role of the CMs). It specifies the evaluation work to be done and serves as an ongoing template for the collaborative evaluation.

You must have a clear and firm understanding with the client (and with each CM as appropriate) of this agreement to protect yourselves from any potentially arbitrary or unethical actions (see Chapter 5 on how to encourage fairness and sincerity). We highly recommend drafting an agreement after the preliminary meetings have taken place early on in the evaluation process.

A formal agreement provides an accurate and implicit understanding of the evaluation vision, and can be renegotiated and modified as feasible. Although a legal or formal contract might only be necessary in large-scale evaluations, it is essential to achieve a clear understanding of the evaluation through some type of written document to ensure that each of the parties (such as you, the CMs, and the client) will adhere to the conditions of the agreement.

In preparing the formal agreement, give special attention to the initial conceptual or verbal agreement. In other words, seriously consider the client's previous comments so that important considerations can be identified. Also, be familiar with the standard formal agreements that the evaluand uses, available conditions, and risks involved with these forms. By signing the formal agreement, the parties indicate acceptance of all the conditions included and approval to begin working on the collaborative evaluation.

A formal agreement is especially important because the collaborative evaluations are dynamic and they have to stay up to date or there will be a risk of losing all the investment made. Once the agreement is signed and the evaluation vision is in place, all new proposed changes to the collaborative evaluation (such as to schedules or the budget) should be accompanied by an update to the agreement. A formal agreement should not allow for unilateral changes during the collaborative evaluation, in order to equally protect each of the parties. Finally, always remember to negotiate the formal agreement with a clear idea of the highest outcome you expect and the lowest you will accept.

Vision and Systems

A **system** is a group of interdependent elements organized to form a whole with a clear and unique purpose, in which the particular way that elements are organized affects the performance of the whole. Thus a system must consist of elements, interconnections, and a function or purpose (Meadows, 2009). Systems ensure that an effective evaluation plan of action is prepared in which all needed information is gathered, considering alternatives and consequences for any given decision.

When establishing a shared evaluation vision, the focus should be on working within the larger evaluation context and understanding the interrelationships among its different parts. As a result, you and the CMs will know how to generate a collaborative evaluation vision that is applicable to action because everyone understands how their work contributes to it.

Systems are essential in a collaborative evaluation because they ensure that all the correct issues are addressed in order to reach better decisions. In response to a problem, the typical approach is to attack it and find people to blame for it; however, focusing on what we want to create, with a systemic perspective, turns out to be a much more meaningful approach (Bellinger, 2011).

An evaluation vision should be seen from a systemic point of view as well, in terms of how it fits within the overall collaborative evaluation. Figure 3.1 shows how systems fit into a broader context in which reality can be viewed from the following multiple levels of perspective:

- **Events.** These are occurrences encountered on a daily basis. They can be vital to organizational survival but not sufficient for sustaining long-term health.

- **Patterns.** These are accumulated "memories" of events. Over a period of time, a problem can reveal recurring trends. Thus patterns generate the events.

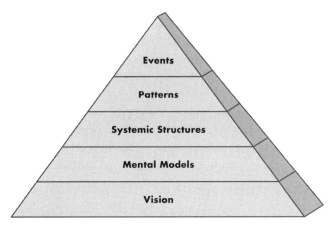

Figure 3.1 Multiple Levels of Perspective. Adapted from
"Introduction to Systems Thinking," Daniel. H. Kim ©1999
by Pegasus Communications (www.pegasuscom.com).

- **Systemic Structures.** These are ways in which the parts or elements of the system are organized. Thus systemic structures generate the patterns.
- **Mental Models.** These are beliefs and assumptions held about how the world works and what is most important. Thus mental models generate the systemic structures.
- **Vision.** This is a picture of what is wanted for the future. It is the guiding force that determines the mental models held as important when pursuing goals.

There are multiple perspectives and a real need for different systems of knowledge, interlinked but each emergent in their own right, in order to deal with a specific situation (Boardman & Sauser, 2008). Because we only see the events or the tip of the iceberg, we often let those drive our decisions. We have to consider that the events are just the result of deeper levels: patterns, systemic structures, mental models, and vision. Fostering an understanding of this will enable us to create an insightful vision.

If you and the CMs clearly define what your aim or vision is going to be, it will be very simple at any time to compare the vision for the future with what the evaluation is now. Moreover, the vision shows the gap between present and future within the evaluation efforts, so you and the CMs can take measures on what you need to do to close this gap.

Establish a Shared Evaluation Vision

Eliot: One of my current clients is a senior program officer at the MNL Foundation. He wants me to work closely with his team, and once the full evaluation
plan, including the vision, has been fully defined and agreed upon, he would
like me to send it to him for his final review and approval. He hasn't attended
any of the meetings because he prefers the team to "own" the evaluation
process and let them create their own shared evaluation vision. Do you think
this is ideal?

Ernest: Well, that's quite different from what my current client prefers. She
has asked me and her whole staff to consider her opinion as another voice
among the whole team—rankings do not exist. In addition, she hasn't missed
one single meeting and is always open and very receptive to what the rest
of her staff has to say. She makes motivating and inspiring comments about
the team and the evolution of the evaluation vision, and she asks questions
without challenging anyone. I think this is a great way to lead by example.
To me, this is an ideal case of a true collaborative effort.

A shared evaluation vision should be motivating and inspiring for you
and all the CMs, where everyone feels a sense of ownership and team spirit
toward it. Everyone has to feel unique because they have been brought together to fulfill this vision and their particular characteristics are needed for
its success. Make sure to reinforce collaboration by providing ongoing opportunities for sharing ideas and feedback (see Chapter 4 on how to ensure
immediate feedback).

ESTABLISH RECOMMENDATIONS
FOR POSITIVE ACTIONS

Recommendations for positive actions are a set of formal suggestions (established by you and the CMs) that facilitate specific change toward more effective actions and social harmony. An **action** can be anything that a person does
(such as thinking, talking, walking, and reading) resulting from an attitude.

The recommendations for positive actions include information of self-
awareness and self-regulation that help strengthen a concept of right and

wrong within the evaluation. These recommendations should reflect specific positive actions that inspire trust (for example, arrive on time, immediately express any concerns, listen to the ideas of others, and look for areas of compromise). They help to plant the seeds of self-control and teach respect for others' rights and feelings.

Boundaries provide a sense of security for everyone involved in the evaluation process. However, you and the CMs have to be balanced because too many boundaries may cause inflexibility, while too few may cause a lack of direction that prevents you from focusing on the critical evaluation tasks. You and the CMs should be involved in setting up the recommendations for positive actions, and continuously report any perceived changes that may influence the collaborative evaluation so that recommendations can be adjusted accordingly.

People's actions can result in positive and long-term performance or just the opposite. You and the CMs have to understand each other's individual differences when setting the recommendations for positive actions. Obviously, these recommendations are adjusted to each particular evaluation context. You and the CMs may periodically review or update some recommendations in order to support and encourage the collaborative effort.

In a collaborative evaluation you and the CMs need to have control over your actions and the consequences associated with them. To enhance cooperation during the evaluation implementation, foster an environment in which everyone finds this opportunity for control useful, or at least not threatening or interfering with the process. The CMs need to feel empowered in order to provide feedback about what they think are needed actions for the evaluation.

To be able to make personal or situational attributions within the collaborative efforts, several authors (for example, Gibson, Ivancevich, & Donelly, 2008; Kelley, 1971) explained that there are three criteria in trying to decide whether a behavior or action should be attributed to the situation or the person:

- **Consensus.** If most other people would do (or not do) the same thing in that particular situation.
- **Distinctiveness.** If the behavior is usual or unusual, or typical or atypical for the person.
- **Consistency.** If the person engages in the behavior consistently or inconsistently.

Establish Recommendations for Positive Actions

Evelyn: One lesson I have learned over my thirty years of professional experience is that it is essential to establish recommendations for positive actions as soon as feasible. One time, I worked with a group who were all about power and ranks within the organization. Once I had a signed contract and we had scheduled our very first CMs' meeting, I introduced the steps for recommendations for positive actions from the MCE. I asked everyone in the room to carefully review the steps and why it was important to follow them. In every single instance, everyone praised the use of these recommendations as one of the key elements to establish a true collaborative atmosphere. Some of the commonly used meeting recommendations, which I always display on a large poster, are: be present; be concrete; listen attentively; speak your truth; seek first to understand; maintain confidentiality; start on time and stop on time; and, of course, have fun.

Eliot: But how do these lead to positive actions?

Evelyn: Well, once they all had provided their recommendations, I made sure they were all followed by each person, including myself, without exception. Interestingly, this simple exercise made my working space a means for a safe environment, encouraging conversation, and more important, very productive sessions. By the way, I always closed my meetings by providing sincere appreciation for people's time, hard work, and exemplary professional actions. Sharing these recommendations, showing everyone how to follow them, publicly acknowledging people, and praising them for following the recommendations will make a significant difference in your team discussions and work. These recommendations draw important lessons that enable everyone to learn together to create the results they really want and to adapt appropriately because there is a desire for continuous improvement. In addition, it eliminates one's tendency to assign blame because it reframes issues into positive actions with a hopeful vision of the future.

The recommendations for positive actions are different in every collaborative evaluation because you and the CMs develop specific group actions as a result of your unique characteristics and interpersonal influence. These recommendations should be clearly understood and easily followed. They should also help to recognize and redirect disruptive moods and actions that may have a negative impact on the evaluation. The goal is to have as few recommendations as possible, and when a recommendation is not needed anymore, then it is eliminated.

At times, you and the CMs may feel negative moods, but with the recommendations for positive actions you may find means to control and channel your negative impulses in useful ways. Picture yourself in a meeting for which the same CM is arriving late for the third time in a row. How do you handle this situation? For this and other nonproductive situations, we suggest the following steps to establish recommendations for positive actions:

1. Hang on a visible wall a poster titled "Recommendations for Positive Actions" and leave it in the same location during every collaborative evaluation meeting (this is for easy reference throughout the evaluation process).

2. Explain to the CMs that every time they observe a controllable action that needs improvement (for example, you or a CM continuously arrive late to meetings), they should write it down as a positive action (such as "arrive to meetings on time").

3. Reassure CMs that each of the recommendations for positive actions will be an optimistic response to a particular undesirable action (and not about a specific individual), to avoid making them demoralizing, too rigid, or overly permissive.

4. Collect all the anonymous recommendation notes (that is, without names or identification numbers so nobody knows who wrote what) at the end of each meeting, taking into consideration that some of those notes may be blank.

5. Read aloud the new potential recommendations (while you remind the CMs not to pass judgment on any of the ideas generated at this point) and provide time for each CM and yourself to clarify, reflect, prioritize, and agree on the final recommendations.

6. Write all the new recommendations on the poster, remembering that they should be precise, limited in their number, and impersonal in order to be more effective. The latter is because the worst types of conflicts are the ones that address personal issues.

7. Agree with the CMs on how the new recommendations for positive actions will be implemented, what type of support or help will be needed, and how those recommendations will be monitored and consistently rewarded throughout the evaluation.

8. Enforce each recommendation respectfully, equally, and consistently, because it would not be fair to skip one at a particular time and impose it at another time. Otherwise, CMs will assume that the recommendations are meaningless, and you will lose credibility.

9. Gather feedback on a regular basis using a previously agreed-upon system (for example, meetings, emails, and surveys as feasible). This will help you and the CMs monitor the suitability of these recommendations and make updates as needed.

10. Provide each CM as appropriate with a summary report of the recommendations for positive actions experience (including actions implemented and the reasons for them) as lessons learned for future similar situations within collaborative evaluations.

The recommendations for positive actions are very helpful because you and the CMs know what is expected throughout the collaborative evaluation. Also, because the CMs helped create those recommendations, they believe in them, accept them, and want to accomplish them. People tend to be very effective at managing relationships when they understand and control their own emotions and empathize with the feelings of others (Goleman, 2004).

Ensure that there are no contingencies surrounding the CMs' efforts to improve their actions. As soon as a particular action-related problem surfaces, identify its cause and how you and other CMs can help to address and solve it. The recommendations for positive actions need to be directly linked to positive reinforcements; in other words, anything that both increases the strength of response and induces repetition of the action that preceded the reinforcement (Gibson, Ivancevich, & Donnelly, 2008).

With the recommendations for positive actions, you and the CMs increase your self-discipline because you are aware and take responsibility for the consequences of your own actions. Through self-awareness, you can understand how your response style is influencing your relationships and how your actions might be keeping you in dependent roles (Hankins & Hankins, 2000). You must remember that the CMs may not always be able to verbalize what they are feeling, but those feelings exist nevertheless, and they appreciate having those recommendations available.

Be aware that CMs with poor self-esteem may continuously try to behave inappropriately in order to confirm their negative self-image with your and the CMs' reactions. For this reason, the recommendations for appropriate actions reinforce positive contributions. People acquire social skills in a variety of ways, especially by imitating the actions of others and by direct reinforcement of their actions (Hankins & Hankins, 2000).

If appropriately used, the recommendations for positive actions help to develop a climate of openness and self-confidence in which people are willing to express their opinions, and to recognize others' achievements among themselves. The recommendations for positive actions encourage CMs to behave in ways that help the collaborative evaluation reach its vision. These recommendations are based on a collaborative approach that induces everyone to proactively learn from each other.

The recommendations for positive actions lead to productive and effective teamwork that is collaborative instead of self-protective within the evaluation. However, specify that you are trying to influence a positive action rather than trying to change the CMs' personalities. In other words, you are trying to ensure that everyone assumes responsibility for their actions within the collaborative effort. These recommendations imply that you and the CMs share a collective commitment to work for the good of the collaborative evaluation as a whole, while maintaining positive feelings and perceptions.

ESTABLISH MEANS TOWARD CONFLICT RESOLUTION

Conflict is an antagonism or a contest of opposing forces within the collaborative evaluation and evidence of a gap between the vision and the current reality. Conflict is inevitable, endemic, and often legitimate, because the individuals and groups are interdependent and need to redefine the nature and extent of their interdependence on an ongoing basis (Owens & Valesky, 2010).

Learning to work through disagreements can be beneficial as long as the parties (such as you and specific CMs) agree on a code of conduct. To strengthen the collaborative evaluation, you and the CMs need to deal with conflict in an open way, so you can work together to identify the source of problems and appropriately solve them. Many of the bad things that happen in our work are related to impulsive behavior. In addition, work-related problems are often created not by what we do, but by what we fail to do (Daniels, 2000).

To get everyone to accept solutions to specific problems, there is a need to continually balance opposing views. Shift distribution of power toward acceptable solutions, so there is appropriate compromising about the conflictive

situation. For example, when there is a disagreement, usually each party focuses on convincing the others of his or her "correct" view (in other words, "I
am right and others are wrong"), and the disagreement escalates until there is a
change of mind-set in which each party attempts to understand others instead
of only expecting to be understood.

Although conflicts may develop due to a lack of understanding among you
and the CMs, some degree of conflict may be needed when diverse opinions
and information are helpful to get tasks completed. Conflict may impede the
attainment of the goals (for example, lengthy delays over unimportant issues),
but the consequences may be beneficial if they produce new information that
enhances the evaluation process.

Clearly, it is important to minimize the destructive aspects of conflict (such
as resentment) and maximize the opportunities within the collaborative evaluation (including problem solving and trust). Leaders have an uncanny ability
(sometimes negative) to awaken transferential processes, during which people
transfer the dynamics of past relationships onto present interactions, causing
conflict (Coutu, 2004). Furthermore, in order to understand conflict, be aware
that there are three basic types of latent conflict (Pondy, 1967):

- **Competition for Scarce Resources.** When the resources (such as space
  or budget allocations) are insufficient to meet the work requirements.

- **Autonomy.** When one party seeks to control the activities that are perceived to belong to another party.

- **Goal Divergence.** When two parties must work together but cannot
  agree on how to do so, perhaps because of differing views.

A conflictive situation within the collaborative evaluation may trigger anger
in the affected parties. **Anger** is a normal, natural emotion that, if communicated constructively, alerts others to your needs, thereby creating an opportunity for reconciliation and support (Hankins & Hankins, 2000). According to
Hankins and Hankins, there are four categories of anger expression:

- **Passive.** Saying or doing nothing.

- **Aggressive.** Retaliating in an obviously hurtful manner such as yell-
  ing at or hitting the abuser, thus being intrusive, hostile, rageful, and
  assaultive.

- **Passive-Aggressive.** Responding in a subtly hurtful manner, such as
  conveniently forgetting, not hearing, being inefficient, gossiping, lying,
  allowing someone to get hurt, and being sarcastic.

- **Assertive.** Confronting in a calm, respectful, nonhurtful, and non-threatening manner.

Conflict occurs when one person frustrates the concerns (goals, values, self-interests, status, or control) of another person. The only way to solve conflict is to break the pattern by getting at least one party in the conflict to abandon the normal behavioral response and do the opposite of what he or she has been doing (Lewis, 1999). For example, if you want to solve a conflict with a specific CM, instead of acting defensive, you can break the pattern by behaving differently than expected, and addressing the conflict in a positive way.

Our actions are shaped by our perception (that is, the interpretation we make) of why an event occurs (Ivancevich, Konopaske, & Matteson, 2010). You may solve conflicts just by changing your perception of a particular situation, or that of others. Learned experiences from similar past conflicts may help you gain awareness of the situation and potential solutions. In addition, the following are some methods for dealing with conflict (Owens & Valesky, 2010):

- **Collaboration.** When the parties work together to define their problems and engage in mutual problem solving (a win-win situation).

- **Bargaining.** When the parties are essentially recognized as adversaries but neither party wins or loses (a no win, no lose situation).

- **Avoidance.** When the latent conflict remains (becoming manifest at any time) due to withdrawal because it is not likely that it can be solved (a lose-lose situation).

- **Power Struggle.** When each party wants to win regardless of the consequences for the other party (a win-lose situation).

A win-win approach (in which both parties win something though not necessarily equally) tends to be the most productive conflict resolution method because people will acquire new skills and understandings. As the evaluator, you should always strive to turn any situation into a win-win situation as a part of reconciling differences among you and the CMs. For example, model the behavior you expect from the affected CMs by leading them from their initial behavior to another more productive one.

Be patient and give the person ample opportunity to respond even if it seems as if it takes an unbearably long time (Hankins & Hankins, 2000). This is because feelings must be processed before facts, so it would be a waste of time if you attempt to deal with facts while people are upset (Lewis, 1999). Keep in mind that conflicts will develop in every evaluation due to lack of understanding or agreement in specific issues, and be ready to solve them as soon as they arise.

We suggest the following steps to establish means toward conflict resolution:

1. Acknowledge the presence of conflict as soon as it appears, and make sure that you (and any affected CMs) are calm and objective in order to be respected. If not, then have a recess to put the conflictive situation into perspective.

2. Meet with the affected CMs and any other relevant individuals (being respectful and approachable yet firm and concise) to explain your good intention to effectively solve the conflict and the specific rationale of the meeting.

3. Promote self-awareness by showing appreciation for positive actions, and immediately respond to cues that signal the escalation of negative actions. For example, you may say that any type of power struggle or manipulation is unacceptable.

4. Encourage the CMs' input by acknowledging their feelings (for instance, look for incongruence between what they say and how they say it) and explain that their input should focus on the behavior or action, their suggested solution, and compromise.

5. Make sure that you understand every CM's feedback. For example, wait for their response without interrupting, paraphrase their comments (limiting this to only what the CM shared with you), and then wait for their reply on this information.

6. Keep the focus on one specific conflictive issue at a time and, when it is appropriate, interconnect all the issues (balancing any opposing views) to form the big picture and later arrive at the most convenient solution within the collaborative evaluation.

7. Analyze the situation against the evaluation expectations and the type of method that can be used for dealing with the conflict, in order to make adjustments to meet the gap (for example, lower the evaluation expectations).

8. Ask CMs for feedback on your analysis, and value any objections because they can improve the process. If you have doubts on some CMs' honesty, ask for written feedback or a private meeting in order to ensure a true conflict resolution.

Establish Means Toward Conflict Resolution

Ernest: There are hundreds, perhaps thousands, of books and professional development sessions on conflict resolution, but is there one single silver bullet or strategy when it comes to having difficult CMs working together?

Evelyn: I wish there was a silver bullet. However, I personally see all conflicts falling into what I call the *three types of conflict buckets.* The first type of bucket is when everyone comes with a collaborative mentality and you find it just slightly difficult to make decisions in a short amount of time. The second bucket is when you have a situation in which at least two CMs do not agree. The third bucket is the worst-case scenario, and it is when you find yourself in an intense and chaotic situation. Anytime I have been involved in the third bucket scenario, I have always suggested the group to take a five- to ten-minute break before moving forward. This strategy not only allows people's energy level to come down a little bit, it also allows you to rethink your strategy or even the agenda you have originally proposed for that day. You could also privately convene with your client and ask for his or her input regarding how to address that conflict and move forward with your meeting.

For example, I once had a CM who felt very insecure and worried that the evaluation results would lead to her losing her job as a result. She was using every opportunity to delay the evaluation by creating conflictive situations. I was working with good intention and under the assumption that this CM reacted in that particular way because she did not have any additional information to make a more informed choice. I gained the CM's trust through clearly showing the transparency of the process and the benefits of the program. She sincerely apologized and assured me she was now ready to help in anything that was needed.

9. Implement appropriate actions to solve the conflict, once it is fully understood. For example, you may choose to work more closely than usual with specific CMs, or you may also reassign those CMs to a less critical evaluation task.

10. Follow up on the conflict resolution progress (perhaps by obtaining continuous feedback) and summarize it in a written format (including source of conflict, how it is being solved, and its specific consequences) that is available to all the affected CMs.

Always remember to balance the needs of all the CMs, yourself, and the evaluation to ensure that the conflict has a positive resolution. Conflict is often the only way to get to where the truth lies (Takeuchi, 2004). Therefore, you should explicitly identify and discuss the conflict with the CMs in an open way, resolve it when possible, and determine whether continued work on particular issues is advisable. Also, you and the CMs have to make clear any significant limitations on the evaluation that might result if the conflict is not resolved. The goal should be to keep the focus of all the CMs on what is truly important: the shared vision of the collaborative evaluation.

A leader who fails to show initiative and deal decisively with conflict will lose esteem and influence (Yukl, 2009). Communicate the need to view conflict as an opportunity to strengthen the understanding of how valuable everyone's contribution is to the evaluation. If a high degree of trust exists between the conflicting groups, this will lead to greater openness and sharing of information (Gibson, Ivancevich, & Donnelly, 2008). Then, to accept solutions to evaluation problems, continually balance their opposing views (see Chapter 5 on how to encourage fairness and sincerity).

Many conflicts can be either reduced or eliminated by constant communication of the objectives to the group members. You cannot always control other people's actions, but you have control over your expectations, and the closer your expectations (goals) are to reality (achievements) the less frustration you will experience (Hankins & Hankins, 2000). You should be able to adjust your expectations if you or the CMs are not performing as you initially expected.

ESTABLISH DECISION-MAKING PROCEDURES

A **decision** is a choice or judgment made from among several alternatives as a reaction to a specific problem within the collaborative evaluation. Furthermore, **decision making** is the process by which the best possible evaluation decision is determined, when you or the CMs, as appropriate, have the opportunity and right to influence such a decision.

Collaborative decision making tends to increase motivation and commitment to carry out the vision. Make sure that you and the CMs understand not only the decisions to be made but also the reasons behind such decisions. Obviously, each person may possess a different degree of knowledge about the decision to be made or may play an equal role in the decision process as feasible.

Everyone involved in the collaborative evaluation should focus their attention on the decision-making procedures (and not only on what decisions to make) in order to understand how to make decisions. When CMs help to formulate the decision-making procedures, then they are more likely to be committed to the evaluation. There needs to be an evaluation atmosphere in which you and the CMs feel comfortable to make decisions and think about solutions in a creative way. Effective partnerships must have a vital sense of ownership of decisions (El Ansari & Phillips, 2001).

Every decision potentially has (a) a merit dimension, which describes whether there is some quantitative way in which one choice is better than another, and (b) an acceptance dimension, which describes whether the people affected by the decision will accept it (Lewis, 1999). Depending on the problem, decisions may be classified as (a) expected, when you know that sooner or later a decision has to be made in order to handle a particular problem, or (b) unexpected, when a particular decision has to be made because suddenly a problem arises without being anticipated. Whether decisions are expected or unexpected, you and the CMs need to prepare a generic procedure for decision making in advance, so that well-thought-out decisions can be made when the need arrives.

By understanding the procedures that will be routinely used to make decisions, you and the CMs avoid unnecessary conflict when a problem arises (see Chapter 6 on how to follow specific guidelines). For example, a CM might feel that everybody is against his or her opinions, so understand every CM's viewpoint (hidden and explicit) and other considerations (such as cost, feasibility, relevance, and acceptability) before establishing a particular decision-making procedure in the collaborative evaluation.

Decisions must be made throughout the collaborative effort because specific resources need to be used to produce a quality evaluation that delivers its results on time. Obviously, not all the evaluation problems have the same priority to be solved. The significance of a problem depends on at least three problem attributes: (a) urgency, which relates to time and how critical time pressures are in dealing with a problem; (b) impact, which describes the seriousness of the problem's effects; and (c) growth tendency, which addresses the likelihood of future changes in problem urgency or impact (Ivancevich, Konopaske, & Matteson, 2010).

The procedures for decision making facilitate the control of everyone's biases, which can skew the decisions within the collaborative evaluation. You and the CMs need to be committed to the decisions that are going to be established, and responsible for the evaluation results. As feasible, involve the CMs in the ongoing evaluation decisions so they can feel useful and valued. In general, the most common styles of decision making (see, for example, Lewis, 1999; PMI Standards Committee, 2008) are the following:

- **Consensus Decision Making.** This occurs when people involved in the process agree to close a particular discussion only when they reach 100 percent support of the decision. If any member has strong objections to the majority position, the group can continue the discussion or overrule a minority member as a last resort.

- **Majority Decision Making.** This occurs when people involved in the process agree that the winning decision will have the majority vote, and the losers will support the decision (even if they do not like it). As a result, each person should be willing to support the majority position even if they do not totally agree with such a position.

- **Hierarchical Decision Making.** This occurs when people involved in the process agree that the decision will be made by the member(s) with the greatest expertise, or by those most directly affected with the decision. In this way, only the expert(s) deal with expert issues.

With a collaborative approach to decision making, you and the CMs are able to share your various points of view and, as a result, there is a lower likelihood that a particular idea is overlooked. Because most decisions surrounding the evaluation are going to be important and complex, CMs can provide very decisive views that many times you could not produce in isolation. Decisions made by groups are superior to those made by individuals, but some aspects of group decision making tend to have negative effects, such as pressure to conform, dismissal of opposing ideas, or exertion of disproportionate influence by a dominant group member (Ivancevich, Konopaske, & Matteson, 2010).

One of the most important advantages of collaborative decision making is that it can assist the identification of creative solutions to evaluation problems (see Chapter 5 on how to encourage flexibility and creativity). However, one tactic favored by manipulative followers is to create a false sense of urgency to rush the leader into uninformed decisions (Offermann, 2004). Therefore, you and the CMs need to reserve your judgment until you believe you will not regret your decision later.

Throughout our professional experience we have noted that most (not all) group decisions have worked better than individual decisions, although those decisions took more time to be reached. Sometimes group decisions are not possible. For example, a decision that must be made in a very short time can't afford long group discussions. The reason for making decisions is to produce the best possible result or outcome for the collaborative evaluation on the basis of specific expectations.

The decision is not an end but a means to the end; once alternatives to solve the problem have been developed they must be compared on the basis of three possible conditions (Ivancevich, Konopaske, & Matteson, 2010):

- **Certainty.** The decision maker has complete knowledge of the outcome probability of each possible alternative (that is, complete data). In general, it is not possible to have complete certainty in most work situations, although there may be some information to make decisions.

- **Uncertainty.** The decision maker does not have knowledge of the outcome probability of each possible alternative (that is, there are uncertain situations). Of course, the decision maker sometimes can reduce the degree of uncertainty by gathering information or studying a situation.

- **Risk.** This is an intermediate condition, when the decision maker can make some probable estimate (for example, investment in a stock), but lacks certainty of the outcomes of each alternative (see Chapter 1 on how to identify potential SWOTs).

Obviously, you and the CMs have to consider that decisions are dynamic and inevitably will influence (positively or negatively) other parts of the collaborative evaluation, increasing the difficulty of the process. For this reason, study all the possible alternative solutions that you and the CMs can think of in order to minimize the risk of triggering any unintended outcomes. Keep in mind that decisions should involve a balance of risks and returns.

You must strictly monitor the collaborative decision-making process because your effectiveness as the evaluator depends on the quality of the decisions made. Remember that each decision will take you one step closer (or farther) from the evaluation vision. We suggest the following steps to establish decision-making procedures:

1. Acknowledge the existence of a decision that needs to be made (for example, which type of data-collection and analysis methods are to be used), and think of initial ideas on its overall significance to the collaborative evaluation.

2. Establish priorities through a structured approach that divides the potential decision(s) to be made into smaller and more manageable parts. Those parts could be interconnected at any time throughout the collaborative evaluation.

3. Select the best style of decision making for the particular situation and choose how outcomes will be measured. For example, use a hierarchical decision-making style when, due to expertise, only you or a few CMs can be involved.

4. Determine the amount of time that will be taken for making a decision (it varies with each type of decision), and establish backup plans if the deadline is not going to be met (such as to postpone the decision or change the decision-making style).

5. Meet with all the appropriate CMs for their feedback (understanding everyone's perspective). For example, ask specific questions on potential decisions, expected consequences, and the probability of occurrence (avoid interruptions).

6. Meet with each of the appropriate CMs, as feasible, in order to share the information collected and use adequate techniques to identify new possibilities. This is because some CMs may find it difficult to publicly express their ideas.

7. Examine every possibility and then present them to all the appropriate CMs (acknowledging your own opinion and being ready to make any changes as needed) in order to agree on the best decision to be made within the collaborative evaluation.

8. Implement convenient and concrete decision-related actions in a timely manner (once they have been agreed upon with the appropriate CMs). Also, keep in mind that you may need to update those actions (and the CMs involved in them) as needed.

9. Use adequate check-out options to know whether or not the CMs feel included in the decision-making procedures and how willing they are to implement the decision. For example, address the issues you or other CMs believe need improvement.

10. Provide each CM and other stakeholders as appropriate with a summary report of the decision-making experience (including actions implemented and the reasons for them) as lessons learned for future similar situations within collaborative evaluations.

Establish Decision-Making Procedures

Eliot: Ernest, what can I do with this group of CMs that takes such a long time to make even the smallest decision? I believe we are still on track, as we are at the initial stage of the process. They showed great commitment with the evaluation vision and they made a unanimous decision to approve and move forward with the evaluation plan they helped draft, which I ultimately proposed. I am not sure what is causing the delay in their decision making. What should I do in this case?

Ernest: Well, it looks like they are all on board with the collaborative evaluation vision, and more important, with the evaluation plan you proposed. If you believe they have all the information they need to move forward with the evaluation plan, then one strategy you may use is to bring them back to where you all are in relation to the overall evaluation timeline. I always encourage a culture of inquiry based on asking questions, reflecting, and using dialogue to move forward. Sometimes people are just afraid to make decisions because it may be the first time they are evaluating their program and they are simply being too cautious about the potential results. It is important to remind them about the need of making timely decisions and that you are there to help through the process.

Everyone will feel more committed and willing to work collaboratively in the implementation of the decision if they feel they truly have been part of it with their opinions valued. Keep in mind that different decision makers may select different alternatives in the same situation because of their individual differences (Gibson, Ivancevich, & Donnelly, 2008). Before a final decision is made, have a clear idea of your own opinion on the potential solutions to the problem and consequences of each alternative. Sometimes good leaders end up making poor decisions because well-meaning followers are persuasive about a course of action (Offermann, 2004).

The quality of the decisions within the collaborative evaluation depends on clearly defining, with the appropriate CMs, the evaluation problem in terms of all the possible ways to solve it. For this reason, foster a true collaborative evaluation atmosphere in which you and the CMs feel comfortable to make decisions and think about solutions in a creative way. Also, timing for the decision is essential, because the "right" decision may not be the "best" decision if it is made too early or too late (PMI Standards Committee, 2008).

ESTABLISH REWARD OPTIONS

Reward options are important ways to recognize and reinforce the ability of individuals (such as CMs) to build upon short- or long-term goals in order to achieve the collaborative evaluation vision. When establishing reward options, it is important to assess individual contributions, in addition to the achievement of everyone as a collective, so that every individual can feel useful, valued, and motivated.

Letting people know that they will be assessed for their individual efforts is essential to group motivation (Irlenbusch & Ruchala, 2008). Clearly understand the CMs' personal needs and values in order to motivate them in an effective individualized way. For example, we show a sincere interest in learning about each of the CMs' lives as appropriate (such as their favorite activities) and reinforce this with sincere, positive comments, in order to appreciate them as individuals.

To have healthy collaborative relationships, give CMs what they need and not just what you would need in their position. As an example, you may encounter particular people with a great hunger for recognition and external affirmation because they are trying to compensate for narcissistic wounds, or blows to their self-esteem, inflicted in past relationships (Coutu, 2004).

Rewards are formal management actions that promote desired actions, and to be effective they must make a clear link between performance and reward (PMI Standards Committee, 2008). Moreover, rewards can be used to improve performance if it is desirable to the person (Ivancevich, Konopaske, & Matteson, 2010). For this reason, establish reward options that are appropriate for the CMs and the specific collaborative evaluation efforts being performed. In this way, you can create genuine interest in the collaborative evaluation and its expected results.

Rewarding contributions urges CMs to stay focused on the shared evaluation vision while continuously working toward accomplishing it. Also, CMs feel encouraged to be proactive because they are recognized for their own ideas within the collaborative evaluation. Hence, rewarding through positive reinforcement is very important for effective collaborative efforts. When possible, have an evaluation environment that ensures an immediate and appropriate type of reward for the particular situation.

The extent to which a reward is motivating depends on how the CM perceives it and how it connects to the particular evaluation accomplishment (see Chapter 2 on how to clarify the expectations). Some rewards are important to

CMs because they lead to other rewards that are more meaningful to them. For example, a CM's responsibility over a large evaluation task may lead to a higher status within the collaborative evaluation. According to Gibson, Ivancevich, and Donnelly (2008), rewards can be classified as one of the following:

- **Extrinsic Rewards.** These are rewards which are external to the job that attempt to improve a person's status: for example, salary and wages, fringe benefits, promotions, and certain types of interpersonal rewards (including expressions of a job well done or letters of commendation).

- **Intrinsic Rewards.** These are rewards associated with doing the job itself, which include such things as a sense of completion, achievement, challenge, autonomy, responsibility, meaningful work, and personal growth. For example, some individuals value the possibility to complete a job or reach a challenging goal.

Both types of rewards satisfy different individual needs, so know each CM in order to understand how they value different reinforcement options within the collaborative effort. For instance, a positive reinforcement occurs when a valued consequence follows a response to a stimulus (Gibson, Ivancevich, & Donnelly, 2008). With a positive reinforcement you and the CMs may feel motivated to continue and even achieve higher levels of performance within the collaborative evaluation.

Each CM may desire a different type of reward (or respond differently to a particular reward) and this desire may also change throughout the collaborative evaluation. You and the CMs need to establish effective reward options such that everyone feels that their collaboration in the evaluation, and continuous improvement of their efforts, will lead to positive and valued consequences. The reward options ensure that you and the CMs will strive to meet and succeed in the evaluation tasks. We suggest the following steps to establish reward options:

1. Ask each of the appropriate CMs for their feedback regarding their evaluation interests and most valued intrinsic or extrinsic rewards. For example, ask how those rewards should be connected to specific levels of evaluation performance.

2. Match the CMs' interests, whenever possible, with specific evaluation tasks assigned to them. This ensures the work is intrinsically desirable enough for CMs to contribute to the collaborative effort, and elevates the possibility of succeeding.

3. Meet with all the CMs in order to share, as appropriate, the information collected on rewards and use adequate techniques (such as brainwriting) to identify new possible ideas. For instance, CMs may find it difficult to publicly express or share their ideas.

4. Examine every reward option's feasibility, and then agree on the best individual and group rewards based on their connection with evaluation achievements. Obviously, those rewards will be expected once they are established.

5. Develop an objective standardized system (to review the CMs' individual and group contributions) and share it with the CMs for their feedback. This increases awareness about how to improve current and future performance so everyone can be rewarded.

6. Use the review system to periodically check the CMs' performance within specific evaluation goals. For example, this review could include asking for the feedback of CMs' colleagues in order to have a full understanding of the surrounding environment.

7. Encourage collaborative work (assessing group and not only individual performance), and as CMs achieve specific milestones, provide immediate and meaningful rewards with available resources (such as a letter of commendation).

8. Be equitable when recognizing CMs for the success of their efforts to avoid dissatisfaction or competition. For example, a reward highly valued by one CM may differ for another CM because its value is in the eye of the beholder.

9. Monitor rewards on an ongoing basis to check if they continue to appropriately motivate CMs, and update them as needed. This is because several kinds of circumstances (for example, personal issues) can alter a CM's response to a particular reward.

10. Provide each CM and other stakeholders as appropriate with a summary report of the rewards experience (including actions implemented and the reasons for them) as lessons learned for future similar situations within collaborative evaluations.

An effective reward system meets the following criteria: (a) it allows for an unlimited number of performers, (b) the performers know what must be accomplished to earn the reward, and (c) the manager's success is tied to the employees' success (Daniels, 2000). Moreover, Daniels explained that when people are working to reach a specific goal, success is determined by whether the person or group reached that goal, independent of what others did.

Always try to work with CMs who are willing to do their best and continuously improve their performance within the collaborative evaluation. Also, aim to have CMs who publicly show their passion for their contributions within the collaborative efforts, so this passion can be spread around. This is why the rewards, if valued by the CMs, can provide an evaluation environment in which everyone feels recognized and an essential part of the group efforts. The important thing is to find ways to recognize contributions that can be effectively received by the CMs.

If you want to identify people who are motivated by the drive to achieve rather than by external rewards, the first sign is a passion for the work itself (for example, those who seek out creative challenges, love to learn and take great pride in a job well done, or have the energy to do things better) (Goleman, 2004). Foster an interesting and challenging work environment in which you are surrounded by CMs who are eager to find better ways to achieve the evaluation vision, and who share satisfaction with you in the resulting accomplishments. People strongly engaged with their work have a more positive attitude toward change (Thamhain & Wilemon, 1996).

The reward options allow the viewing of evaluation risks from a positive perspective. Instead of viewing only the potential for failure and negative consequences in every task, the reward options encourage CMs to look at the positive side as well. With reward options, everyone feels empowered to take primary responsibility for the evaluation progress and looks after their own contributions. This is because CMs are willing to take responsibility for moderately risky tasks to achieve the potential positive consequences. For example, CMs may be interested in specific rewards that will come from the task's success and will directly reflect the capability of the CMs.

The use of rewards reinforces a desirable action within the collaborative evaluation, in which people feel encouraged to achieve higher-quality goals. However, be aware that the relationship between rewards and satisfaction changes because people and the environment change (Gibson, Ivancevich, & Donnelly, 2008). Make sure that you and the CMs develop reward options that meet everyone's needs while having a positive impact on the commitment within the collaborative effort. Depending on the relative importance rewards have for particular CMs, they can serve as a motivator to improve the CMs' skills for performing specific evaluation tasks.

Rewards, if appropriately administered, are a very effective way of motivating CMs to do their best. Rewards increase self-worth within the collaborative evaluation when people feel appreciated for their contributions. Recognize CMs (individually and as a group) for their successes within the evaluation. In this way, you are assuring them that you believe in their own abilities. Also, other CMs feel encouraged to trust that they can commit to the evaluation because there is a nurturing or can-do environment (see Chapter 5 on how to encourage effective practices).

Rewards should always suit the specific evaluation situation and be provided to only those who deserve them. For this reason, focus on the particular

Establish Reward Options

Ernest: This is the first time in my twenty-something years working in evaluation that I not only get to work with a very large group of CMs, but with all women. I worry that it might be intimidating to be the only man in the group, but I find it challenging and interesting at the same time. I think I need to be extremely careful when offering or suggesting a reward system in this circumstance. How would you recommend I approach this situation?

Evelyn: I don't think you should be concerned at all about this and especially not about the gender situation. Whether you are working with a group of men or of women, or a mixed group of men and women, it is important to get to know your group well. People love to be rewarded, whether it is through intrinsic or extrinsic rewards. For example, you can simply ask this group to write on a piece of paper something like the following: "In my previous (or current) job, I always did ABC-related activities. For this collaborative evaluation, I would love to do XYZ-related activities." With something as simple as that, you may be able to give people from this group an opportunity to be rewarded with the types of activities they would like to do. Another strategy you may want to explore, and this depends on the scope of work and how much time you will really spend with this group, is to ask your client how she or he feels about creating together a reward system and then think about feasible reward options.

expected actions that will lead to the consequent performance you desire within the collaborative evaluation. Then, provide only rewards that recognize CMs who have exceeded the evaluation expectations; otherwise you will be devaluing rewards by using them excessively. This is a perfect way to stimulate above-average performance within the collaborative effort that sets an important example to follow.

Throughout our evaluations, we have always marked the end of each collaborative effort with a celebration in recognition of everyone's hard work. We believe it is a great way to show our appreciation for all the people who collaborated in the evaluation. This celebration allows every CM to share their learned lessons, realize others' achievements and capabilities, and say their farewells, giving closure to the collaborative process. Then, we reinforce what was said in the public celebration by sending an individualized note of recognition to every CM, in which we emphasize our appreciation and thank them for their contributions to the collaborative evaluation.

In this chapter, we emphasized the importance of establishing a collective commitment to meet the evaluation obligations. In particular, we focused on a shared evaluation vision of everyone involved in the collaborative evaluation. We also discussed how recommendations for positive actions are necessary to facilitate effective social harmony. In addition, we presented means toward conflict resolution and procedures for decision making. Furthermore, we provided guidance on how to establish reward options to recognize and reinforce the ability of everyone involved. Finally, as in other chapters, we incorporated examples in order to reinforce interdependence among the MCE elements, such as ensuring open communication throughout the collaborative evaluation, the topic discussed in Chapter 4.

Ensure
Open Communication

Communication is a process of social interaction (such as speaking, listening, or writing) used to convey information and exchange ideas in order to influence specific actions within the collaborative evaluation. Also, it involves presenting a message in a way that is understood and accepted. In other words, communication implies an attempt to share meaning by transmitting messages among people (Owens & Valesky, 2010).

Both formal (evaluation-related) and informal (personal) communication strategies must be planned to reflect the diverse styles of you and the CMs (and other stakeholders) within the collaborative evaluation. Good communication helps build trust, and trust is the intangible that makes a collaboration cohesive (Austin, 2000). You and the CMs have to interact effectively so that openness and trust in sharing information are valued and enhanced within the collaborative effort.

The goal is for you and the CMs (and other stakeholders when appropriate) to be able to communicate in ways that are understood and accepted, permitting such communication to have a positive impact on the collaborative evaluation. Obviously, communication is a very complex process, because even the most expertly fashioned message will not accomplish its purpose unless it is understood (Kreitner, 2009). Also, effective communication involves understanding others as well as being understood (Gibson, Ivancevich, & Donnelly, 2008).

The essence of the MCE is to encourage open communication among a diverse group of individuals with a common evaluation purpose. You and the CMs need to work together to transform the evaluation environment into an open one for exchanging information. To assist with that, the MCE component presented in this chapter is divided into the following subcomponents: (a) ensure active participation, (b) ensure careful listening, (c) ensure the message is clear, (d) ensure immediate feedback, and (e) ensure the need for change is justified (see Figure I.2).

ENSURE ACTIVE PARTICIPATION

Active participation is when individuals (such as you and the CMs) take part and contribute with reciprocal input in the collaborative evaluation process to enhance it. You and the CMs may perceive the evaluation "reality" in a different way, due to the presence of multiple realities, and this requires the creation of an environment in which it is safe to take turns transmitting messages between one another in order to express your diverse opinions (such as ideas, uncertainties, and dissenting points).

Active participation is essential in a collaborative evaluation if everyone is to understand it. All the information to be used in an evaluation is normally considered to be very sensitive and should be treated with the highest confidentiality levels. As feasible, your responsibility is to make sure there is an open communication flow and an ongoing monitoring process of the collaborative effort. Socially skilled people work on the basis of the assumption that nothing important gets done alone (Goleman, 2004).

For the evaluation to be a true collaborative process, everyone's interests and opinions relevant to the evaluation efforts should be exchanged in a balanced way. The basics of democracy are that all those who have legitimate interests should be included in decisions that affect those interests (House & Howe, 2000). Make sure that there is a balance of power within the collaborative evaluation so that everyone feels represented in an appropriate and fair way (see Chapter 5 on how to encourage fairness and sincerity).

The CMs' input is needed for diversity of opinions and to build support by listening to each individual. Make important decisions when every CM, as appropriate, has been heard and can agree to support a particular choice as the best course of action. A leader who automatically rejects others' opinions can be as unwise as one who unthinkingly goes along with them (Offermann, 2004).

Active participation allows you and the CMs to provide, react to, and prove new ideas generated within the evaluation. It builds the evaluation effort by avoiding the risk of biased interaction toward just the individuals who have their own specific agendas or interests. Deliberation should be based on the discussion of merits instead of the social status of participants (House & Howe, 2000). Therefore, foster a group dialogue of openness and exploration that continues among the CMs themselves (even outside formal meetings), in which everyone uses the ideas raised in order to obtain sincere reactions.

Encourage every CM to interact in the ongoing evaluation efforts. Each meeting is an opportunity to exchange ideas and to observe and acknowledge everyone's own needs. The goal is that you and every CM are able to provide ideas or express any concern as feasible. Besides meetings, there are other means to encourage active participation in ways that are useful for the purposes of the collaborative evaluation. For example, you may use emailing, blogging, and tweeting.

You and the CMs must understand how the information you send and receive (for example, in sessions or meetings) will affect the collaborative evaluation effort as a whole. Also, everyone's communication needs have to be met as fully as possible if the communication process is to be a successful one. For this reason, we suggest the following steps to ensure active participation within the collaborative evaluation:

1. Verify that all the CMs understand their roles (without perceptions of rankings) and the reason for their involvement in the evaluation. When CMs understand the implications of their contributions they actively support the evaluation efforts.

2. Identify CMs who might have developed informal alliances and how those affect, positively and negatively, the integrity of the evaluation process. For example, as opportunities arise, you may consider interacting in those alliances (such as lunch invitations and parties).

3. Determine the communication needs (for instance, the type of information required or the communication style) of each of the CMs and how they expect those needs to be addressed during the session to facilitate an open discussion.

4. Distribute a preliminary outline of the agenda at the beginning of each session (this gets CMs into the subject matter of the proposed agenda), and throughout it, encourage CMs to offer their input (for example, suggestions and challenges).

5. Break the group into subgroups, as appropriate, whenever you encounter CMs who feel too shy to express their opinions to large groups, or who try to monopolize the session. This gives all the CMs an opportunity to have their ideas heard.

6. Acknowledge and understand everyone's position on the issue discussed in the session. For example, privately ask any CM who appears unhappy whether there is anything you or other CMs may do to gain their support or involvement.

7. Seek opinions with an open mind by using alternative mechanisms to ensure active participation (such as focus groups, interviews, observations, questionnaires, and records review) that are appropriate to the specific situation.

8. Test the commitment of each of the CMs, perhaps demonstrated in writing, to ensure they are willing to fully support the outcome of the session (for instance, if you suspect a particular CM does not fully support a decision).

9. Gather feedback on a regular basis using a previously agreed-upon system (for example, meetings, emails, and surveys as feasible). This will help you and the CMs monitor the participation process and make updates as needed.

10. Keep a journal with information from the session (such as minutes) to follow up, and circulate it as appropriate so that CMs feel fully involved. As a result, you and the CMs can use the information to bring evaluation improvements.

An effective communication involves transmitting information that is understood by the receiver. Ideally, the communication needs to be enthusiastic and meaningful to everyone involved in order to be effective. Also, it is necessary to have a neutral, inclusive, and supportive environment to encourage active participation.

In personal communications, perceptions are more powerful than intentions (Carter & Minirth, 1993). Thus trust is very important in order for active participation within the evaluation to be effective. However, trust is present only when you and the CMs dedicate enough time to developing open communication. There are many ways to foster trust, such as setting an example by demonstrating interest and appreciation for the CMs. Also, the matching and mirroring techniques improve communication because individuals build rapport when they are using the same representational system.

Active participation requires commitment from both you and the CMs within the evaluation process. It means that everyone is allowed to make important contributions from their own perspective to meet the evaluation expectations. Remember that if you expect participation, you must also participate (with enthusiasm and respect) and ensure that the message has reached everyone so that they are all informed as appropriate. As a consequence, you and all the CMs will know your ideas are influential and valued within the collaborative evaluation.

Ensure Active Participation

Eliot: In my seven years as an evaluator I have seen CMs who are actively engaged, but I know a CM who simply can't stop talking and overtaking our meeting time. Some of the CMs have already approached me and asked me to confront him, but of course I am sure there may be an easier way to address this behavior without any kind of confrontation. What would you suggest I do in this case?

Evelyn: Have you ever used the "parking lot" strategy? I also had a CM who never stopped talking during her first meeting until I suggested we should take her idea or concern and place it on the "parking lot." Simply put, the parking lot strategy involves writing down an idea or concern, placing it either on the table or on a wall, and letting her know we would come back at the end of the session, and before our time was up, to see whether her comment was still applicable to the conversation at hand.

At the end of the session, we did come back to three items I had placed on the "parking lot." As I expected, she openly admitted that her comments didn't apply any longer to the conversation. I publicly thanked and appreciated her for following the guidelines we had set early on for our collaborative evaluation effort. Interestingly enough, at the end of that specific meeting she came and thanked me for helping her realize, in a very positive way, that encouraging active participation does not mean that each CM needs to share every single idea that comes to mind. Also, several meetings later, she shared with me that after that first meeting she started writing down her ideas during our meetings and then determining whether or not they should be shared openly or simply be considered by her as an *interesting thought*.

ENSURE CAREFUL LISTENING

Careful listening is when individuals (such as you and the CMs) pay full attention and show a desire to understand what others have to say (letting go of personal ownership of ideas). Listening is a challenge because it shows that you and the CMs have the humility to accept that you do not have all the answers within the collaborative evaluation.

To improve the ability to listen, a person needs to be motivated to change, and then he or she needs practice and feedback from others (Goleman, 2004).

By listening carefully, you and the CMs demonstrate your care and respect for others throughout the collaborative evaluation. Also, you show that you are willing to receive information that may conflict with your own interests or biases.

Ineffective listening can create misunderstandings. Listen to the "whole" message, not just to the part of the conversation that is of particular interest (only what you want to hear). For this reason, be aware of the differences among stakeholders (including education and culture) when selecting them to collaborate in the evaluation. Many people have asked, "What do I do to improve my ability to listen to what other people have to say?" We suggest the following steps to ensure careful listening:

1. Use appropriate techniques to ensure complete listening (including mirroring gestures, eye contact, and friendly expression) and wait patiently during pauses, because generally the most important information follows them.

2. Observe the speaker's nonverbal actions (such as body language or tone of voice) to better understand the message and the speaker's feelings about it. For example, what the CM is saying should be in congruence with how the CM is saying it.

3. Provide short and encouraging responses or statements to show that you are attentively following the conversation. At this point, you should ask only open-ended questions and avoid giving any unrequested judgments or advice.

4. Pause for a few seconds after the speaker has finished talking, to reflect on what was said and how it was said before you respond. This shows that you are interested in the issue and considering carefully its meaning and implications.

5. Summarize the information received without deeper analysis and wait silently for the speaker to validate if your summary was correct. For example, "I believe what you are saying is that you would like to add another evaluation question."

6. Think carefully and, if needed, use the speaker's responses to ask other specific questions in order to gain further detail from the new information. You may ask the speaker to provide a nontechnical example to illustrate the point being made.

7. Get the speaker's perspective on the next possible steps and then help in respectfully guiding toward an adequate solution. For example, ask, What do you feel I should do now in order to help you meet the evaluation objectives?

8. Send a friendly email to the speaker (and other appropriate members) with a summary of the meeting. For example, describe what happened in the meeting, who interacted, the information discussed, and the points agreed upon and not agreed upon.

9. Gather feedback on a regular basis using a previously agreed-upon system (for example, meetings, emails, phone calls, and surveys as feasible). This will help you and the CMs monitor the listening process and make updates as needed.

10. Provide each CM and other stakeholders as appropriate with a summary report of this experience (if it is a particularly illustrative experience) as lessons learned for future similar situations within collaborative evaluations.

Listening helps the individual feel worthy of making contributions (Ivancevich, Konopaske, & Matteson, 2010). You and the CMs inspire confidence in others within the collaborative effort when you carefully listen, because everyone feels they are being acknowledged. However, have an open mind in order to recognize your own biased ideas and avoid listening to only what you want to hear. By understanding the needs of others, you have the power to align what they want with what the collaborative evaluation needs itself.

Some of the advantages of careful listening are that people know you are sincerely interested, you obtain feedback, and acceptance is fostered (Kerzner, 2009b). Also, being a good listener is actually a more effective way of making a good impression than being a gifted speaker (Lewis, 1995). For example, you can start a conversation by saying that you are interested in learning about the CMs' perceptions of the evaluand and what the evaluation can do for it. By stating a general request like this one, you will be able to receive unexpected responses potentially helpful for the collaborative evaluation.

By listening attentively to others, you and the CMs will gain very important information that will help you determine the sensibility and importance of particular issues. You and the CMs also need to understand that people may interpret the same message in different ways, when things that conflict with preconceived notions may be either ignored or distorted (Gibson, Ivancevich, & Donnelly, 2008). For example, due to previous negative experiences with a specific CM, you may not believe (or even listen to) all the information this person is providing you. Be aware of this possibility when you and the CMs listen to each other, because everyone brings perceptions of "their reality" into the collaborative evaluation.

People who communicate their evaluation ideas on an ongoing basis will feel important and confident if they know those ideas are being carefully heard. However, take into consideration that often the person who makes the most noise is also the neediest in the group and the one you have to beware the most (Bennis, 2004). Also, focusing your attention on this type of individual will distract you from working with the entire group on accomplishing the shared vision.

One of the greatest challenges is to be able to discriminate between what is meaningful to the collaborative evaluation effort (what you need to use) and what should be disregarded. In our experience, people (such as CMs) who feel someone is listening to and understanding them tend to be more open to constructive criticism and respond more positively. Also, they tend to evaluate their own ideas more objectively, and they are more ready to incorporate others' ideas as well. This is because they feel important and respected and, in addition, they tend to respect others as well.

You and the CMs should have a sincere interest in listening to others, truly valuing their opinions and making sure of your own needs and biases before you make judgments about the information received (or provide what you believe will be useful feedback). Also, by listening to others, you and the CMs may learn information that will help you make important improvements, both individually and to the collaborative evaluation tasks.

Careful listening has benefits for both you and the CMs. Everyone gains broader information (and potentially useful ideas) on specific issues related to the collaborative evaluation. Also, everyone feels more confident and able to communicate, because all the opinions are being heard and interpreted as originally meant, given that you (or the CMs) are paying attention to the whole message rather than just to what you want to hear. In other words, you and the CMs know that all the information will be rephrased and repeated back among you until the intended message is clearly understood. Careful listening is a way of showing that you and the CMs have paid full attention and tried to understand the message.

Ensure Careful Listening

Ernest: Eliot, I invited you to this initial meeting with our client not just to expose you to a negotiation meeting in a collaborative evaluation but also to ask you to observe how I practice *careful listening*. I tell you this because about four years ago, another colleague who will remain nameless almost led us to lose a big evaluation contract because of his poor listening skills. I once read that people spend around 80 percent of their active time involved in one of four types of communications activities: reading, writing, speaking, or listening. From these four activities, listening accounts for a high percentage of our communication time. Sadly, most people take this for granted and simply assume that everyone knows how to listen.

Eliot: Can you give me a little more background about what happened and how you dealt with that situation?

Ernest: As we are doing this morning, I always make sure that we, the evaluation team, understand the *meeting strategy* prior to visiting with our client. In this instance, our meeting started very well until my colleague thought our client needed a full lecture on collaborative evaluations. He would go on for periods of five-to-seven minutes without even stopping and asking the client and other participants whether they understood and were in agreement with his ideas. To make a very long story short, the client followed up with me and told me that the main condition for continuing to work with her would be excluding my colleague from our evaluation team. I explained the situation to my colleague and offered him work in a different project that didn't require significant interaction with the client. That helped and saved my contract. That also helped to build my professional relationship with my client because I carefully listened to her feedback.

ENSURE THE MESSAGE IS CLEAR

A **clear message** implies providing information that everyone accurately understands as intended. This also involves considering how to overcome potential communication barriers within the collaborative evaluation. Moreover, it means that you and the CMs will provide the same basic information in several or redundant forms to ensure that if one part of the message is not understood, other parts can still carry the same message. Information must be adequate and accessible to intended users. To ensure a clear and complete understanding of the message as it was intended, communicate it in a simple language. A clear message ensures a source of control within the collaborative evaluation.

In addition to the language itself, body posture can assist in communicating your message within the collaborative process. For example, make a positive and confident impression from the first moments of your encounter by using a positive and warm attitude, a genuine smile, eye contact, and straight posture. If you intend to gain cooperation, a right-angle orientation when sitting is most effective (for confrontations, select a face-to-face position).

A clear message allows you and the CMs to accurately link new information received to the collaborative evaluation vision (see Chapter 3 on how to establish a shared evaluation vision). Among others, some of the tools for enhancing communications are review schedules, status meetings, and reporting systems (Kerzner, 2009b). Remember that the message you communicate may be received in a totally different way than you intended, because CMs and you may have different points of view on the issue. Thus we suggest the following steps to ensure the message is clear:

1. Analyze the message (for example, its meaning and possible interpretations) in a systematic way in order to clearly determine what you want to accomplish by it, and how it reflects on other CMs and the overall collaborative evaluation.

2. Carefully choose each of the words of the message you want to communicate, while being completely direct and sincere, so your nonverbal gestures will be in complete harmony with your words, helping to clearly convey the message.

3. Select the most appropriate way to communicate the message (such as verbally) in an understandable and timely way. For example, use appropriate and simple language (avoid technical words), stories, pictures, graphics, or audiovisuals.

4. Provide the same basic information in several reinforcing ways (including copies of materials) to ensure that the full message is communicated, as thoroughly as possible, even if there are different perceptions between you and the CMs.

5. Verify that the CMs (or other participants) understand the message communicated and its parts to make sure of its clarity. Have a relaxed atmosphere within the collaborative evaluation so CMs feel free to communicate.

6. Overcome any potential communication barriers (for instance, written versus oral or formal versus informal) and make adjustments as needed to ensure the message is totally understood by the specific CMs. Where necessary, use additional examples.

7. Determine the CMs' level of receptiveness of the message (demonstrated by verbal and nonverbal gestures or by signing their approval on formal agreement documents) and the future steps related to it within the collaborative evaluation.

8. Devote time for communicating regularly with individual CMs in order to determine if everyone is sufficiently informed (such as regarding the latest key issues) and provide a vehicle for learning about their evaluation needs and concerns.

9. Follow up with CMs on the ongoing communication of the message (for example, agree on deadlines for specific activities) and make updates as needed on the clarity of the message throughout the collaborative evaluation.

10. Provide each CM and other stakeholders as appropriate with a summary report of this experience (if it is a particularly illustrative experience to share) as lessons learned for future similar situations within collaborative evaluations.

Show CMs (and other relevant stakeholders) that you are always willing to listen in order for them to freely express any concerns or doubts about your message. If you experience some resistance from a CM (or CMs) about the message, then take some time to reframe it. This will help you think about a different way to present your message. For example, maybe it will be more appealing for the CMs if you add a little more feeling while explaining your ideas, instead of basing them solely on rationale. However, keep in mind that the message should be based on factual content rather than on your individual opinions.

A great danger is when evaluators do not fully understand stakeholders' views and interests, or that they misrepresent them in the evaluation (House & Howe, 2000). For this reason, in all the evaluations we have conducted, we have always scheduled time for regular dialogue with CMs (and other stakeholders) in order to keep an open communication. This is because uncertainties within the evaluation decrease the motivation of CMs. Thus, continuously ask for the CMs' points of view on the message in order to verify their support.

Problems within the collaborative evaluation are considered important (or not) depending on how you and the CMs approach them. In many evaluations, we have observed that CMs react in a more positive light when they receive information from people with a positive attitude. Therefore, ensure an atmosphere within the collaborative evaluation in which everyone feels involved through open dialogue, and feels free to air their views in their own way (see Chapter 5 on how to encourage effective practices).

The use of humor can make problems seem more manageable or, conversely, it can have a catastrophic effect on the evaluation. A sense of humor helps you maintain enough perspective and humility to keep on learning (Maccoby, 2004). People who use their sense of humor usually convey a sense of willingness to be open to other's opinions. However, you and the CMs need to be careful and only use this type of approach (and even the use of a simple smile) if it is appropriate to the evaluation situation. Smiling inappropriately can create as negative an impression as not smiling at all (Lewis, 1995). Humor can relieve a tense situation but should be used carefully so it does not interfere with the evaluation process.

Understanding the CMs' interests, needs, and perspectives on the evaluation issues is a very complex task that can only be accomplished with effective communication. Keeping CMs up to date through a clear message on the information they need to know generates good will toward the collaborative evaluation. Also, it shows an interest in what CMs need to say, specifically when you meet with each of them, if possible, on a one-on-one basis. For this reason, every CM must have accurate and immediate information as appropriate. This is a very positive way to overcome opposition because CMs feel that they are being part of a friendly atmosphere.

We believe that the more planning you and the CMs put into communicating the message (for example, determining how you will make logical transitions among issues), the more clarity it is likely to achieve. Also, it prepares for any potential strong reaction against the message (see Chapter 3 on how to establish means toward conflict resolution). The message needs to be understood (for instance, how it will affect others) to get a sense of commitment on future changes that will result from it. The success of the collaborative evaluation depends on your ability (and the CMs' ability) to transmit and receive clear information with confidence and take appropriate action on such information.

Ensure the Message Is Clear

Ernest: I would love to hear what you have to say about my client, with whom I am having a very hard time communicating. Our meetings normally go very well, but it is when I send him my notes about what we just discussed during the meeting that he starts disagreeing and challenging some of the ideas or tasks I am reporting back to him. What would you recommend me to do?

Evelyn: Well, I believe you are doing the right thing of writing back to him as soon as feasible after your meeting with a summary of what was discussed and agreed upon. One strategy you may try is probing what he has just said or suggested by rephrasing his same statement and saying it back to him. You may say something like, "Just to make sure I clearly understand what you are suggesting us to do: I am hearing that we should do XYZ by this ABC day and time; am I correct?" Then wait until he agrees. If there isn't a full agreement you may then ask him for further clarification. Then you may continue with your meeting. I am confident this will help you improve your communication with your client.

ENSURE IMMEDIATE FEEDBACK

Feedback is the response to an inquiry that, if done well, ensures a high level of sharing and understanding for a meaningful communication within the collaborative evaluation. Because the root of feedback is factual information, you and the CMs need to provide feedback in a behavioral way (based on actions) in order to provide clear suggestions for improvement without threatening anybody's self-esteem.

Leaders must end secrecy and keep people informed (Block, 1993). In general, we give feedback that begins with a description of the accomplishment met, the expected goal, and then a discussion of ways to meet the resulting gap. This type of feedback mechanism allows everyone to be more open to the message received and to move forward with the steps for improvement. For example, for a fundraising shortfall, you might start by saying that currently the CMs have collected $200 for a particular purpose for which they were attempting to raise $1,000, and that you would like to suggest some ideas on how to raise the remaining $800.

You and the CMs should feel comfortable in giving feedback, or it will be skewed out of fear of retaliation. In other words, facilitate an open and non-threatening evaluation environment. The goal is to have a collaborative evaluation in which everyone is willing to say how things are working from their perspective. Any feedback request must be treated with respect and in a timely fashion because, if useful knowledge is uncovered, it can help in making important improvements to the evaluation plan.

The right feedback opens the door to knowledge and understanding of the collaborative evaluation efforts. Thus we suggest the following steps to ensure immediate feedback:

1. Establish a friendly atmosphere in which any feedback (positive or negative) is viewed as a constructive opportunity for improvement so there is no intimidation from undesirable repercussions within the collaborative evaluation.

2. Agree on a methodology to make sure you and the appropriate CMs, and other stakeholders as needed, are informed of the evaluation and its progress (for example, through meetings, minutes, emails, draft reports, suggestion boxes, videos, and brochures).

3. Ask periodically for suggestions and ideas regarding the collaborative evaluation (such as about general or specific procedures). In this way, you and the CMs will be encouraged to reflect on your feelings and particular improvement ideas.

4. Listen carefully, respectfully, and enthusiastically to all the suggestions received. This transmits confidence that each suggestion is being taken seriously and will be followed up as appropriate in the collaborative evaluation.

5. Give a regular update on the progress of specific evaluation tasks and their relationship to the overall collaborative evaluation. For example, schedule specific evaluation milestone meetings (such as weekly, monthly, or as required).

6. Be available to meet at nonscheduled times in order to share unexpected issues or concerns that have arisen in the collaborative effort. For example, a CM may need to meet with you to talk briefly and make an evaluation decision.

7. Take CMs aside (either as individuals or in small groups) and solicit information by asking how they think the collaborative evaluation is

doing and how it might be improved. For example, use questionnaires and telephone interviews.

8. Ask for others' individual comments (for instance, from colleague evaluators or experts) or feedback regarding similar evaluation circumstances to learn from them. For example, what would they do if facing the same situation?

9. Thank every specific individual with a written note for the help offered through their feedback. For example, you may say that you appreciate their comments on a particular issue, and then explain how you will proceed on them.

10. Provide each CM and other stakeholders as appropriate with a summary report of this experience (including a report of the feedback and its viability) as lessons learned for future similar situations within collaborative evaluations.

When you share a summary of the lessons learned from the feedback to the CMs (as needed), everyone is able to learn from what others have experienced within the collaborative evaluation. Even though feedback may be available, you and the CMs need to understand it as it was intended in order to successfully apply it. The best feedback is that which takes into consideration the individual receiving it, and is fair (based on facts), straightforward, nonjudgmental, and simple.

Figure 4.1 and Table 4.1 show examples of how you and the CMs can use visual aids to provide feedback as the evaluation progresses. Feedback should always be delivered as soon as the information emerges (and not just when the evaluation is ending). With the use of visual aids (such as pictures and graphics) individuals can immediately understand the situation and react to it. In this way, everyone will have time to make adjustments to the evaluation efforts as needed. Always balance the needs of all the CMs, yourself, and the evaluation itself when you provide feedback.

One simple test of whether you're getting the feedback you need is to count how many people challenge you at your next meeting (Offermann, 2004). Open channels of communication in order to obtain feedback that is based on complete and accurate information. In other words, facilitate an open atmosphere within the collaborative evaluation. Self-aware people are comfortable talking about their limitations and strengths, and they often show a thirst for constructive criticism (Goleman, 2004). Make sure that any feedback concerns with behavior are within the control of the individual (Bennis & Nanus, 2003).

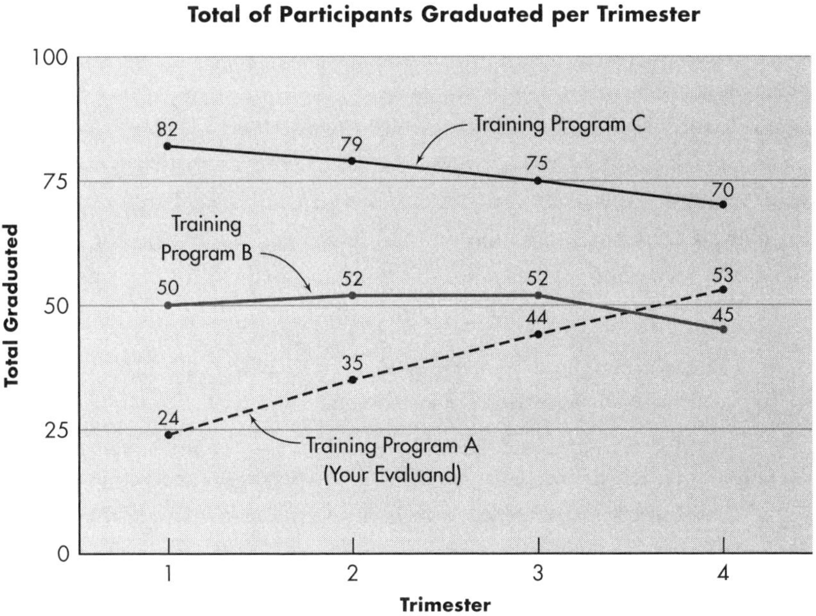

Total of Participants Graduated per Trimester

Figure 4.1 Example of Feedback Using a Figure

Table 4.1 Example of Feedback Using a Table

Training Program	Total of Participants Graduated per Trimester			
	I	II	III	IV
Training Program A (Your Evaluand)	74	63	45	24
Training Program B	51	63	78	87
Training Program C	42	71	79	82
Training Program D	60	62	66	79

The goal is to have people within the collaborative evaluation who are will-ing to say how things are from their perspective. You and the CMs should treat any feedback request with respect and respond in a timely fashion, because the right feedback facilitates a greater understanding of the evaluation process. Act on the premise that CMs consider it useful and important to be informed on specific issues, and that this generates trust on the achievement of a common evaluation goal (see Chapter 6 on how to follow the collaboration guiding principles).

Evaluation knowledge increases when you and the CMs receive continuous feedback (with points of view other than your own) that strengthens your common experience and stimulates your thinking. Therefore, be sure to follow a feedback methodology that details (depending on the various types of information and responsibilities established within the evaluation)

Ensure Immediate Feedback

Eliot: For the past several years I have been using a few online applications that allow you to keep track of your tasks during the evaluation and also keep all team members informed about any new document that has been uploaded to the website, any task finished, and all milestones reached. I mention this because one of my clients continues to emphasize how she believes immediate feedback is one of the most important aspects of an evaluation. Is there anything else you would recommend to me in this regard?

Evelyn: As a matter of fact, yes there is. Feedback comes in two ways, expected or unexpected. Expected feedback can be based on your evaluation plan, contract specifications, or verbal agreements. Unexpected feedback can be tricky at times but when provided properly can become an added bonus for your client-evaluator relationship. For example, sometimes people ask you for unplanned conference calls or even meetings, and what I normally do, right after each of these, is to write an email summarizing what was covered and agreed upon in that call or meeting. I also make sure I share that document with the team and, as needed, save it on the website or platform we are using to maintain our own documentation.

In regard to solicited feedback via email, for example, my rule of thumb is to reply within twenty-four hours and, if I believe I need more time, I will still email the person or team and let them know I will get back to them once I have more information. Last, if you will be with limited email access for a few days, I strongly recommend that you use an auto-reply message letting people know you will reply to them as soon as feasible. Never assume people know you are busy and for that reason you haven't replied to their emails or phone calls.

to whom the feedback is going to be provided and how it is going to be distributed or updated.

Feedback can be highly motivational to you and the CMs if everyone believes that the information received is objective and will help improve what is being done. Be aware that in some cases misunderstandings can occur. For example, CMs' feedback could follow their personal agendas and even be ill-intended. Instead of waiting for an ambush, determine who will be shooting, from where, and with what, and arm yourself accordingly (Weiss, 2009). Always make sure you and the CMs understand the reasons for the feedback you are receiving (or potentially will receive) so you can react appropriately to it (for example, establish improvement options).

There are times when informal meetings could be the best source of feedback because verbal ideas are shared more effectively (with opportunity to clear up misunderstandings immediately) than through written means. However, keep in mind that written feedback is needed in most day-to-day circumstances. Do your best to address letters and faxes requiring a response on the same day when you are in the office or as soon as feasible. Feedback is essential in a collaborative evaluation because it ensures the quality of the evaluation efforts by informing appropriate individuals of the evaluation status (what is going well and what needs to be modified). Moreover, it shows early on areas that need to be addressed in a different way in order to meet the evaluation vision.

ENSURE THE NEED FOR CHANGE IS JUSTIFIED

Change is a process for substituting current patterns of behavior or actions for new ones in the hope of benefiting the collaborative evaluation. An adaptive capacity is what allows people to make decisions that bring success, to transcend setbacks and losses, and to reinvent themselves again and again (Bennis, 2004). Because the evaluation is always changing and evolving, its elements (such as resources) also change over time. You and the CMs need to deal with those new conditions by having advance information to be able to adjust.

There are six change forces: (a) bureaucratic forces, which are the rules and other requirements intended to provide direct supervision; (b) personal forces, which include personalities and interpersonal skills; (c) market forces, which include the competition and incentives; (d) professional forces, which include standards of expertise and other norms intended to build professional community; (e) cultural forces, which include shared values, goals, and ideas; and

(f) democratic forces, which include social contracts and shared commitment to the common good (Sergiovanni & Starratt, 2006). Therefore, learn to distinguish when you and the CMs really have to change or when to preserve things as they are within the collaborative evaluation.

Shift goals in a systematic way, so when you and the CMs show that change is a positive alternative to current issues, everyone involved is more prone to want the change. Obviously, the key to achieving change is to convince others that the change is in their best interest. Consequently, people need to have information that enables them to know what is to happen and why (Gibson, Ivancevich, & Donnelly, 2008). You and the CMs will show commitment to change once you understand the importance of it and how it will affect you. For instance, people don't resist change if the change provides immediate positive consequences for them (Daniels, 2000).

Change is never easy, because it involves moving from a state of knowing to not knowing (Owens & Valesky, 2010). Obviously, this can affect the sense of trust and safety. When you and the CMs are conscious of the need to change, then you can take responsibility for implementing actions to achieve the desired change. People will accept change when proper incentive is available and when satisfaction results from goal attainment (House, 1971). You and the CMs need to spend time recognizing each other's contribution to the collaborative evaluation, so you can feel fulfilled and satisfied.

Change requests may occur in several forms, such as oral or written, and externally or internally initiated. When trying to obtain everyone's agreement on the need for a particular evaluation change, it is very valuable to have data that support the argument. In addition, humor humbles, and creates insights that make it a very powerful instrument for change (Coutu, 2004). In implementing effective change, an optimistic outlook is very important, along with many other elements, such as vision, communication, and understanding. Therefore, we suggest the following steps to ensure the need for change is justified:

1. Recognize the need for change due to a diagnosis of the evaluation situation and everyone affected by it. For example, after identifying the gap between the present and ideal state, ask the CMs what should be done differently.

2. Ask for feedback from others in similar evaluation circumstances (including colleague evaluators and experts) in order to accumulate relevant information. For instance, what would they do if facing the same evaluation situation?

3. Choose the best type of information (such as figures, tables, documents, or reports) that can justify a rational argument for the proposed change. For example, map out the previous relevant processes that led to the need for change.

4. Anticipate negative responses to or criticism about your argument (which may be completely rational and well founded) by preparing several detailed and well-supported possible alternatives or plans to help explain your argument.

5. Use a two-way communication to present the suggested step-by-step plan for change (such as showing concrete, attainable goals and results) with clear facts on how the proposed change is linked to the collaborative evaluation vision.

6. Acknowledge and understand everyone's position, including yours, on the need for change. For example, ask any CMs who appear unhappy with the change how they will be affected by it, and how you (or others) may gain their support.

7. Seek additional ideas with an open mind (be willing to modify your own ideas) by using alternative mechanisms to ensure participation (such as questionnaires, interviews, or records review), and clear up misunderstandings.

8. Check the commitment of each of the CMs to ensure they agree (in writing if the changes are significant) to fully support the change. This is especially important if you suspect that a CM who perhaps is silent does not fully support the decision.

9. Agree with the CMs on the next steps or procedures to follow within the collaborative evaluation (for example, in areas in which more support or training should be offered or other main priorities) as a result of the approved change.

10. Gather feedback on a regular basis using a previously agreed-upon system, such as meetings, and summarize it in a written format (including specific facts on progress measures) so it is available to each CM and other stakeholders as appropriate.

For the evaluation to be realistic, individuals need to enter into dialogue and understand the complexities of the changes introduced (Pawson & Tilley, 1997). In the most successful collaborative evaluations, change is understood as a natural and inescapable process. However, to help people move with the changes, provide hard evidence for every change needed, because in this way everyone knows what you are doing and why you are doing it (see Figure 4.2). Obviously, useful evaluations are the ones producing findings that fit into the evaluand change agenda.

Most change requests are the result of an external event, such as an error or omission in scope definition, or a value-adding change (PMI Standards Committee, 2008). When you or the CMs present what needs to be changed, also reassure everyone about what is working well and does not need to be

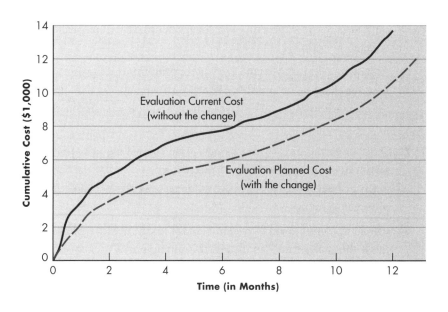

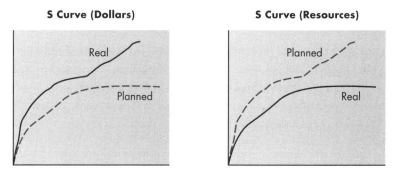

Figure 4.2 Example of Evidence of Change Needed

changed. You and the CMs have to show that change is a positive experience so the change is welcomed, but it is just as important to acknowledge as well what is already right within the collaborative evaluation. The goal is to turn change into something that everyone should look forward to (and not be afraid of) because it is something good for the evaluation, so everyone will be highly committed to it.

You and the CMs have an important responsibility to improve the quality of any change within the collaborative evaluation by positively influencing the way everyone thinks and performs their evaluation tasks. For example, understand each CM's point of view when planning for change and use this information to obtain optimal results within the collaborative evaluation. Each CM can make a more positive contribution when you involve them in planning the change while making sure they know exactly what is expected from them.

Change is a challenge that inevitably will affect the evaluation and its stakeholders. The roots of resistance to evaluation go very deep, so it is wise not to underestimate their strength (Scriven, 1993). To implement change within the collaborative evaluation, examine the CMs' (and your own) needs and values in order to realign them with any revision of the evaluation plan. Also, make sure everyone involved in the evaluation is appropriately informed of the changes required in order to work toward the same goal. Change is likely to stabilize over time, when the new, more effective level of performance can be maintained without coercion (Owens & Valesky, 2010; Sergiovanni, 2004).

You and the CMs should only consider the possibility of change after addressing all the potential positive and negative consequences (for example, worries that may lead specific individuals to resist the change, or areas in which change will have more impact) so they can be approached as opportunities. Make sure you and the CMs speak openly about how any updates will provide advantages that will outweigh the current ones, as well as the possible adverse effects. Also, develop contingency plans to foresee unwanted situations as a consequence of the changes to be made. Then, together you can decide the most appropriate changes after you and the CMs have thoroughly analyzed the critical needs of the collaborative evaluation.

The important thing is to make changes in an orderly way, following a standard procedure (Lewis, 1999). Then, unexpected deviations may be prevented from what you and the CMs had initially expected because you understand any underlying causes. Obviously, for a change to occur flexibility should be built into the collaborative evaluation to cope with how changes might affect the original plan (see Chapter 5 on how to encourage flexibility and creativity). As a result, updates may be needed in the evaluation plan (for instance, with new milestones and timelines), implementation, and then measures of its impact.

To understand the implications that any modifications will have on the collaborative evaluation (and stakeholders in general), you and the CMs need to know who will be directly affected by those modifications. The more people are affected by the proposed change, the more complex it is to combine the evaluation tasks into a shared vision that works well for them. Therefore, make

Ensure the Need for Change Is Justified

Cheryl: Ernest, I just received the preliminary evaluation results from another consulting firm about our printing unit; it came back with very negative results. In short, it leads to the possibility of closing the unit. I have never seen a team so committed to our work as the printing unit team. All previous evaluation results have always been positive, but I have never requested such a rigorous evaluation as this one. As the evaluation client, how do you think I can approach this situation?

Ernest: Well, perhaps the external evaluators have also mentioned some alternatives for you and your team to consider before closing the unit. Let me just think out loud here for a minute and raise some questions: (1) For how many more months does your current budget allow you to run your operations? Are the evaluators providing you with a transition plan for your current team? (2) Can you cross-train your current team, reclassify their job descriptions, and relocate them in other positions? (3) Should the evaluator recommend you to outsource the printing service, will there be a need to still have an in-house coordinator of such service? (4) Should you offer your current staff the opportunity to create their own and external business, would you consider them as an attractive service provider for your printing services? and finally, (5) Have you considered sharing the report with the team from the printing unit?

As you think about the answers to these questions, I am sure you will see some ideas you may use to address this situation. If you need more assistance, let's schedule a time so we can think of more specific strategies to ensure the need for change is justified.

sure that everyone affected is part of the change process because this is the best way to buy their ownership into it. Change should be seen as an opportunity to make improvements to the evaluation efforts, when everyone's valuable ideas are considered important and are being heard.

The clarity with which you and the CMs perceive the potential results of change has great implications for its success in the collaborative evaluation. Everyone involved in the evaluation change should understand the reasons for it (backed with hard evidence) and how the implications for their roles can affect the evaluation at every stage. In this way, you and the CMs can feel positively committed to your work because you understand, with greater clarity and detail, the meaningfulness of your contributions. By communicating on an ongoing basis within the collaborative evaluation, you and the CMs are building trust, which will help everyone to have a more positive response toward change.

In this chapter, we emphasized the importance of ensuring open communication in a way that is understood and accepted within the collaborative evaluation. We focused on active participation in order to promote a balanced and relevant exchange. We also discussed how careful listening helps everyone involved feel worthy of making contributions. In addition, we presented benefits of a clear message and immediate feedback to build a greater understanding of the collaborative effort. Furthermore, we provided guidance on how to ensure the need for change is justified to be able to explore the implications of new conditions and adjust to them. Finally, as in other chapters, we incorporated examples to reinforce interdependence among the MCE elements, such as encouraging effective practices throughout the collaborative evaluation, the topic discussed in Chapter 5.

Encourage
Effective Practices

Effective practices are sound established procedures or systems for producing a desired effect within the collaborative evaluation. For example, this can be accomplished by balancing needs among evaluation resources. Also, fostering an atmosphere in which everyone is supportive of everyone else's capabilities increases recognition that each individual provides important input to the evaluation process.

Throughout the collaborative evaluation, create opportunities to increase knowledge and skills in you and each CM (for example, resource sharing and mentorship). In this way, everyone effectively takes action toward the accomplishment of the evaluation vision (see Chapter 3 on how to establish a shared evaluation vision). As a result, everyone feels empowered and able to actively interact in the collaborative evaluation activities because (by focusing on strengths and capabilities) there is a belief that each contribution makes a difference.

Encouraging effective practices should be done on an ongoing basis in order to facilitate collaboration throughout the evaluation. For this reason, the MCE component presented in this chapter is divided into the following subcomponents: (a) encourage appreciation for individual differences, (b) encourage fairness and sincerity, (c) encourage benchmarking, (d) encourage teaching by example, and (e) encourage flexibility and creativity (see Figure I.2).

ENCOURAGE APPRECIATION FOR INDIVIDUAL DIFFERENCES

Individual differences refers to the mixture of characteristics among individuals (such as you and the CMs) within the collaborative evaluation that account for variation on how they react to the same experiences. By encouraging appreciation for individual differences, you and the CMs can build relationships and use those differences to improve the evaluation process.

If you and the CMs want to predict everyone's particular actions with increased precision (for example, a CM's preference to remain socially withdrawn) and create a better evaluation environment, each individual's differing contribution must be clearly understood and appreciated so you can all work toward an improved overall effort. Be aware of the degree to which one set of observations about a person may lead to erroneous conclusions about other actions (Prentice, 2004). Therefore, be cautious and understand that the individual differences, in addition to your interpretation of those differences, may have a major effect on the collaborative evaluation.

People may be similar in some aspects, but they are also unique, and the study of individual differences helps explain variances in performance levels (Gibson, Ivancevich, & Donnelly, 2008). People are different from each other in many ways (for instance, they want different things). If you and the CMs appreciate each other in terms of your differences (such as motivation, perception, personality, and values) you will be able to make the best possible evaluation-related decisions.

Avoid being biased or judgmental toward particular individual characteristics within the collaborative evaluation. Specifically, avoid labeling some individual characteristics as good and others as bad (for example, age, gender, and race), holding stereotypes, or refusing to associate with people with different characteristics from your own. Also, keep in mind that each characteristic influences a particular action within the collaborative evaluation, depending on the situation.

If you and the CMs understand the differences among individuals, you can use those differences productively within the evaluation. It is important to understand that you and the CMs are not the only ones with a vision, and that everybody sees the collaborative evaluation in their own way. Try to appreciate the differences everyone brings to the joint evaluation effort. We suggest the following steps to encourage appreciation for individual differences:

1. Learn as much as you can about each of the CMs' individual characteristics. For example, ask the CMs for a biographical sketch or get information from them on specific issues relevant to the collaborative evaluation.

2. Create a summary list of the most important features that reflect the individual characteristics among the CMs. With this list in mind, you may be able to fit the CMs' characteristics to the needs of the collaborative evaluation.

3. Meet with each of the CMs to discuss their (and your) individual characteristics and the relationship of these to the evaluation. Understanding of these characteristics can provide evaluation opportunities that will stimulate you and the CMs.

4. Seek clarification (with a courteous and positive attitude) about their individual characteristics when meeting with each of the CMs, as convenient. For example, if doubts arise after the meeting, you might follow up to clarify them all.

5. Listen, rather than just making statements or educating CMs about their individual characteristics. For example, wait silently and patiently during pauses in a conversation, because generally the most important comments come after them.

6. Request feedback from each of the CMs to add or delete information from the initial individual characteristics list. In other words, identify any contrasting points of view through the generation of alternative ideas or possibilities.

7. Agree with the CMs, as appropriate, on a final list that clearly describes everyone's (yours and the CMs') individual characteristics (such as how these complement yours or other CMs' and how they could be linked to the evaluation expectations).

8. Align the CMs' main characteristics with the collaborative evaluation expectations. For instance, a CM whose characteristics are "fair" and "skillful in quantitative or qualitative methods" could collaborate with the data-collection design.

9. Gather feedback on a regular basis using a previously agreed-upon system (for example, meetings, emails, and phone calls as feasible). This will help you and the CMs monitor the appreciation for individual differences and make updates as needed.

10. Provide each CM and other stakeholders as appropriate with a summary report of this experience (including an updated list with everyone's biographical sketch) so they are able to understand how everyone's differences can be helpful for the evaluation.

The goal is to gain everyone's confidence in the collaborative evaluation by understanding each other's strengths and weaknesses in their contributions toward the joint effort. To appreciate individual differences, you and the CMs must understand the characteristics that everyone brings to the evaluation, and try to establish relationships among those characteristics and the evaluation vision. In a collaborative effort everyone can learn from each other, and this knowledge can be used to conduct an evaluation that is relevant to the context of the evaluand.

To show a sincere appreciation toward every person involved in the collaborative evaluation, also know your own characteristics and how those may affect the evaluation. For example, after you understand every CM's individual characteristics, you may choose to behave in ways different from usual to show appreciation toward other's differences. You may choose to respect a particular CM's need for emotional distance, while responding appropriately to other CMs' quests for attention. Also, a specific evaluation task within the collaborative effort may be uninteresting for a particular CM, while it may be exciting for other CMs. Therefore, use your knowledge of those differences to best support the CMs.

In a collaborative evaluation the efforts of each individual depend on the efforts of all the other members. You and the CMs should recognize and proactively use each other's unique combination of strengths and limitations. This will lead to an increased appreciation of the essential role each of you plays in the collaborative effort, and for how you link your personal goals with the overall evaluation goals. Appreciating the individual differences means ensuring that everyone's roles and contributions are considered highly, and their opinions are heard.

By getting to know and recognize the characteristics that each CM brings to the evaluation, you can determine reasonable means to make decisions while maintaining the integrity of each individual. It is obvious that you will differ from the CMs in many ways, and the decisions about who will perform a particular evaluation task will lead to some challenges if you do not have a clear understanding on this issue. For this reason, the major individual differences that you may consider in any evaluation include (a) diversity, (b) motivation, (c) perception, (d) personality, and (e) values.

Diversity

Diversity is the variety existent among individuals (such as you and the CMs) on particular dimensions that clearly differ from our own. The core dimensions of diversity include age, ethnicity, gender, physical attributes, race, and sexual orientation (Gibson, Ivancevich, & Donnelly, 2008). Other dimensions include educational and work experience, language, and socioeconomic status.

It is important that you and the CMs acknowledge that everyone (in one way or another) is different from each other in order to appreciate and respect those differences. As a result, everyone involved can understand how beneficial it is to identify diversity and integrate it into the collaborative evaluation. Obviously, this leads to an increased awareness of potentially conflictive differences. For example, members with different ethnic backgrounds may have different ways of socializing or value different rewards.

Throughout our experience as evaluators, we have learned that some dimensions of diversity can be more important than others—in terms of more frequently leading to conflict—and this of course depends on every particular situation (see Chapter 3 on how to establish means toward conflict resolution). Obviously, this is taking into consideration that a collaborative evaluation depends upon positive personal relations and effective emotional connections between you and the CMs.

There needs to be a sense of awareness, appreciation, and celebration of the existing diversity surrounding us. Your actions in certain situations will depend on the knowledge basis you have on how to behave in those situations, such as when exposed to urban versus rural environments. Diversity is learned through exposure (for example, traveling, reading, and sharing), so the more practice you and the CMs have in diverse environments and with different types of people, the better you will be able to understand and appreciate diversity. Value diversity because it enriches the collaborative evaluation by the influence it has on self-perception and the perception of others.

Motivation

Motivation is a force that affects individuals' actions (such as yours and the CMs') and explains why people behave in a particular way within the collaborative evaluation. You and the CMs are motivated by individual needs that depend on many factors (social, cultural, economic, hereditary, and so on) and lead to your goals. A **need** is a deficiency or something wanted at a point in time that acts as a motivator to generate a particular action or behavior.

When a need is present, you and the CMs seek to fulfill that need and may be more susceptible to managers' motivational efforts (Gibson, Ivancevich, & Donnelly, 2008). Understand the CMs' individual needs in order to understand their motivation within the collaborative evaluation effort. When you recognize the CMs' diverse needs and help them to meet those needs through adequate evaluation roles, their commitment increases.

There are at least three distinct motivational components: (a) direction, which is the pattern of choices made when a person is confronted with alternative actions; (b) intensity, which is the strength of a person's attention to the response once the choice is made; and (c) persistence, which is the staying power of behavior, or how long a person will continue to devote effort (see, for example, Ivancevich, Konopaske, & Matteson, 2010; Owens & Valesky, 2010). In addition, there are two major approaches or views that have dominated the thinking about motivation in organizational behavior (Owens & Valesky, 2010):

- **Extrinsic View.** This view emphasizes the external control of the individual. It tends to view motivation as something that one does to people through a combination of rewards and punishments.

- **Intrinsic View.** This view emphasizes that motivation lies within the individuals themselves. It tends to view motivation as tapping inner drives by creating growth-enhancing environments.

People are neither motivated only by their own internal perceptions and characteristics nor only by external demands and environmental conditions but by an interaction of the two (Porter & Lawler, 1968). Recognize the different motivation views in order to accurately apply this knowledge in the evaluation effort. There are several theories of motivation that can help you and the CMs focus on each of the needs that affect your actions within the collaborative evaluation. Some of the most common theories are as follows:

- **Alderfer's Theory.** Alderfer's theory of motivation involves a three-level need hierarchy, in which there is a satisfaction-progression and frustration-regression process. The needs are (a) existence, including food and working conditions; (b) relatedness, including social relationships and external esteem; and (c) growth, including internal esteem and self-actualization (Alderfer, 1969).

- **Herzberg's Theory.** Herzberg's two-factor theory of motivation describes these factors in the workplace: (a) hygiene and (b) motivation. Extrinsic conditions (such as salary) are hygiene factors because they do not motivate, but without them there is dissatisfaction. Intrinsic conditions (such as interest in the job) are motivators that drive people to achieve (Herzberg, Mausner, & Snyderman, 1993).

- **Maslow's Theory.** Maslow's need hierarchy model is one of the most popular motivation theories. It explains that people have a need to develop and grow. In ascending order, the needs are (a) physiological,

(b) safety and security, (c) social, (d) esteem, and (e) self-actualization (Maslow, 1991). This theory emphasizes that once a need is satisfied then it is not a stimulus anymore.

- **McClelland's Theory.** McClelland's learned needs theory of motivation proposes that many needs are acquired over time from the society's culture (your own life experiences). Hence, understand the actions associated with the need for (a) achievement, (b) affiliation, and (c) power (McClelland, 1962).

By fostering a positive collaborative evaluation environment (for example, inquiring about the CMs' evaluation needs and acting on those findings), you can establish a solid base for the CMs' motivation. Because motivation varies among the CMs, try balancing the individual needs and the collaborative evaluation needs to perform at your best. Because trust is an important form of motivation, once you understand the CMs' needs, address them as feasible to increase their trust in you and the collaborative evaluation.

Perception

Perception is the act by which individuals (such as you and the CMs) give meaning to, experience, or interpret stimuli from the collaborative evaluation environment or context. Perception helps you to give your own (individualized) interpretation to stimuli in a coherent way. To organize the information experienced from the surroundings, you and the CMs use the five senses: sight, touch (feel), hearing, smell, and taste.

The same evaluation task may be perceived in different ways by different people within the collaborative effort. For example, you may imagine that you are empowering the CMs with the freedom you are giving them to make choices within the collaborative evaluation. However, some of the CMs who need a more rigid environment may feel frustrated because of the excessive freedom you are giving them to make choices within the collaborative evaluation. In contrast, some other CMs may believe that you are not giving them enough freedom to use their judgment about how to perform the evaluation tasks.

The perception of reality is in the mind of the beholder, so something is real only if you or the CMs perceive it to be real. People create "maps" of the world to help make sense of the environment, forming the basis for memories and expectations (Dilts, 1983). These maps help everyone deal with the evaluation environment by learning from past experience and avoiding the same types of mistakes in the future. As a result, you and the CMs create your own maps or definitions of reality in accordance to your own interpretations of such reality.

There are several tools and techniques that help you and the CMs understand how each individual perceives their collaborative evaluation environment. A very useful example is **Neuro-Linguistic Programming** (NLP), which is a model of the neurological processes used to create the maps of how individuals (such as you and the CMs) experience and communicate their environment.

NLP can help you and the CMs gain more control of the unique representation each of you gives to the collaborative evaluation environment according to those individual perceptions. With the use of NLP, you and the CMs can also improve communication with other evaluation stakeholders and reach a more harmonious relationship (see Chapter 4 on how to ensure open communication). This is because NLP shows you how to recognize the verbal and nonverbal information necessary to understand individual differences.

There are two important ways, derived from the five senses, to understand the individual patterns used in the thought process (see, for example, Harris, 2003; O'Connor & Seymour, 2011):

- **Eye Accessing Cues.** These are particular eye movements (in certain directions) that indicate visual, auditory, or kinesthetic thinking. This technique is used to determine which representational system an individual uses, or accesses, to process particular information.

- **Predicate Accessing Cues.** This technique is used to determine the preferred individual representational system by listening to the predicates used during communication. For example, (a) visually: "I *see* what you mean"; (b) auditory: "this *sounds* like a good idea"; or (c) kinesthetic: "I don't *feel* this is clear."

These accessing cues can help you and the CMs establish rapport within the collaborative effort by understanding how people process information and then matching or mirroring those patterns. NLP can also be a useful tool to help you and the CMs be more open to changing particular actions. For example, the accessing cues may reveal that a particular CM tends to favor the visual representation system rather than the auditory or kinesthetic. As a consequence, you may change your own style and mirror this visual representational system by conveying the evaluation information through pictures and graphs.

By accurately understanding the CMs' and other stakeholders' perceptions, you can facilitate the communication needed to meet mutual (and not just your perceived) evaluation expectations. Also, your decision-making skills improve as a result of fostering appreciation for everyone's decision-making style. Furthermore, you gain a broader understanding of the thought processes and comprehension levels of the CMs, and all this helps you to be respectful in the way you overcome objections within the collaborative effort.

Personality

Personality is the combination of distinctive behavioral, cognitive, and emotional characteristics that shape each person (such as you and the CMs) as a unique being within the collaborative evaluation. Moreover, personality is a stable set of characteristics, temperaments, and tendencies that determine commonalities and differences in the behavior of people (Gibson, Ivancevich, & Donnelly, 2008).

By recognizing various types of personalities, you and the CMs can understand and appreciate the similarities and differences that shape each other. The way you and the CMs behave and relate to each other depends on your unique personality. Personality is the complex mixture of desirable and undesirable psychological traits that are manifested by our distinctive method of relating to others and coping with our emotions, thoughts, and perceptions (Hankins & Hankins, 2000). Personality can vary depending on our particular genetics or hereditary factors, and environmental factors, such as people around us.

Freud identified specific types of personalities, although he recognized that there are an almost infinite variety of personalities. In his work, Freud explained that usually one personality dominates the others and makes us react differently than others to the same situation. Several authors (for example, Maccoby, 2004; Rothgeb, 2003; Sandler, Spector, & Fonagy, 1991) studied Freud's work and summarized the following three types of personalities:

- **Obsessive.** Self-reliant people ruled by their severe conscience, these people like to maintain order around them. They are critical and cautious, and are great team players. However, they lack vision, and they may end up rigidly adhering to regulations without flexibility.

- **Erotic.** This is not meant as a sexual personality but rather describes people for whom loving and being loved is most important. They are generally helpers and facilitators at work. However, their main weakness is that they tend to need too much approval from others.

- **Narcissistic.** These are independent people who want to be admired (not loved). They are creative strategists and risk takers who want to learn everything of interest to them. However, they are poor listeners, they have a lack of empathy for others, and they have a tendency toward grandiosity and distrust.

Because you and the CMs have a unique combination of characteristics, take the time to recognize your different personalities. In this way, you may be able to understand everyone's potential behavior (for example, their reactions to particular collaborative evaluation situations) and use this information to identify and establish individualized evaluation roles. The following are some types of personalities (see, for example, Friedman & Schustack, 2010; Hankins & Hankins, 2000):

- **Actively Withdrawn.** People who tend to be quiet, pleasant, and creative. They want others to like them, but they fear rejection so they appear emotionally distant because of their self-doubt, low self-esteem, and shyness.

- **Ambivalent.** People who tend to be initially charming and friendly. However, they have conflictive feelings (independency versus dependency) and sabotage their relationships because of their fear of intimacy and rejection.

- **Compulsive.** People who tend to be hard workers, dependable, meticulous, and punctual. However, they need to feel in control, and, unable to reach many of their goals, they feel dissatisfied with their achievements.

- **Dependent.** People who tend to be friendly, loyal, positive, and generous because they strongly need acceptance. They already reject themselves and fear others' rejection so they strive to keep harmony and please others.

- **Dramatic.** People who tend to be socially outgoing and charming. However, they are overly dramatic (for example, prone to exaggeration), self-centered, shallow, lack empathy, and have an insatiable need for attention.

- **Egotistical.** People who tend to be ambitious, hardworking, and proud of their achievements. However, they tend to have a fragile self-esteem; be self-centered, presumptuous, and envious of others; and overrate their own abilities.

- **Mistrustful.** People who tend to be objective, energetic, and persevering. However, they are pessimistic, suspicious, argumentative, and overcritical of others' mistakes, while having difficulty accepting responsibility for their own errors.

- **Oppositional.** People who tend to be analytical, loyal, and strong advocates for justice. However, they tend to feel unappreciated and to be habitually discontented, unpredictable, stubborn, impatient, irritable, and resentful.

- **Passively Withdrawn.** People who tend to be calm and peaceful, and prefer to work independently in solitary activities. However, they lack enthusiasm and initiative, and are unintentionally indifferent and underresponsive to others.

- **Self-Serving.** People who tend to be energetic, self-confident, outgoing, and friendly. However, they are selfish, arrogant, non-empathic, immature, irresponsible, exploitive, manipulative, aggressive, hurtful, and vindictive.

By addressing the subject of personality in this book, we are not encouraging you to label others but to better understand them in the context of the collaborative evaluation. If you understand your personality and those of the CMs you will be able to address and respond constructively to many types of unavoidable situations. Because each individual's personality is a combination of many characteristics, the more aware you and the CMs are of those characteristics the easier you all can avoid any potential conflict within the collaborative evaluation.

Values

Values are the beliefs, convictions, and ways of thinking considered important or right that guide your (and the CMs') actions regarding particular choices within the collaborative evaluation. Values are those preferences that help create your identity. In general, some examples of values are dedication, ethics, fairness, honor, loyalty, responsibility, and sincerity.

Values can also be defined as the guidelines an individual uses when confronted with a situation in which a choice must be made (Ivancevich, Konopaske, & Matteson, 2010). They are a basic part of an individual's thoughts, and profoundly influence which alternative is chosen when making decisions.

Therefore, you and the CMs should identify and treat with appreciation and respect each other's individual values throughout the collaborative evaluation.

Values are beliefs that you and the CMs use as a baseline for behaving when you face an evaluation problem that requires a particular choice or decision. You and the CMs may select the technique of brainwriting when identifying the values, for example, using these questions: (a) Who is the evaluation client? (b) What does the evaluation client value? (c) What do I or we (the CMs) value? and (d) What does the evaluand (if applicable) value?

Values will guide the decision-making procedures and also promote consistent actions throughout the collaborative evaluation. As you and the CMs become more diverse, learn about each other's value systems and how those can be potentially applied to the evaluation. In this way, you and the CMs can address (and even avoid) early in the evaluation any type of potential conflict that could surface (see Chapter 3 on how to establish a collective commitment).

Values are linked to attitudes, because a value serves as a way of organizing attitudes (Gibson, Ivancevich, & Donnelly, 2008). Specifically, an **attitude** is a positive or negative feeling or mental state of readiness that exerts specific influence on a person's response (such as to people, objects, and situations). An attitude is a general way of thinking (for example, being liberal or conservative), often used to mean the same as opinion, belief, preference, feeling, and value (Fink, 2003).

Both attitudes and values establish our predisposition toward specific tasks (for example, satisfaction with the CMs' evaluation roles) and interpersonal relations within the collaborative evaluation. They allow you and the CMs to address any misunderstandings or redirect your efforts. By clearly understanding the different values (or attitudes) among the CMs, you can recognize how those are shaping the approach taken in the evaluation.

It is possible to change everyone's values because those are learned predispositions and can be relearned. However, this is a very delicate and difficult process because they are strong determinants of your (and the CM's) actions. Be very careful about how your values are influencing the decisions made in a biased way (for example, how the evaluation information should be collected and analyzed).

The first step to appreciating the CMs' values is to truly recognize that each CM has different values from your own. Then you can be able to understand those personal values, have the ability to respect why those values are in place, and address them in the most appropriate way for the collaborative evaluation.

Everybody is worthy of appreciation, and values are very important because, as already noted, you and the CMs use them as a baseline throughout the collaboration.

Acknowledge all the different types of values that you and each CM bring to the joint effort. Most people use three types of values (see, for example, Wigfield & Eccles, 2002). Obviously those values may be combined at different levels during the collaborative evaluation, and may change from task to task.

- **Interest Value.** People easily and quickly choose to do what interests them. In other words, they tend to choose what they are curious or concerned about, or something that attracts their attention. For example, you may choose to collaborate in this evaluation because you like the topic being evaluated and you want to learn more about it.

- **Skill Value.** People seem more willing to do those things that they believe challenge their special skills or talents to perform a task. For example, you may quickly observe that the CMs with a strong technological background will prefer to do tasks (for instance, analyzing quantitative or qualitative data) using up-to-date computer software.

- **Utility Value.** People choose something in particular because they want the benefits that come when they finish that task. The focus is shifted from means to ends because of the usefulness of a particular goal. For example, you want to be part of this evaluation because of the professional recognition you will get, or because the findings will help improve the evaluand.

It is taken as a given that you and the CMs have specific values. The goal is to find ways to appreciate those values in order to maximize a productive performance in the collaborative evaluation. In addition, you and the CMs need to keep in mind that an evaluation is designed and implemented to determine the value (such as merit or worth) of an evaluand. Hence, this value can only be carefully and rationally established when you and the CMs appreciate and respect its importance.

Summary of Differences

Individual differences are now recognized as crucial to consider when designing jobs (Gibson, Ivancevich, & Donnelly, 2008). Everyone has different characteristics, so you and the CMs should be able to use those differences proactively

Encourage Appreciation for Individual Differences

Eliot: Hi Ernest, I need your advice. I am working with a nice group of CMs and would like to encourage wide appreciation of all the group members. There is one CM who has a very strong accent; sometimes it is hard to understand him when he is speaking, but some of his colleagues have told me he has amazing drawing skills and, more important, he is a great listener. He can take a large amount of information and then visually represent people's concepts and ways of thinking. He is always very quiet and distant; when I asked him why, he mentioned that sometimes he believes people do not appreciate his opinion because of his accent. I would really welcome your thoughts and some ideas about how to address this situation.

Ernest: It is important in any collaborative effort to build on people's strengths instead of their limitations. This particular person may be your best ally when it comes to developing logic models or other management tools. For example, one important skill needed to develop logic models is the ability to take large and sometimes complex ideas and processes and build a graphical representation so others can easily understand what the evaluation is trying to accomplish. You should ask him to help you with that. Then, make sure to publicly acknowledge his contributions with the other CMs. I am sure they, and more important he, will change their perceptions; they may even consider him as the in-house facilitator for the development of future logic models.

in the interest of the collaborative effort. Obviously, disagreements may occur, but the important issue is to be prepared to settle them immediately with no harm to the evaluation.

You and the CMs need to specifically encourage and increase your appreciation for each other's characteristics. Moreover, you and the CMs have to be prepared to deal with the profound differences that may be faced within the collaborative evaluation, and to use those differences to the evaluation's advantage. This creates willingness to address the concerns, belief structures, and needs of everyone involved. As a consequence, there is higher respect, collaboration, and ownership within the evaluation efforts. Finally, remember that a good way to get people to like you is to show that you like them (Offermann, 2004).

ENCOURAGE FAIRNESS AND SINCERITY

Fairness means that individuals (such as you and the CMs) are trustworthy, just, credible, and equitable. There is neither prejudice nor favoritism toward particular individuals and tasks. Also, it means that there is a balanced distribution of rights between you and the CMs within the collaborative evaluation. **Sincerity** means that individuals (such as you and the CMs) are genuine, straightforward, honest, and candid when communicating with each other. Empathy and compassion have to be balanced with sincerity (Bartz, 2004).

A fair work environment is necessary in order for you and the CMs to trust each other and feel comfortable providing sincere information or ideas. The CMs' trust (and your own trust) toward others and the evaluation is difficult to gain but, at the same time, very easy to lose. A good starting point in fostering trust is to build credibility by setting the example, such as keeping your promises and demonstrating that you are worthy of trust yourself (Bennis & Nanus, 2003; Kouzes & Posner, 1995).

The collaborative evaluation's credibility increases when you and the CMs are not afraid to make it visible to others, because it is based on accurate facts that make it believable. Credibility comes from the image of a sound decision maker and can be enhanced by the relationship to other key people who support the group's efforts (Kerzner, 2009b).

From the moment you and the CMs agree to do a collaborative evaluation, you are showing a biased opinion toward that type of effort. Obviously, you all have to believe in the positive aspects of the evaluation, otherwise you would not be willing to work on it. From the beginning of the evaluation, do your best to take an unbiased look at the information that later should also lead to unbiased conclusions about whether the evaluation is achieving what it is intending to achieve. By being aware of these limitations, everyone can openly address them in a systematic light in order to point out credible evaluand strengths and weaknesses.

Any evaluation is going to be biased (to a certain extent) in one way or another. The decisions you make (for example, which approaches and tools to use), and even your own personal background and experience, are going to influence the evaluation results. Although no evaluation can be free of bias, you and the CMs can improve the evaluation quality by including others' feedback, for example, on how to use appropriate procedures and techniques. To do this, be sincere with the CMs if you want to get sincere answers back. This interaction should be done in a professional yet sensitive manner.

Take adequate measures to protect the rights of everyone involved in the evaluation effort (such as know the laws regarding protection of human subjects). Perceptions of fairness are different among stakeholders so, when considering how best to treat the CMs (and other people in general), remember to behave toward others as you wish others would behave toward you, while understanding their own individuality.

You and the CMs need to be aware of how to deal with evaluation information (for example, confidentiality versus anonymity) and how this may affect the well-being of others' and your own value judgments. We suggest the following steps to encourage fairness and sincerity:

1. Exhibit fairness and sincerity toward the CMs (and other stakeholders) at all times to encourage them to follow this example as well. For instance, ensure excellent working conditions (such as an open-door policy) for each of the CMs.

2. Use a clear and rational system to communicate the evaluation information to each of the CMs from the beginning of the collaborative process. Keep in mind that this system has to be congruent with the evaluation vision.

3. Be consistent in avoiding ambiguity to increase the CMs' sense of knowing what is expected throughout the evaluation. For example, use the same assessment procedures, so the same type of performance earns the same type of outcome.

4. Ask each of the CMs, as appropriate, general questions that encourage total sincerity on an ongoing basis. For example, give each of the CMs an opportunity to express their true feelings related to the collaborative evaluation process.

5. Identify, with the CMs' help, the advantages and disadvantages associated with each collaborative evaluation task and any available alternative assumptions in order to select the least biased defensible option(s) for completing the task.

6. Encourage constructive criticism and act on it. For example, ask the CMs for their opinions on other evaluation tasks, invite them to present divergent perspectives, and ask them to provide suggestions for improvement throughout the evaluation.

7. Have frequently updated information and resources available while making sure that you and the CMs have the expertise to use them. For

example, ensure that the CMs know how to use the technology available (such as the Internet and databases).

8. Thank each of the CMs, publicly or privately as appropriate, by consistently letting them know that their fairness and sincerity exhibited throughout the collaborative evaluation is highly appreciated and valued.

9. Gather feedback on a regular basis using a previously agreed-upon system (for example, meetings, emails, and surveys as feasible). This will help you and the CMs monitor the fairness and sincerity process and make updates as needed.

10. Provide each CM and other stakeholders, as appropriate, with a summary report of this experience (if this is a particularly illustrative experience of fairness and sincerity) as lessons learned for future similar situations within collaborative evaluations.

To encourage a sincere evaluation environment, make sure that the CMs, and yourself, feel (when being comparted with others in similar situations) that there is a fair or equitable relationship between what they do and the rewards they get as a result of their efforts. Individuals are motivated by a desire to be treated equitably at work and there are four important terms to consider (Ivancevich, Konopaske, & Matteson, 2010):

- **Person.** The individual for whom equity or inequity is perceived (such as a specific CM). For example, to restore equity, the CM may simply change his or her attitude toward the work to be done (see Chapter 2 on how to clarify the role of the CMs).

- **Comparison Other.** Any group or persons used as a reference regarding the ratio of inputs and outcomes (such as specific CMs being used as a comparison by other CMs). For example, to restore equity the CM may change the reference group by making comparisons with some other individuals.

- **Inputs.** The individual characteristics or efforts brought by the person to the job. These may be achieved (skills, experience, learning, and so on) or ascribed (age, sex, race, and so on) attributes. For example, to restore equity the CM may decide to invest less effort or time into a particular task.

- **Outcomes.** What a specific person received from the job (such as recognition, fringe benefits, or pay). For example, to restore equity the individual may decide to produce a better product since a reward is being used (see Chapter 3 on how to establish reward options).

Encourage Fairness and Sincerity

Eliot: I am working right now with the most interesting group of CMs. They are very diverse in gender, culture, and organizational background, and they seem to work very well together. There is only one issue: two of them have been very good friends for almost thirty years, and they both hold the highest seniority within this group. A couple of days ago, two different CMs approached me, individually, and told me that at some point I will see that people's thoughts and opinions will become more cautious and could even be withheld. When I asked why, their comments pointed to this conclusion: if you want to see transparency, honesty, and candid conversations about our program, your best strategy will be not to have these two friends working together and present with other CMs at the same time. So, what would you recommend I do?

Evelyn: It looks like this group of CMs has already told you what they consider to be ideal: not to have these friends together. I always ask CMs to *be present* and *speak their truth* during our meetings; however, it sounds like this may not be possible in this situation if some of the CMs are coming directly to you. One thing you can do is to encourage sincerity through individual feedback from every CM and create opportunities for them to speak privately with you. For example, I have individtual follow-up phone calls with each CM after each meeting. Also, during our meetings, I pay specific attention to what areas or topics from the evaluation in particular each member is most interested in and enjoys doing the most. Then, when I call them, I initiate my conversation by focusing on these points. Next, I pose questions about issues I noticed that were not fully disclosed during our meeting time. Finally, when we all are back together, I am very sensitive and try to address the most important issues they shared, in a respectful and collaborative way, protecting confidentiality.

Sincere answers to questions create opportunities for further refinements and improved results (Winer & Ray, 2002). When you and the CMs believe that people around you (whether in formal or informal groups) are nonbiased, you tend to express your viewpoints more freely and feel less compelled to protect yourselves from potentially nonsupportive or retaliatory responses.

Also, to win the CMs' commitment, sometimes you may have to intentionally choose to defer to their wishes in order to demonstrate fairness and openness (Offermann, 2004).

In our experience, when the CMs work in a fair and sincere environment, their anxiety regarding the collaborative evaluation process decreases while their openness and optimism increase. This is because they know they are surrounded by an open (nonsecretive) evaluation environment in which they can feel a sense of trust toward others. In addition, because this is instilled in all the CMs from the beginning of the evaluation, everyone knows from an early stage in the proceedings how their actions may affect others and the evaluation itself.

You must be seen as a fair individual by every CM, because showing any favoritism can also lead to loss of confidence and respect for your abilities as the evaluator. Keep in mind that you may be used as the comparison person by some of the CMs, and this will have a direct effect on their morale and productivity (see "Encourage Teaching by Example" later in this chapter). The CMs will commit to do their best effort (such as being fair and sincere individuals) in every single aspect of the evaluation only if they see the same type of commitment from you.

ENCOURAGE BENCHMARKING

Benchmarking is the process of determining an outstanding point of reference or benchmark that serves as a standard for comparison or judgment. Specifically, performance data are used to measure benchmarks for comparative or improvement purposes. For example, a benchmark can be a similar evaluand that is considered the best, a related evaluation model or approach, or an individual who functions particularly well when performing a similar evaluation task.

Benchmarking involves analyzing how a particular initiative (such as an evaluand or an evaluation) is doing against what others (benchmarks) are doing well in similar situations. You and the CMs may compare different aspects of the evaluation to similar examples of these aspects in an attempt to improve its quality.

Benchmarks may (or may not) belong to the same organization and knowledge field. The goal is to study how others have effectively handled similar situations and the potential effects it had on their work. Keep in mind that it is not only what you and the CMs know but also what you do not know that often makes the difference between success and failure in the collaborative evaluation.

You and the CMs have to analyze the initiative, processes, and performance levels thoroughly before doing benchmarking. For small-scale evaluations it is not going to be necessarily feasible to do benchmarking, mainly due to the limited amount of resources available. Benchmarking is a costly task, so it is better to focus on the most important processes that affect the overall evaluand and its goals. For this reason, oversee the benchmarking process in a way that ensures that it is in line with the initiative as a whole.

Once you and the CMs decide against what the initiative, such as the evaluand, is going to be compared, everyone has to understand how that benchmark got to be the best, and how your evaluand can get to a successful position too. However, remember that the evaluand will not necessarily follow those same steps because they may not be applicable. Thus, benchmarking will help you identify your own performance patterns, and whether it is possible to achieve a similar level of success.

By encouraging the use of benchmarking, you and the CMs can find very important information relevant to other similar initiatives and what has been learned from those experiences. Keep in mind that by relating those benchmarks to your particular experience they may be able to offer you valuable suggestions for the collaborative evaluation (perhaps some that you have overlooked or not considered). It is a very important investment in time and effort to get this type of feedback. We suggest the following steps to encourage benchmarking:

1. Make sure that you and the CMs have a clear understanding about the evaluand and the evaluation before you approach the benchmarking process. In this way, everyone can agree on what is needed and how the information will be used.

2. Study all the information available on specific benchmarks (such as any area in which their performance is better). Among other things, you may use the Internet or request brochures to identify and review all the perceived benchmarks.

3. Identify key people (both internal and external to the evaluation) whose input would be important, and periodically update names, addresses, and contact numbers. For instance, you might cross-reference those names if possible.

4. Contact those specific individuals who may be helpful for the benchmarking and find out the lessons they have learned (such as mistakes and how they solved them). For example, contact people who possess a desired evaluation skill.

5. Compare the benchmark practices (including products, services, models, and instruments) in order to apply them to concrete action plans. For example, apply the learned information in recommendations of how to reach particular objectives.

6. Participate in relevant national or international events, such as presentations, seminars, and conferences. These offer a wide range of opportunities to develop particular knowledge for you and the CMs to use in the collaborative evaluation.

7. Solicit information on similar collaborative evaluation reports from national or international evaluation centers or institutions. This may help you develop local and overseas contacts that can be able to give variety to your benchmark focus.

8. Present the information collected as a result of this benchmarking process in a formal meeting in order to agree with the CMs on relevant options (such as valuable areas that can be used) to update the collaborative evaluation activities.

9. Gather feedback on a regular basis using a previously agreed-upon system (for example, meetings, emails, and surveys as feasible). This will help you and the CMs monitor the benchmarking process and make updates as needed.

10. Provide each CM and other stakeholders, as appropriate, with a summary report of this experience (including actions implemented and the reasons for them) as lessons learned for future similar situations within collaborative evaluations.

By encouraging benchmarking you and the CMs are able to identify, understand, and adapt sound practices from others to improve the collaborative evaluation. Benchmarking is now a widespread practice that attempts to answer the question, How are we doing in terms of strategy, quality of product, compensation program, job design, or teamwork? (Gibson, Ivancevich, & Donnelly, 2008).

In benchmarking, you and the CMs should not limit your search locally but apply information from other countries as well (as feasible). The international evaluation marketplace is going to continue to grow, and for this reason, you and the CMs may consider ideas from it. However, be aware of cultural differences and learn to value diversity within evaluations. By encouraging benchmarking, you and the CMs can build advantageous networks with others

Encourage Benchmarking

Eliot: I have been invited to submit a proposal on how I can help an organization improve internal evaluation practices through benchmarking. With my limited experience, I know the basic principles of benchmarking, but I am struggling a bit on conceptualizing the overall process and creating a simple, easy-to-understand framework. The biggest challenge I see is framing the macro level and then moving into the micro-level process. I already found some interesting resources, but do you have any specific ideas to meet my client's needs and help me define the benchmarking scope of work?

Ernest: Today is your lucky day! Several days ago, I was reorganizing my electronic library and remembered seeing an article describing benchmarking in a very easy way. If I recall correctly, we should look at different types of benchmarking on the basis of the various levels of activities undertaken. For example, one type of benchmarking helps organizations or units diagnose in a holistic way which processes are worthy of detailed consideration. Another type of benchmarking focuses on improving specific organizational processes by comparing them with exemplary practices. A final thought before you start writing your proposal: to avoid proposing a complex scope of work, recommend a maximum number of similar organizations you will approach to seek comparative information. Let me know if I can help you more once you have drafted a proposal. I will be more than happy to read it and help you further refine it.

and integrate a number of viewpoints and areas of interest within the collaborative evaluation (see Chapter 6 on how to follow the collaboration guiding principles).

Different perspectives on the same evaluative issue provide a new and more well-rounded approach to the evaluation tasks to be performed. This powerful process of creating reasonable comparisons increases the effectiveness of the evaluation. In this way, you can accurately determine what you need to know about the evaluand (and the evaluation) and how you can obtain this information before any type of evaluative judgment can be made.

Benchmarking helps to set priorities within the collaborative evaluation (and justify them through comparative means), by sorting out which of the alternative sources will provide the best information. To gain the best information possible from the benchmarking process, you and the CMs should communicate extensively with each other so that everyone clearly understands the intent of the evaluation and becomes familiar with the issues pursued with benchmarking. For example, through benchmarking you and the CMs may conclude that the use of external consultants for future efforts may be needed to provide a more neutral view on particular evaluand issues.

By encouraging benchmarking you and the CMs can learn from other's successes and failures in an ongoing pursuit to benefit the collaborative evaluation. Keep in mind that everyone may be potential evaluation stakeholders, so they can make valuable suggestions about the evaluation. This learning can be done through several means (for example, direct or indirect interpersonal relations, telephone, email, and mail). What is valuable to others can be used as an interesting example to improve the evaluand value itself. For example, by studying the major differences between the benchmarks and your evaluand, you will have the opportunity to reduce the gap between them and become closer to meeting the evaluand ideal goal.

ENCOURAGE TEACHING BY EXAMPLE

Teaching by example is when an individual (such as you or the CMs) illustrates and fosters learning through knowledgeable modeling, guidance, and support. In particular, it capitalizes on your (and the CMs') own willingness to improve others' developmental performance and help them cope with any source of frustration or uncertainty within the collaborative evaluation.

You and the CMs essentially observe and interpret each other's actions. The goal of teaching by example is to build on people's existing strengths and develop new skills to be used in the collaborative evaluation. In other words, the goal is to bring out people's potential so that they can take on higher evaluation challenges. However, it is necessary to understand that this process needs to be collaborative (instead of competitive) through proactively responding to others' reactions in order to be effective in the long run.

Setting an example is very important for organizational effectiveness and a way to foster credibility (Bennis & Nanus, 2003; Kouzes & Posner, 1995). The quality of the example set is measured by how you and the CMs learn and are able to apply that learning as a result of this example. For instance, it is not so significant how knowledgeable or intelligent the individual who sets the example is, but how much you and the CMs are able to learn and potentially accomplish within the collaborative evaluation as a result of that teaching.

A drive to surpass goals can be contagious, and leaders with these traits often can build a team around them with the same traits (Goleman, 2004). If you exemplify appropriate traits needed in the evaluation, the CMs will most likely follow this example themselves. Teaching by example is effective when you or the CMs provide opportunities for the learning to occur through dialogue and reflection of insights. Obviously, this is a very time-consuming factor necessary to increase the evaluation quality through understanding, trust, credibility, and commitment. We suggest the following steps to encourage teaching by example:

1. Exemplify general appropriate behavioral characteristics (including enthusiasm, responsibility, sensitivity, and dedication) so others understand what is expected from them as well and relate with one another in a similar manner.

2. Encourage active learning by consistently opening the opportunity for everyone (such as you and the CMs) to talk about what they are learning, relate it to their past experiences, and apply it to the collaborative evaluation.

3. Help CMs become more comfortable with their evaluation roles and responsibilities by introducing repetition to the teaching efforts. For example, rely on multiple approaches to provide stimuli and enrich the learning process.

4. Identify external individuals who are not part of the collaborative evaluation but who could be able to perform a critical role (such as a coach, a mentor, or a model) in order to further specific evaluation knowledge or skills.

5. Become attuned to learning opportunities, and use them to show your own commitment. For example, improve the CMs' efforts in needed areas by being ready to provide opportunities in training (or development) and implementation.

6. Promote interaction among key individuals (both inside and outside the evaluation) to facilitate learning in specific areas. This ensures that everyone (such as you and the CMs) is a facilitator rather than just an evaluation spectator.

7. Assess individual and group performance to monitor continuous learning progress (for example, what you and the CMs should have learned) and change the teaching methods to reflect the feedback concerning what everyone still needs to learn.

8. Organize a reading library that helps you and the CMs, as feasible, to be in touch with contemporary evaluation writings (for instance, evaluation journals). This is an excellent way of acquiring new evaluation skills and enhancing competencies.

9. Gather feedback on a regular basis using a previously agreed-upon system (for example, meetings, emails, and surveys as feasible). This will help you and the CMs monitor the teaching-by-example process and make updates as needed.

10. Provide each CM and other stakeholders as appropriate with a summary report of this experience (including actions implemented and the reasons for them) as lessons learned for a better or more innovative way of improving the teaching-by-example process.

For the collaborative evaluation to excel, you and the CMs must constantly learn from each other's experiences. For example, this means learning from past lessons in order to improve the evaluation and avoid the same mistakes in the future (such as wrongly considering current practices as set in stone). With this type of learning experience, you and the CMs can achieve high productivity in the evaluation on the basis of high expectations (see Chapter 2 on how to clarify the expectations).

Teaching by example is not only your job but the CMs' as well. Often the CMs make very effective teachers, either by helping less experienced colleagues or by sharing with the group specific evaluation skills. These help key individuals have a deeper understanding of a particular evaluation issue, and it is a great example of empowering through transferring new skills. Also, it ensures that everyone involved in the collaborative evaluation learns how to develop and implement solutions and turn them into action.

Ways of Teaching by Example

There are several ways teaching by example can take place within the collaborative evaluation. These include (a) coaching, (b) mentoring, (c) modeling, and (d) training.

Coaching

Coaching is the individualized tutoring that makes it easier for individuals (such as you and the CMs) to learn by creating purposeful relationships that lead to growth and support within the collaborative evaluation. Coaching could be a sole situation, focused on solving one-time evaluation problems or deficiencies. Leaders must assume roles as coaches in organizations that are willing to become learning organizations (Ellinger, 2003).

You will find that some CMs do not perform their evaluation tasks as you expected, and this is not for an absence of ability but may be their inability to understand the task. Therefore, be the understanding person with the ability to clearly communicate with each particular CM, as feasible, in order to help them accomplish their evaluation goals (see Chapter 4 on how to ensure the message is clear). Great leaders take risks initially on talent they perceive. Those risks do not always pay off, but the willingness to take them appears to be absolutely essential in developing leaders (Zaleznik, 2004).

Mentoring

Mentoring is the individualized overall guidance by a knowledgeable and trusted advisor (such as you) that has an ongoing impact on the individual's development of new collaborative evaluation knowledge, skills, and abilities. It has repeatedly been shown that coaching and mentoring pay off not just in better performance but also in increased job satisfaction and decreased turnover (Goleman, 2004).

To build a mentoring relationship you need to first establish a trusting environment (see Chapter 6 on how to follow the collaboration guiding principles). An important step to foster trust is to build credibility with the CMs. Also, establish a relationship characterized by a sincere interest, care, respect, and appreciation for the people you are helping. Mentors sense how to give effective feedback, and they know when to push for better performance or hold back (Goleman, 2004).

Modeling

Modeling is the process of teaching others through showing the correct or appropriate behavior, with the goal of having the learner observe and imitate these actions. Models can be people with whom you actually interact (peers and other colleagues) or they can be fantasy figures (Hankins & Hankins, 2000). Modeling occurs when someone behaves similarly to a particular individual (or model) to imitate (or show) a specific behavior.

Leaders can take care of their companies by setting good examples, because followers tend to model themselves after their leaders (Offermann, 2004). However, take into consideration that as people mature and develop their own sets of values, they become more discriminating about whom they choose to model (Hankins & Hankins, 2000). To keep the morale high, always behave appropriately, because fewer bad moods at the top mean fewer throughout the organization (Goleman, 2004).

Training

Training is a systematic instruction in which activities are designed and facilitated by an expert (inside or outside the collaborative evaluation) with the purpose of enhancing specific skills and knowledge. Some authors distinguish among training, education, and development, but the distinctions are neither consistent nor widely accepted (PMI Standards Committee, 2008).

Training may be facilitated formally (for example, instruction taught in a particular room) or informally (for example, feedback between you and the CMs, or among the CMs). You, the CMs, or outsiders can train others, which is a very useful way to encourage learning by example. In particular, we have wonderful results with peer training because the CMs identify with or relate to each other's responsibilities within the collaborative evaluation. As a result, they are more willing to listen, exchange ideas, and learn more effectively from other CMs' points of view.

To encourage teaching by example, you and the CMs should take into consideration that your working style and actions are constantly observed and imitated by others. The evaluation atmosphere has to be right for the collaborative work, in which the information shared is meaningful for you and the CMs. In this way, everyone's example can be successfully used to teach and encourage good evaluation practice.

An open-door policy aids teaching by example, because everyone knows you can be approached for advice or information at any time. In addition, you should be able to approach the CMs whenever necessary for an informal encouraging discussion on how the evaluation tasks are going. However, keep in mind that if the CMs visit you too often (or vice versa), either the clarification of expectations has been inadequate (perhaps the CM is insecure about the responsibility scope) or inappropriate (for example, the CM is not the right person for the job to be done).

The biggest surprise we have found is how easy it is for the CMs to buy into the collaborative evaluation after they learn how to do it themselves. It is when they understand the evaluation process that their confidence in it improves, and they are willing to take more initiative in meeting the agreed-upon evaluation

Encourage Teaching by Example

Evelyn: I am truly convinced that from time to time unique opportunities knock at your door, whether you sought them or not. Have you ever seen or experienced something like this? My new client, Dr. Coleman, would like me to help him develop internal evaluation capacity in his organization that is based on the MCE. He asked me to mentor each of the five evaluation staff members and would like this to be a six-month engagement process in which I can share my experiences and teach each member by example. I can accomplish part of that task by asking each person to colead some of the activities of their current evaluation projects, but I am wondering whether this would be too limited because of the small evaluation portfolio they have. What else do you think I can do?

Ernest: Another idea you might consider is bringing them, individually, to activities you are completing for some of your other evaluations. You should explain that they are junior evaluators assisting you, the senior evaluator, with specific evaluation tasks. But it is of paramount importance to obtain prior approval from your client. Of course, try this only with clients who have known you and the quality of your work for a long time; I would discourage you from doing this with new clients. If you like this idea let me know how it goes; I would love to hear from you.

vision. Then, by observing and patterning others' actions, everyone can improve their evaluation performance on the basis of highly developed skills.

ENCOURAGE FLEXIBILITY AND CREATIVITY

Flexibility is the capacity to willingly consider new options for accomplishing the collaborative evaluation tasks, even though those options might differ from one's own views or evaluation style. Obviously, flexibility requires plasticity in attending to differing options, and a high level of discernment in order to appreciate the relevant features within those options.

Being flexible implies that you and the CMs will be able to adjust easily to necessary changes within the collaborative evaluation, ultimately allowing yourself to be more collaborative in the evaluation (see Chapter 4 on how to ensure the need for change is justified). Indeed, flexibility is important when a change is needed in the way the evaluation tasks or activities are being accomplished, how resources are being shared, and your (and others') own working style.

Creativity is the quality of being able to produce original ideas and fruitful collaborative evaluation work. Creative decision makers share some common characteristics, such as (a) they persevere or stay longer attacking problems; (b) they take moderate to high risks and stay away from extreme risks; (c) they are open to new experiences and are willing to try new approaches; and (d) they can tolerate a lack of structure, some lack of clarity, and not having complete information, data, and answers (Ivancevich, Konopaske, & Matteson, 2010).

In a flexible environment creative improvements are bound to happen, for example, in the way tasks are being accomplished and resources are being shared. Therefore, with a flexible work environment, you and the CMs feel comfortable to generate, discuss, and agree on creative ideas. Also, you and the CMs are able to commit to action, promoting a sense of shared responsibility while adjusting to changes within the collaborative evaluation (see Chapter 3 on how to establish a collective commitment). We suggest the following steps to encourage flexibility and creativity:

1. Facilitate an evaluation environment in which you and the CMs feel welcome to apply your expertise in other areas outside specific responsibilities. For example, continuously look for opportunities to invite others' expertise as needed.

2. Encourage proactivity among you and the CMs by searching on an ongoing basis for new alternatives in the collaborative evaluation. For example, look at the upcoming evaluation tasks from a different and original perspective.

3. Avoid criticizing new ideas or assumptions ("Yes, but . . .") before they, or any other alternative, have been fully described. For example, consideration of ideas should be done afterward, when all the options have been discussed.

4. Clarify any doubt (with respect and sensitivity) in order to ensure that every idea is designed to meet the needs of the collaborative evaluation. For example, prepare answers to common objections (such as, Why should we follow this idea?).

5. Reframe a seemingly meaningless idea by looking at the situation from another perspective and encouraging fresh thinking (using the appro-

priate flexibility and creativity technique) to understand how the idea relates to specific priorities.

6. Assess each of the proposed ideas in order to summarize the most important options. For example, avoid rushing into any negative decision until understanding if some minor adjustments can make a positive difference.

7. Agree on an initial tryout or pilot of strong ideas and how they should be implemented (for example, how the new ideas can address current evaluation problems). This is done to make a clear balance between imagination and logic.

8. Adjust for external factors that affect the collaborative evaluation to apply updated information as feasible. Although you and the CMs have your own ideas, you should remain open to other new ones and be willing to adapt to change.

9. Conduct periodic meetings with the CMs to communicate advances in the latest evaluation implementations and to obtain ongoing feedback on other ideas (one idea at a time to avoid confusion) in order to make updates as needed.

10. Provide each CM and other stakeholders as appropriate with a summary report of this experience (if it is a particularly illustrative experience) as lessons learned from success and failures for future similar situations within collaborative evaluations.

Organizations can help develop creativity by (a) buffering, when you look for ways to absorb the creative decision risks of employees; (b) organizational time-outs, when you give people time off to think things through; (c) intuition, when you give unsophisticated or uncompleted ideas a chance; (d) innovative attitudes, when you encourage everyone to think of ways to problem solve; and (e) innovative organizational structures, when you let employees interact with managers and mentors (Yong, 1994).

You and the CMs need to keep up to date and improve the way you conduct the collaborative evaluation constantly. The evaluation is not linear, and because of this, to be effective in this field you and the CMs have to be prepared to change the plan as needed (such as when planned meetings get postponed without your being able to avoid it). Also, allow room for new opportunities and provide a mechanism for discarding ideas that are not appropriate anymore. As previously mentioned, although the new ideas are vital for the evaluation, there has to be a balance between imagination and logic.

Flexibility and Creativity Techniques

Many people are frightened by complete independence and need to feel the security of a system that provides boundaries. Hence, it is your task to understand and address those differences among the CMs (see Chapter 6 on how to follow the collaboration guiding principles). Also, provide the maximum opportunity for growth to each individual without creating anarchy (Prentice, 2004).

The techniques presented in this chapter are very useful when specific judgments (such as yours and the CMs') need to be unified in order to achieve a satisfactory collaborative evaluation vision. These techniques help the CMs to generate ideas in an organized way and also build on the ideas of others to reach better evaluation decisions. We frequently use the following techniques to encourage flexibility and creativity: (a) brainstorming, (b) brainwriting, (c) Delphi technique, and (d) Q-sort.

Brainstorming

Brainstorming is an idea-generation technique that promotes the spontaneous sharing of collaborative evaluation ideas through nonjudgmental discussion between you and the CMs (or other stakeholders). Through brainstorming, you and the CMs can quickly and collaboratively solve an evaluation problem through the generation of a list of ideas or possibilities that is refined later on in the collaborative evaluation.

In brainstorming, you and the CMs contribute to problem solving during the process without previously taken notes and avoid criticizing any suggestions to enhance the generation of imaginative solutions. To brainstorm, (a) explain in advance that the purpose of brainstorming is to generate as many ideas as possible in a verbal and nonjudgmental way, (b) ask open questions so the CMs can share their ideas (one by one) without allowing them to focus on particular problems, (c) record each of the ideas (for example, on a flipchart) as they are produced without any specific order and without rejecting any, and (d) present your own ideas (but without dominating the session) when the CMs are satisfied or have no further ideas to share.

As a result of the brainstorming session, (a) invite the CMs to assess each of the ideas provided during the session before a vote is made, (b) carry out (with the CMs' help) a clearing and synthesis by dropping the weakest ideas, and

(c) agree with the CMs on a short list of the strongest idea(s) by together ana-lyzing the implications of the ideas left. In this way, you and the CMs have removed your inhibitions and contributed to making decisions through the collaborative use of your own range of approaches and expertise.

Brainwriting

Brainwriting is an idea-generation technique that promotes the spontane-ous sharing of evaluation ideas in writing, when little verbal communication is allowed (also called nominal group technique). The final decision is made later by counting the outcome of the individual votes. It is useful when the evaluation problem will lead to fewer ideas if you and the CMs (or other stake-holders) would have to share those ideas verbally rather than in writing. In addition, brainwriting can remove the biasing effects that might occur during brainstorming.

To brainwrite, (a) explain in advance that the purpose of brainwriting is to write as many ideas as possible on a paper without speaking to one another; (b) ask each of the CMs to submit an idea (or list of ideas) relevant to the col-laborative evaluation decision being made; (c) collect each of the notes with their anonymous, if needed, ideas; (d) record each of the ideas (for example, on a flipchart) including your own, in an identifiable order (such as by letters) as they are read, without rejecting any idea; and (e) ask the CMs to read the list and add in writing new ideas to that list. This process will continue until the CMs have no further ideas to add to the list.

As a result of the brainwriting session, (a) invite the CMs to individually assess and prioritize each of the ideas provided during the session before a vote is made, (b) select in writing an individualized choice/s by directly ranking or voting, (c) count the outcome of the individual votes, and (d) agree with the CMs on a final decision by together analyzing all the implications of the idea(s) selected. As in brainstorming, every CM has contributed to making decisions within the collaborative effort by writing ideas that result from their individu-alized range of approaches and expertise (see Chapter 3 on how to establish decision-making procedures).

Delphi Technique

Delphi technique is an idea-generation technique used to gather ongoing writ-ten feedback from anonymous individuals (such as you and the CMs) through questionnaires (mailed, online, and so on) until a reasonable consensus is reached. Generally speaking, it is a technique in which the CMs (or other Delphi participants) are anonymous to each other and can be physically apart, because there is not direct communication among them.

To use the Delphi technique, (a) send out or administer the first questionnaire soliciting anonymous opinions about a specific evaluation topic, (b) send out sequential questionnaires with an anonymous statistical summary from earlier responses of all the CMs on the first questionnaire, (c) ask the CMs to individually evaluate their own opinions or judgments on the basis of earlier summary responses (the CMs can change their previous response or justify their same response), and (d) agree with the CMs on the final decision once you have done at least two rounds of anonymous group judgment. Throughout our experience as evaluators we have found that the CMs' results are essentially similar after the second round of questionnaires.

Q-Sort

Q-Sort is anza-generation technique used for the purpose of obtaining ratings in which individuals (such as you and the CMs) have to prioritize or rank, by a series of sorting procedures, a list of cards with descriptive statements. Although similar to the Delphi technique, the Q-sort does not use questionnaires and does not require consensus among its participants.

Q-sorts are used to establish priorities for statements that answer questions, such as, Which strategies have the most collaborative evaluation support? Which strategies best fit the collaborative evaluation? and, Which strategies are most feasible with the available resources? To use the Q-sort technique, (a) distribute cards (for example, that contain evaluation need statements) to the CMs clearly identified by numerals, (b) ask the CMs to prioritize or rank-order their individual preferences (according to their perceptions) by sorting cards in a certain number of piles, (c) analyze the ordinal data from the sorts on the various options solicited, and (d) share with the CMs the Q-sort statistical results.

Using these flexibility and creativity techniques, you and the CMs can produce better ideas and share them with one another for improvement. However, be careful not to use agreement or consensus as an excuse to kill creative initiatives. CMs need to be able to stand back and make their own (independent) choices on how to perform their evaluation tasks. However, CMs also need to count on your support as they handle different situations within the collaborative evaluation.

Encourage Flexibility and Creativity

Cheryl: You have worked for me as an external evaluator for many years. I am always delighted to speak with you because you are very approachable and insightful, and you embrace our collaborative evaluation philosophy. This time I would like to ask you how I can promote a working environment in which flexibility and creativity are always present and appreciated.

Ernest: By now, after so many years working with your staff, you may have a good idea who can handle more ambiguity, perform specific tasks better than others, and tend to suggest new ideas. Once you have identified that small group of creative thinkers, foster what some people call a *buffer zone*. This means eliminating instances when policies or other work pressures interfere with or discourage creative practices. Please note that when people learn how to become comfortable with ambiguity, they can develop complex thinking skills. They tend to become more reflective and open-minded to the thoughts of others. They also come to understand that it is not only possible, but acceptable, to hold contradictory or opposite ideas and feelings in their minds at the same time. Provide this group with opportunities to play with ideas that may be uncertain. Then try new things at a very small scale and, if they are proven logical, feasible, and productive, you may consider scaling up those practices. Finally, make sure you acknowledge the work of the group and methodology used, and even more important, celebrate any new ideas.

In this chapter, we emphasized the importance of encouraging effective practices to produce a desired effect within the collaborative evaluation. In particular, we focused on the appreciation for individual differences (diversity, motivation, perception, personality, and values). We also discussed how fairness and sincerity help to support credibility in the collaborative evaluation. In addition, we presented various aspects of benchmarking and teaching by example to build on existing strengths within the collaborative effort. Furthermore, we provided guidance on how to encourage flexibility and creativity in the work environment. Finally, as in other chapters, we incorporated examples in order to reinforce interdependence among the MCE elements, such as following specific guidelines that support sound collaborative evaluations, the topic discussed in Chapter 6.

Follow
Specific Guidelines

Guidelines are principles that direct the design, use, and assessment of the collaborative evaluations, their evaluators (such as you), and their CMs. Guidelines provide direction for sound evaluations, although they alone cannot guarantee the quality of any collaborative evaluation.

By identifying and addressing where the collaborative evaluation meets the necessary guidelines, the evaluator(s) and the CMs demonstrate a clearer understanding of what the process is about and how it should be carried out. Evaluators continuously benefit from guidelines developed by various associations regarding appropriate activities that need to be followed and met. For example, the guiding principles of the American Evaluation Association (AEA) refer to an expected professional lifestyle that permeates across the evaluators' actions on all evaluations they may conduct, while the Joint Committee on Standards for Educational Evaluation (JCSEE) focuses on the soundness of a particular evaluation.

The guidelines described in this chapter provide a shared vision about good collaborative evaluations, and (if adopted and internalized) may serve as a model for you and the CMs to assess and improve them. The MCE component presented in this chapter is divided into the following subcomponents: (a) follow guiding principles for evaluators, (b) follow evaluation standards (such as program, personnel, and student evaluation standards), and (c) follow the collaboration guiding principles (see Figure I.2).

FOLLOW GUIDING PRINCIPLES FOR EVALUATORS

Around the world, several principles are available to guide the evaluators' professional practice. As an example, we are focusing on the principles published by the American Evaluation Association (2004). The **AEA's guiding principles for evaluators** were developed to guide the professional practice of evaluators and to inform evaluation clients and the general public about the principles they can expect from professional evaluators. (A full description of these principles is available on the AEA's website at http://www.eval.org).

These guiding principles need to be proactively used to guide your (and the CMs') actions in everyday evaluation practice. This is because several factors could influence and bias the collaborative evaluation, as individuals are actively involved in this process. The evaluator also has interests in the evaluation, on the one hand satisfying the evaluation sponsor, and on the other hand doing excellent work and getting professional recognition and appropriate compensation for it (Weiss, 1998).

The AEA's guiding principles for evaluators represent the diversity of perceptions about the primary purpose of evaluation, as well as the diverse background of the evaluators (for example, training, experience, work, and settings). Therefore, the following are the guiding principles for evaluators: (a) systematic inquiry, (b) competence, (c) integrity and honesty, (d) respect for people, and (e) responsibilities for general and public welfare. These five principles are not independent, but overlap in many ways, and their order does not imply priority among them because the priority will vary among evaluations.

Systematic Inquiry

Systematic inquiry is when evaluators (such as you) conduct a systematic, data-based inquiry (quantitative, qualitative, or both) of the evaluand, adhering to the highest technical standards for an accurate and credible outcome.

Within this guiding principle, it is expected that you explore with the client the strengths and weaknesses of the evaluation questions and approaches that might be used in the evaluation. Also, the evaluation information (such as methods, approaches, and results) needs to be communicated accurately and in sufficient detail to allow others to understand and provide feedback on it.

Competence

Competence is when evaluators (such as you) provide effective performance to stakeholders due to their background (for example, appropriate education or abilities) regarding the evaluation tasks.

Within this guiding principle, it is expected that you decline to conduct evaluations that fall outside the limits of your professional training and competence. Also, you should ensure that individuals working with you in the evaluation (such as the CMs) demonstrate cultural competence. Moreover, be able to provide your highest level of performance by continually maintaining and improving your evaluation competencies (formal education, workshops, self-studies, working with other evaluators, and so on).

Integrity and Honesty

Integrity and honesty is when evaluators (such as you) attempt to ensure honesty and integrity in their own behavior and the entire evaluation process. Also, it is expected that evaluators attempt to negotiate honestly with stakeholders in order to clarify all the evaluation matters, for example, costs, tasks undertaken, and limitations of methodology.

Within this guiding principle, it is expected that changes should be recorded and communicated in a timely fashion. Also, disclose your or others' interests in the evaluation (for instance, financial or political), and any role, relationship, or activity that might pose a significant conflict of interest (or seem likely to produce misleading information). Moreover, you should attempt to prevent or correct any substantial misuses of your work by others, and disclose all sources of financial support (and the source of the request) for the evaluation.

Respect for People

Respect for people is when evaluators (such as you) respect the security, dignity, and self-worth of the respondents, clients, and other stakeholders with whom you interact during the evaluation. Also, abide by current professional ethics and standards (for example, in terms of scope and limits of confidentiality) regarding issues that might be engendered to those involved in the evaluation.

Within this guiding principle, it is expected that you must explicitly state justified negative or critical conclusions from the evaluation, and carefully judge when the evaluation benefits should be foregone because of the risks or harms. Moreover, you should conduct the evaluation and communicate its results in a way that clearly respects the stakeholders' dignity and self-worth. Furthermore, you have the responsibility to identify differences among evaluation stakeholders (for example, in gender, disability, and ethnicity), and to be alert to potential implications of these differences throughout the evaluation.

Responsibilities for General and Public Welfare

Responsibilities for general and public welfare is when evaluators (such as you) consider the different interests and values that may be related to the

Follow Guiding Principles for Evaluators

Evelyn: I see you are working once again with the RTS Foundation. As I recall, you stopped working with them two years ago because you didn't agree with some of their practices. I heard the program officer with whom you worked just left the foundation. I have also heard their board has approved the dismissal of other people at the foundation. I am not sure what is happening, but I hope it is for the best for the foundation, its staff, and the thousands of people their programming benefits. Do you know what's going on?

Ernest: As a matter of fact I do. I have gone back to work because they have a new director of evaluation. She heard about me not long after she started and invited me to meet with her. The main reason I stopped working with the foundation's former director of evaluation was because of his unusual and unethical approach to evaluation. The last two invitations I received from him to submit a proposal marked a clear point of departure for me. In one instance he said he needed to complete this evaluation at any cost, and when I asked him why, he said, "It is a matter of personal responsibility; I need to complete a minimum number of evaluations a year in order to receive a positive performance evaluation and a good salary increase." I declined immediately. The second time, he said he needed to complete this evaluation before the end of the fiscal year. This time he was very careful not to share the reason for it, but at some point he mentioned that he also needed to meet this level of "evaluation expenditure" before June 30. In both cases, there was no intention of using the evaluation results. He was only interested in his own benefit. I guess those may be some of the reasons why he is no longer with the foundation!

general and public welfare. When planning and reporting evaluations, you should consider the full range of stakeholders and their perspectives and interests relevant to the evaluand.

Within this guiding principle, it is expected that you consider not only the immediate evaluation outcomes but also implications and potential side effects of the evaluand. In general, you should allow all relevant stakeholders to have access to evaluative information, and should actively disseminate that information to stakeholders (if possible) in an easy-to-understand way. You are also expected to maintain a balance between client needs and other needs. If conflict arises, identify (and try to resolve) its source, and make clear any significant limitations that might result if the conflict is not resolved. In addition, you may have to go beyond an analysis of particular stakeholder interests by considering society's welfare as a whole.

We suggest these steps to follow the AEA's guiding principles for evaluators:

1. Provide a copy of the American Evaluation Association's (AEA's) guiding principles for evaluators to the CMs and other relevant stakeholders, as appropriate. (A full description of these principles is available on the AEA's website at http://www.eval.org).

2. Discuss with all the CMs each of the AEA's guiding principles for evaluators, to make sure there is a clear understanding of their meaning and implications (or make any clarifications as feasible) within the collaborative evaluation.

3. Use check-out procedures on each of these guiding principles for evaluators. As an example, a full description of the guiding principles checklist for evaluating evaluations is available at http://www.wmich.edu/evalctr/.

4. Follow the AEA's guiding principle for evaluators, systematic inquiry. It is when evaluators (such as you) conduct a systematic, data-based inquiry of the evaluand, adhering to the highest technical standards for an accurate and credible outcome.

5. Follow the AEA's guiding principle for evaluators, competence. It is when evaluators (such as you) provide effective performance to stakeholders due to their background (for instance, appropriate education or abilities) regarding the evaluation tasks.

6. Follow the AEA's guiding principle for evaluators, integrity and honesty. It is when evaluators (such as you) attempt to ensure honesty and integrity in their own behavior and the entire evaluation process, for example, in areas related to tasks undertaken.

7. Follow the AEA's guiding principle for evaluators, respect for people. It is when evaluators (such as you) respect the security, dignity, and self-worth of the respondents, clients, and other stakeholders with whom you interact during the evaluation.

8. Follow the AEA's guiding principle for evaluators, responsibilities for general and public welfare. It is when evaluators (such as you) consider the

different interests and values that may be related to the general and public welfare.

9. Gather feedback on a regular basis using a previously agreed-upon system (for example, meetings, emails, and surveys as feasible). This will help you and the CMs monitor each of these guiding principles and make updates as needed.

10. Provide each CM and other stakeholders as appropriate with a summary report of this experience (including how these guiding principles for evaluators were applied to specific issues) as lessons learned for future similar situations within collaborative evaluations.

FOLLOW EVALUATION STANDARDS

Several standards are available to guide the conduct and use of evaluation. As an example, we are focusing on the evaluation standards developed by the Joint Committee on Standards for Educational Evaluation (JCSEE). The **evaluation standards** are the commonly agreed-upon principles of professional practice in the conduct and use of evaluation, that when implemented will lead to greater evaluation quality. The JCSEE was founded in 1975 in order to develop standards that guide the design, implementation, assessment, and improvement of an evaluation. Since then, the JCSEE has developed a set of standards for the evaluation of personnel, programs, and students. (A full description of these standards is available on JCSEE's website at http://www.jcsee.org/).

The **personnel evaluation standards** are a set of twenty-seven standards for designing, conducting, and judging personnel evaluations and personnel systems (Joint Committee on Standards for Educational Evaluation, 2009). The **program evaluation standards** are a set of thirty standards, and their goal is to ensure useful, feasible, ethical, accountable, and sound evaluation of programs, projects, and materials (Joint Committee on Standards for Educational Evaluation, 2011). Finally, the **student evaluation standards** are a set of twenty-eight standards for use in a variety of educational institutions (Joint Committee on Standards for Educational Evaluation, 2003).

The most important insight provided by the JCSEE is the concept that the following attributes are necessary and sufficient for sound and fair evaluations: (a) utility, (b) feasibility, (c) propriety, and (d) accuracy. Hence, each of the program, personnel, and student standards are grouped according to their potential contribution to each of these attributes. In addition, the latest edition of the program evaluation standards (JCSEE, 2011) includes one more attribute, **evaluation accountability,** which refers to the responsible use of resources to produce value. The program evaluation standards placed under this attribute are (1) evaluation documentation, (2) internal metaevaluation, and (3) external metaevaluation.

Utility Standards

The **utility standards** are intended to ensure that the evaluation will be useful (for example, informative, timely, and influential) (JCSEE, 2003, 2009, 2011). Judgments about utility are made on the basis of the extent to which stakeholders find evaluation processes and products valuable in meeting their needs. In other words, these utility standards address components that could affect the usefulness of the information obtained from the collaborative evaluation. The standards can be described as follows:

- **Personnel Evaluation Standards.** The personnel evaluation standards placed under utility are (1) constructive orientation, (2) defined uses, (3) evaluator qualifications, (4) explicit criteria, (5) functional reporting, and (6) follow-up professional development (JCSEE, 2009).

- **Program Evaluation Standards.** The program evaluation standards placed under utility are (1) evaluator credibility, (2) attention to stakeholders, (3) negotiated purposes, (4) explicit values, (5) relevant information, (6) meaningful processes and products, (7) timely and appropriate communicating and reporting, and (8) concern for consequences and influence (JCSEE, 2011).

- **Student Evaluation Standards.** The student evaluation standards placed under utility are (1) constructive orientation, (2) defined users and uses, (3) information scope, (4) evaluator qualifications, (5) explicit values, (6) effective reporting, and (7) follow-up (JCSEE, 2003).

Feasibility Standards

The **feasibility standards** are intended to ensure that the evaluation can be implemented as planned (JCSEE, 2003, 2009, 2011). Judgments about feasibility are made on the basis of the extent to which evaluations can take place with an adequate degree of effectiveness and efficiency. Feasible evaluations need to be practical, viable, diplomatic, adequately supported, and efficient in their use of resources. The standards can be described as follows:

- **Personnel Evaluation Standards.** The personnel evaluation standards placed under feasibility are (1) practical procedures, (2) political viability, and (3) fiscal viability (JCSEE, 2009).

- **Program Evaluation Standards.** The program evaluation standards placed under feasibility are (1) project management, (2) practical procedures, (3) contextual viability, and (4) resource use (JCSEE, 2011).

- **Student Evaluation Standards.** The student evaluation standards placed under feasibility are (1) practical orientation, (2) political viability, and (3) evaluation support (JCSEE, 2003).

Propriety Standards

The **propriety standards** are intended to ensure that the evaluation will be conducted legally, ethically, and with due regard for the welfare of those involved in it, or affected by its results (JCSEE, 2003, 2009, 2011). Judgments about propriety are made on the basis of what is proper, fair, legal, right, acceptable, and just in evaluations. The standards can be described as follows:

- **Personnel Evaluation Standards.** The personnel evaluation standards placed under propriety are (1) service orientation, (2) appropriate policies and procedures, (3) access to evaluation information, (4) interactions with evaluatees (people being evaluated), (5) comprehensive evaluation, (6) conflict of interest, and (7) legal viability (JCSEE, 2009).

- **Program Evaluation Standards.** The program evaluation standards placed under propriety are (1) responsive and inclusive orientation, (2) formal agreements, (3) human rights and respect, (4) clarity and fairness, (5) transparency and disclosure, (6) conflicts of interests, and (7) fiscal responsibility (JCSEE, 2011).

- **Student Evaluation Standards.** The student evaluation standards placed under propriety are (1) service to students, (2) appropriate policies and procedures, (3) access to evaluation information, (4) treatment of students, (5) rights of students, (6) balanced evaluation, and (7) conflict of interest (JCSEE, 2003).

Accuracy Standards

The **accuracy standards** are intended to ensure that the evaluation will produce technically sound, accurate, and credible information (for example, valid interpretations or conclusions linked logically to the data) about the features that determine the evaluand value (JCSEE, 2003, 2009, 2011). Judgments about accuracy are made on the basis of what is truthful of evaluation representations, propositions, and findings, especially those that support judgments about the quality of programs or program components. The standards can be described as follows:

- **Personnel Evaluation Standards.** The personnel evaluation standards placed under accuracy are (1) valid judgments, (2) defined expectations, (3) analysis of context, (4) documented purposes and procedures, (5) defensible information, (6) reliable information, (7) systematic data control, (8) bias identification and management, (9) analysis of information, (10) justified conclusions, and (11) metaevaluation (JCSEE, 2009).

- **Program Evaluation Standards.** The program evaluation standards placed under accuracy are (1) justified conclusions and decisions, (2) valid information, (3) reliable information, (4) explicit program and context descriptions, (5) information management, (6) sound designs and analyses, (7) explicit evaluation reasoning, and (8) communication and reporting (JCSEE, 2011).

- **Student Evaluation Standards.** The student evaluation standards placed under accuracy are (1) validity orientation, (2) defined expectations for students, (3) context analysis, (4) documented procedures, (5) defensible information, (6) reliable information, (7) bias identification and management, (8) handling information and quality control, (9) analysis of information, (10) justified conclusions, and (11) metaevaluation (JCSEE, 2003).

You and the CMs need to continually exercise professional judgment in order to correctly use these evaluation standards, and reflect best practice within the collaborative evaluation. Evaluation is the process whose duty is the systematic and objective determination of merit, worth, or value and, without such a process, there is no way to distinguish the worthwhile from the worthless (Scriven, 1991). As a general summary, we suggest these steps to follow the evaluation standards:

1. Provide a copy of the evaluation standards (such as the program evaluation standards) to the CMs and other relevant stakeholders, as appropriate. (A full description of these standards is available on the JCSEE's website at http://www.jcsee.org/).

2. Discuss with all the CMs each of the evaluation standards, to make sure there is a clear understanding of their meaning and implications. Keep in mind that the program evaluation standards also includes the attribute evaluation accountability.

3. Provide a copy of the metaevaluation (evaluation of an evaluation) checklists to the CMs and other stakeholders, as appropriate. (A full description of these checklists is available on the Evaluation Center's website at http://www.wmich.edu/evalctr/).

4. Discuss with all the CMs and other relevant stakeholders each of the metaevaluation checklists, to make sure there is a clear understanding of their meaning, application, and implications within the collaborative evaluation (or make clarifications as needed).

5. Follow the evaluation standards grouped under the attribute, utility. They are intended to ensure that the evaluation will be useful (that is, informative, timely, and influential), when stakeholders find evaluation processes and products valuable in meeting their needs.

6. Follow the evaluation standards grouped under the attribute, feasibility. They are intended to ensure that the evaluation is practical, diplomatic, adequately supported, and efficient in the use of resources, and can be implemented as planned.

7. Follow the evaluation standards grouped under the attribute, propriety. They are intended to ensure that the evaluation will be conducted legally, ethically, and with due regard for the welfare of those involved in it, or affected by its results.

8. Follow the evaluation standards grouped under the attribute, accuracy. They are intended to ensure that the evaluation will produce technically sound, accurate, and credible information (such as valid interpretations or conclusions linked logically to the data).

9. Gather feedback on a regular basis using a previously agreed-upon system (for example, meetings, emails, and surveys as feasible). This will help you and the CMs monitor the suitability of the evaluation standards and make updates as needed.

10. Provide each CM and other stakeholders as appropriate, with a summary report of this experience (including how these evaluation standards were applied to specific issues) as lessons learned for future similar situations within collaborative evaluations.

Follow Evaluation Standards

Eliot: When I started this evaluation, I was very happy to see that all the CMs were very enthusiastic about it; they all assured me I would have their full support throughout the evaluation. I told them that I would be following the program evaluation standards. I also explained what each standard meant and how I would be using them. However, as the data-collection process ended and I completed the first draft of the evaluation report for my client, I learned that one of the CMs, who had helped us with a portion of the data-collection process, had failed to give us a set of survey results that apparently point out clear weaknesses of the program we are evaluating. My meeting with my client is next week; how do you think I should address this issue?

Evelyn: From the evaluation practice point of view, I see several program evaluation standards being affected. However, first you need to verify whether this claim is real and if there is physical evidence to support such a claim. If it is true, you have to find out whether you can recover the surveys or survey results; then you need to learn how this happened, so you can prevent it in the future. Once you have gathered and verified all the information, speak openly and honestly with your client. Also, look into the timeline in which you are working. You will obviously need to include these data in your analysis and review any conclusions or recommendations you may have considered. What is important is your full transparency with this information and your client. This will indeed be something he will appreciate and will help him regard you as someone who follows high personal and professional standards.

FOLLOW THE COLLABORATION GUIDING PRINCIPLES

The **collaboration guiding principles** are established tenets that guide the professional practice of collaborators. We have found several commonalities across our experience with collaborative efforts, and we have summarized those into specific principles. The principles have been implicitly present throughout this book, helping to blend together the six MCE components.

The collaboration guiding principles represent the diversity of perceptions about the primary purpose of collaboration. These principles proactively guide the everyday collaborative practice. Hence, they are conceptualized here as general ideals or expectations that need to be considered in collaborative efforts. The following are the collaboration guiding principles: (a) development, (b) empathy, (c) empowerment, (d) involvement, (e) qualification, (f) social support, and (g) trust.

Development

Development is when you and the CMs use training (such as workshops or seminars) or any other mechanism (for example, mentorship) to enhance learning and self-improvement. Everyone involved in the collaborative effort should continuously develop through education and communication.

This principle implies that everyone has the responsibility to acknowledge and appreciate other people's differing learning styles and address those according to the particular situation. Also implied is that you and the CMs will take active steps to stay current regarding any strategies that will provide better collaboration opportunities. This might involve reading particular literature, attending workshops and conferences, and so on. Furthermore, it implies a responsibility to contribute to the development of the CMs, at least in the context of the collaboration, and to avoid inadequate actions (such as unfairness) that detract from their development.

Empathy

Empathy is when you and the CMs show sensitivity, understanding, and a thoughtful response toward the feelings or emotions of others. Consequently, when you and the CMs are able to empathize with other people, you also are better able to skillfully manage a positive reaction to your collaborative environment. For example, when you can empathize with the feelings of others, then you can find a common ground to build rapport.

This principle implies that you and the CMs acknowledge and deal in a positive way with topics found to be sensitive or discomforting. It also implies that you and the CMs are able to identify your own perspectives and biases in a particular situation, and compare them with other interpretations in order to gain a full understanding of the situation's complexity. Furthermore, empathy also implies that you and the CMs provide a safe and open environment for discussion, in which everyone is able to state their position on the issue in a thoughtful manner even when it is necessary to disagree.

Empowerment

Empowerment is when you and the CMs develop a sense of self-efficacy by delegating authority and removing any possible obstacles (such as negative feelings) that might limit the attainment of established goals. For example, when you share information, the CMs feel a sense of control over the collaborative effort and ownership over the subsequent recommendations for improvement.

You (and other evaluators as feasible) are the only one who has responsibility for the overall collaboration and its results. However, this principle implies that everyone involved has responsibilities and authority to make decisions on specific tasks and accountability for the subsequent results. As a motivational boost, openly encourage the CMs to use their own initiative for deciding and taking action at different levels of the collaborative effort, as appropriate. As a result, everyone would be voluntarily committed to their roles, because they consider those important and pleasant.

Involvement

Involvement is when you and the CMs constructively combine forces throughout the collaboration in a way that is feasible and meaningful for everyone. In other words, involvement is when you and the CMs voluntarily complement each other's strengths and weaknesses by working together to understand the collaboration picture. Obviously, the level of involvement varies among everyone who collaborates in the effort.

This principle implies that you and the CMs are actively engaged in making decisions and taking action by recognizing the need to join efforts for a mutual cause. For example, everyone is able to provide ideas on how to solve particular problems (and take action to solve those problems), by combining their own talents and resources in order to implement solutions. Hence, a proactive involvement is essential to establish collaborative processes throughout any type of effort and to strengthen its results.

Qualification

Qualification is when you and the CMs have a high level of knowledge and skills needed to achieve an effective collaboration. It means that you and the CMs are prepared for dealing with relevant performance issues that are directly affected by the individual's background. A specific example of failure to fulfill this principle is when you and the CMs have insufficient knowledge to provide support in the collaboration.

This principle implies that you and the CMs are responsible for maintaining the personal and professional qualifications needed. These qualifications have to be theoretical and practical so that you are able to accomplish multiple collaboration tasks (for example, provide technical information, resolve conflicts, and deal with diverse issues). Also, you and the CMs need to be qualified on alternative collaboration approaches or strategies and to select methods that are effective in helping others achieve the mutual objectives.

Social Support

Social support is when you and the CMs manage relationships with others in order to establish a sense of belonging and a meaningful and holistic view of social-related issues. This principle implies that you and the CMs have the ability to develop productive networks in order to enhance the capacity of solving problems in a collaborative way.

Through social support you and the CMs can meet important collaboration needs such as solidarity and validation of everyone's role and contribution. Therefore, this principle implies that obtaining support from a broad array of people (for example, from different backgrounds and disciplines) is central to a collaborative work. Obviously, you and the CMs need to avoid conflict of interest or people who are likely to detract from, bias, or compromise the collaborative effort. It is everyone's responsibility to prevent any risk of conflict of interest from materializing as a result of the collaboration.

Trust

Trust is when you and the CMs have a firm confidence in or reliance on the sincerity, credibility, and reliability of everyone involved in the collaboration. Although a high level of trust among you and the CMs must exist for a successful collaboration, trust takes time to build and can be eliminated easily.

The CMs' trust in you and the collaboration is highly dependent on how much they perceive you trust them. It is the impression you make as the evaluator at any particular time (such as demonstrating interest in and appreciation for them) that will determine how trust is perceived by the CMs. Hence, for them to trust you, show that you sincerely trust them as well. This principle implies that a high level of mutual trust facilitates collaboration between you and the CMs, because misunderstandings can be easier to solve.

As a general summary, we suggest these steps to follow the collaboration guiding principles:

1. Provide a copy of the collaboration guiding principles to the CMs and other relevant stakeholders if appropriate. (A full description of these collaboration guiding principles is also available on our website at http://www.collabeval.com).

2. Discuss with all the CMs each of the collaboration guiding principles, to make sure there is a clear understanding of their meaning, application, and implications (or make clarifications as needed) among everyone involved in the collaborative effort.

3. Follow the collaboration guiding principle, development. It is when you and the CMs use training (such as workshops or seminars) or any other mechanism (for example, coaching or mentoring) to enhance learning and self-improvement.

4. Follow the collaboration guiding principle, empathy. It is when you and the CMs show sensitivity, understanding, and a thoughtful response toward the feelings or emotions of others, therefore better managing a positive reaction to your collaborative environment.

5. Follow the collaboration guiding principle, empowerment. It is when you and the CMs develop a sense of self-efficacy by delegating authority and removing any possible obstacles (such as negative feelings) that might limit the attainment of established goals.

6. Follow the collaboration guiding principle, involvement. It is when you and the CMs constructively combine forces (complementing each other's strengths and weaknesses) throughout the collaboration in a way that is feasible and meaningful for everyone.

7. Follow the collaboration guiding principle, qualification. It is when you and the CMs have a high level of knowledge and skills needed to achieve an effective collaboration. For example, be prepared for dealing with issues directly affected by your background.

8. Follow the collaboration guiding principle, social support. It is when you and the CMs manage relationships with others (such as productive networks) in order to establish a sense of belonging and a meaningful and holistic view of social-related issues.

9. Follow the collaboration guiding principle, trust. It is when you and the CMs have a firm confidence in or reliance on the sincerity, credibility, and reliability of everyone involved in the collaboration evaluation (trust takes time to build and can be eliminated easily).

10. Gather feedback on a regular basis using a previously agreed-upon system, such as meetings, and summarize it in a written format (including

Follow the Collaboration Guiding Principles

Evelyn: I am just coming back from a meeting with several CMs for the evaluation on the literacy program. I received your message and was a bit disappointed to learn we will not be able to work on this collaborative evaluation together; I was certainly looking forward to it. What happened?

Ernest: Well, I was looking forward to working with you on this new evaluation, too. Here's what happened: I was planning on conducting another evaluation locally. Now, after further discussion with my new client, it makes more sense for me to travel to their location instead. They have agreed to provide the funds to cover the additional expenses. This client, who has not worked in a collaborative evaluation before, requested me to observe how his staff follows the collaboration guiding principles in their daily operations. His goal is to create expanded opportunities to work collaboratively in future projects as well. Obviously, this is a very interesting endeavor because each of the collaboration guiding principles will have different relevance throughout different stages in the evaluation. For example, the *empowerment* principle could be more relevant when there is a need for specific individuals to develop a sense of self-efficacy. Then, the *social support* principle could be more relevant when there is a need to develop productive networks in order to enhance the capacity of solving problems in a collaborative way. I am ready to start this new collaborative effort!

the current use of each principle) so it is available to each CM and other stakeholders as appropriate.

Consider providing orientation and professional development opportunities to the CMs to develop awareness of each of the guidelines presented in this chapter. In addition, make available follow-up training, if feasible, for those CMs who would like to gain a better understanding of these guidelines. For example, you and the CMs can closely examine how the different guidelines fit together to support collaborative evaluations.

In this chapter, we emphasized the importance of following specific guidelines that direct the design, use, and assessment of the collaborative evaluation. We focused on guiding principles expected from professional evaluators in general. We also reviewed the evaluation standards as an example of commonly agreed-upon principles of professional practice in evaluation. In addition, we discussed the collaboration guiding principles intended to guide the professional practice of collaborators. All these specific guidelines should be continuously evaluated in terms of their applicability as sound systems for specific collaborative evaluations. Finally, as in other chapters, we incorporated examples in order to reinforce interdependence among the MCE elements.

Afterword

THIS BOOK ILLUSTRATES the interesting potential of collaborative evaluations and the manifold opportunities of achieving new insights. The greatest strengths of the Model for Collaborative Evaluations (MCE) are that it gives focus to collaborative evaluations and provides a strong basis for establishing long-term relationships. This model assumes that important decisions can be made collaboratively at early evaluation stages and that ongoing alternatives can be easily incorporated as necessary. Therefore, the MCE is an evaluation tool that helps you and the CMs better understand how to develop priorities in order to achieve a high level of support within a collaborative evaluation.

The MCE has been shown (in the business, nonprofit, and education sectors, among others) to establish formality by being methodical and forming a great alignment among its six components. This model promotes constant sources of information for collaborative efforts, because it constitutes a simple and innovative way of consultation that standardizes the activities to be carried out. Also, it provides direction on sensitive topics, to help avoid unnecessary tensions among you and the CMs. Furthermore, the MCE facilitates instruction, reducing the costs for the training process and induction of new members.

Every time we have used the MCE we have observed that CMs and other stakeholders identified more with the evaluation and were motivated to continuously improve it. This is because the MCE allows a systematic examination of the elements that influence the success of collaboration in evaluations. Also, the MCE helps you and the CMs to better appreciate the complex nature of the collaboration process. This model has been used as a part of a wide variety of efforts, both in single and multiple-site evaluations. Also, it has been used in collaborative evaluations at the national and international level. Furthermore, it has been used for both formative and summative purposes. Therefore, if properly conducted, the MCE has great potential for being used across virtually every area of society in which a collaborative evaluation is needed and feasible.

It is important to emphasize that different elements of the MCE will be more useful than others depending on the situation. This model does not pretend to establish a unique way to achieve collaborative evaluations. It would be interesting to carry out the same type of evaluation with another approach that could address issues in a different way. A comparative analysis of results could then be made in order to deepen and share new knowledge, contributing to and benefiting the collaborative effort. It would also be helpful to evaluate your own collaborative evaluations in order to establish their value and learn from them. In addition, the MCE can be used outside the evaluation field by transforming it to a more general collaboration model.

Many stakeholders use evaluation results to improve the effectiveness of their evaluands. The MCE can help you understand and account for the nature of the work and the full range of stakeholders in the collaborative evaluation process. Hence, the evaluation results are able to provide a useful basis for guiding the decision-making process because people work collaboratively while respecting the evaluand and its interactions within its total system.

This model provides an important learning opportunity so you and the CMs can gain knowledge on how to conduct collaborative evaluations step-by-step. We are convinced that a well-developed collaborative evaluation leads to better questions, answers or results, and use of those results. With this book, we hope to have clarified issues about collaboration in ways that illustrate the interesting possibilities that need to be addressed in a sound collaborative evaluation.

The MCE provides an increased shared ownership that also leads to an increased quality of information for decision making and receptivity of findings. As a consequence, it enhances the likelihood that evaluation findings will be used, providing a crucial basis for learning and development. Obviously, there is a continuous possibility of achieving new insights (every time you apply the MCE to new settings) because the application of this model is vast. It is our goal that this book will be a valuable source for your collaborative evaluations!

Finally, the information contained in this book was drawn from our professional evaluation experience and designed as a reference to conduct collaborative evaluations. This book aims to connect the theory and practice of collaborative evaluations through steps so you can immediately apply the MCE. We are very interested in receiving feedback about the usefulness of the stories throughout the book and your experiences with this model. You are welcome to contact us at http://www.collabeval.com.

Reference Matter

Model for Collaborative Evaluations (MCE) Checklist

Table A.1 Identify the Situation

Model for Collaborative Evaluations (MCE) Checklist
The checklist includes several checkpoints to be scored as follows:
1 = Addressed, 2 = Partially Addressed, 3 = Not Addressed, and 4 = Not Applicable.

Identify Stakeholders (General)	1	2	3	4
1. Be clear that your responsibility is to meet, or even better, exceed your client's expectations while ensuring that particular interests of all relevant stakeholders are considered throughout a balanced collaborative evaluation.				
2. Learn as much as you can about your evaluation client, and later about other potential stakeholders, in order to establish a beneficial relationship. For example, read from the evaluand's or client's website and other sources of information.				
3. Think carefully and write down all the questions you need the client, and later other potential stakeholders, to answer (for instance, who needs to be informed, who is to receive the evaluation results, and whose collaboration is crucial).				
4. Seek clarification (with a courteous attitude) to your questions when meeting with the client, and later with other potential stakeholders, as feasible. For example, if doubts arise after a meeting, then seek to clarify all those doubts.				
5. Listen rather than just making statements or educating about the evaluation process (avoid interrupting). For example, wait silently and patiently during pauses, because generally the most important information follows them.				
6. Identify diverse points of view (such as strongest supporters and opponents) in order to diffuse any resistance toward the collaborative evaluation and ensure that everyone's contributions will be adequately considered.				
7. Make a preliminary list with the client's assistance (and others as applicable) of the key stakeholders affected by the evaluation. For example, distinguish who would gain or lose the most from the evaluation under different scenarios.				

Table A.1 (continued)

	1	2	3	4
8. Invite your client to review and add or delete names from the preliminary stakeholders list. By doing this, you can have a better idea of who the key stakeholders really are and their possible contributions to the evaluation as future CMs.				
9. Gather feedback on a regular basis using a previously agreed-upon system (including, meetings, emails, and surveys as feasible). This will help in monitoring the stakeholders' identification process and making updates as needed.				
10. Provide the client and other stakeholders as appropriate with a summary report of this experience (for example, an updated list of the stakeholders) as a baseline for identifying the situation of the collaborative evaluation.				
Identify Stakeholders (Collaboration Members)	**1**	**2**	**3**	**4**
1. Make a preliminary list of essential characteristics that are desirable in the CMs. With this goal in mind, you will be able to later match specific stakeholders to this list while being prepared to be flexible in the selection process.				
2. Agree with your client, and other key stakeholders as feasible, which stakeholders from the list can have the most active involvement in the collaborative evaluation, becoming potential CMs (including the client or not, as appropriate).				
3. Create, with the potential CMs' help, a calendar that shows their availability during the different evaluation stages and how they see themselves fitting into the collaboration. For example, determine who will be available and when.				
4. Learn about each potential CM in terms of their individual characteristics (such as strengths and weaknesses) before making a decision on which individuals you are going to officially invite to become CMs of the evaluation.				
5. Identify which of the potential CMs may require special training to enhance their evaluation skills. Sometimes you may not find enough qualified CMs, so they will need appropriate training to build specific evaluation skills.				
6. Agree on the final CMs with the client, once you have met with all the key stakeholders, as feasible. Be sure that major stakeholders are represented (that is, specific characteristics) across the main areas affected by the evaluation.				
7. Ensure that you and the client are making a fair decision on the CMs' selection (for example, that you have all the relevant facts to make a decision) and how to match their skills and abilities to the expectations of the collaborative evaluation.				

Table A.1 (continued)

	1	2	3	4
8. Determine if the selected CMs agree to formally collaborate as such in the evaluation, and get started with those who are willing to do it. In other words, find who is genuinely interested to collaborate in the evaluation efforts.				
9. Consider the morale of the non-selected stakeholders, who may feel disappointed with the selection. For example, ensure open communication with them, because they can provide important feedback for the collaborative evaluation.				
10. Gather feedback on a regular basis using a previously agreed-upon system, such as meetings, and summarize it in a written format (including an updated list of the CMs) so it is available to each CM and other stakeholders as appropriate.				
Identify Logic Model Elements	**1**	**2**	**3**	**4**
1. Make sure that you and the participants (CMs and other key stakeholders) have a clear understanding of the initiative's characteristics and the organization or institution as a whole (including the vision and mission).				
2. Share with participants a summary comparison of similar initiatives and their logic models (this is done for obtaining new ideas). For example, refer to information from the literature, Internet sites, and other experts in the area.				
3. Establish a clear logic model scope that is based on the informational requirements of the initiative and the agreement of participants. For instance, are the logic model elements going to represent the entire initiative or just a part of it?				
4. Agree with all the participants on the most convenient arrangement of the logic model elements. For example, use a priority order or an alphabetical order arrangement for each of the inputs, activities, outputs, and outcomes.				
5. Assist participants in identifying the logic model elements following this order: (a) most essential outcomes, (b) outputs needed to generate outcomes, (c) activities needed to generate outputs, and (d) inputs needed to generate activities.				
6. Solicit participants to outline the logic model connections (perhaps using arrows or labels) in order to show the relationships between its elements. For instance, how do the outputs link with the outcomes? How do the activities link with the outputs?				
7. Delete all those elements and connections that are duplicates, seem unreasonable, or irrelevant. For example, check with participants that each of the boxes is connected with other(s) and make sure the connections are logical.				

Table A.1 (continued)

	1	2	3	4
8. Write a brief description that clearly reflects the meaning of each of the boxes in the logic model. Otherwise, only the people who have collaborated in the development of the logic model will have a complete understanding of it.				
9. Agree with all the participants and other stakeholders as appropriate (for example, board members) on a definitive logic model. This final version of the logic model should be clearly aligned with the initiative's vision and mission.				
10. Gather feedback on a regular basis using a previously agreed-upon system, such as meetings, and summarize it in a written format (including an updated logic model) so it is available to each participant and other stakeholders as appropriate.				
Identify Potential SWOTs	**1**	**2**	**3**	**4**
1. Create a SWOT matrix on a flipchart (poster or other similar option) and have available a variety of color-coded, self-adhesive cards (such as blue for strengths, yellow for weaknesses, green for opportunities, and red for threats).				
2. Review relevant data (for example, historical information on this and other evaluands) to have some examples that could be identified as SWOTs, such as technology and information availability, assigned budget, and time considerations.				
3. Divide the participants (including CMs and other stakeholders as needed) into four teams representing strengths, weaknesses, opportunities, and threats. Then provide each team the color adhesives identifying their particular SWOT.				
4. Instruct each team to write one specific idea per adhesive, under their specific team SWOT, until they run out of ideas. Then the team leader will read to their members each of the ideas and, with their feedback, eliminate any overlap.				
5. Place the color adhesives on the flipchart, under the specific team SWOT, so the rest of the teams can read them. In the case of the opportunities and threats, only leave those that have at least a 50 percent chance of occurrence.				
6. Solicit participants to each make note of their own new ideas about the SWOTs (to make sure all the most important ideas are addressed) and share each of those ideas while adding them to the SWOTs matrix as appropriate.				
7. Ask for ideas or feedback from other stakeholders who may help identify additional realistic SWOTS (such as unintended results or areas that may have been overlooked). Question every alternative before adding it to the SWOTs matrix.				

Table A.1 (continued)

	1	2	3	4
8. Agree with all the participants and other specific stakeholders, as feasible, on a definitive SWOTs matrix. This final version of the SWOTs matrix should be clearly aligned with the evaluand vision and mission to understand which issues deserve attention.				
9. Design with the participants emergency procedures (for example, risk analysis, predefined action steps, or contingency plans) and plan for timely feedback throughout the evaluation to provide early warning signs of specific problems.				
10. Gather feedback on a regular basis using a previously agreed-upon system, such as meetings, and summarize it in a written format (including an updated version of the SWOTs report) so it is available to each CM and other stakeholders as appropriate.				
Identify the Evaluation Scope (Questions)	**1**	**2**	**3**	**4**
1. Ask the client (the CMs and other key stakeholders as appropriate) about the history of the evaluand and, specifically, if it has previously been evaluated. If so, ask what evaluation questions were used at that time and what results were found.				
2. Identify the amount of resources (such as time, people, materials, and funds) available for the evaluation. This will determine the feasibility of increasing or reducing the number of evaluation questions that can be manageable.				
3. Ask the client directly for an initial draft of evaluation questions (if the client is able to give you a direct answer). For example, what are the main questions he or she wants the evaluation to answer? Are those questions consistent with specific needs?				
4. Ask the client indirectly for an initial draft of evaluation questions (if the client is not able to give you a direct answer). For example, what should be accomplished as a result of this evaluation? What problem should the evaluation address?				
5. Listen rather than make comments about any of the evaluation questions at this point (avoid interrupting). For example, wait silently and patiently during pauses, because generally the most important information follows them.				
6. Recognize and address any type of insistence on including potentially biased or unanswerable questions. For instance, find out who would be affected by a particular question (and why), especially if the answer is different than expected.				
7. Assist the client (with the CMs' or other stakeholders' feedback as appropriate) in narrowing down the original list to a manageable number of preliminary questions (for example, those that are realistic depending on budget, time, and feasibility).				

Table A.1 (continued)

	1	2	3	4
8. Invite the client to select, as a result of a previous thorough analysis, all the final evaluation questions that will be addressed throughout the collaborative evaluation (with the CMs' or other stakeholders' feedback as appropriate).				
9. Agree with the client (in writing) on the final evaluation questions that will be answered by the collaborative evaluation. This is only done after solving any possible concerns on the feasibility of those evaluation questions.				
10. Provide the client, each CM, and other stakeholders as appropriate with a summary report of this experience (including a list of the evaluation questions) as lessons learned for developing questions in similar collaborative evaluations.				
Identify the Evaluation Scope (Work Breakdown Structure)	**1**	**2**	**3**	**4**
1. Identify the long- and short-term evaluation goals in order to put into context what needs to be achieved and the option(s) to make it happen within the collaborative effort. For example, determine what should happen in the evaluation.				
2. Provide a summary or example with a definition of the WBS to the CMs, and other relevant stakeholders if appropriate, and discuss it with them in order to make sure there is a clear understanding (or make clarifications as needed).				
3. Divide each of the evaluation questions (or any other main evaluation components) into groups, with the help of the CMs, and give each evaluation question a unique identification number for record-keeping purposes.				
4. Break down each of the evaluation questions into smaller, concrete activities (and sub-activities if required) to show an increasingly in-depth description. Thus an element in a higher level is equal to the sum of all its sub-elements in the next lower level.				
5. Stop when the WBS reaches a level, such as an activity, that is conveniently measurable and manageable (for example, when the responsibility of an activity and authority over it can be assigned to a particular, skillful CM).				
6. Determine a logical order for each activity (within each group) and assign an identification number to each. This makes it easy to understand later how one activity may affect the timing of other activities and the evaluation as a whole.				
7. Check with the CMs that all the required activities per group have been considered (without any gaps). In other words, check with the CMs that there is a logical subdivision of the evaluation work against the reporting requirements.				

Table A.1 (continued)

	1	2	3	4
8. Write a brief description that clearly reflects the meaning of each of the boxes (work components) in the WBS. Otherwise, only the people who created the WBS (for example, you and the CMs) will have a complete understanding of it.				
9. Gather feedback on a regular basis using a previously agreed-upon system (such as meetings, emails, and surveys as feasible). This will help you and the CMs monitor the suitability of the WBS and make updates as needed.				
10. Provide each CM and other stakeholders as appropriate with a summary report of this experience (including the WBS with each of its descending levels) as lessons learned for future similar situations within collaborative evaluations.				
Identify Critical Evaluation Activities	**1**	**2**	**3**	**4**
1. Determine with the client when the evaluation should begin and end in terms of calendar or real dates (taking into consideration breaks for nonworking days and unrelated meetings, among others) to avoid different perceptions later.				
2. Identify with the CMs all major activities from the WBS and their possible duration. For example, use historical information on similar activities, or estimate how many hours (or dates by which) each activity needs to be completed.				
3. Use the best scheduling technique available (such as a network diagram) to draft the collaborative evaluation schedule on the basis of its deadline(s), the number of resources available, and backup strategies in case problems occur.				
4. Identify the critical evaluation activities (those without slack time) and verify that each of them is manageable and realistic (for instance, in terms of time and effort). These overall critical activities must be completed within the scheduled time.				
5. Divide every critical evaluation activity into categories (for example, you or the CMs control it; you or the CMs indirectly control it; you or the CMs do not control it), and try to move the not-controlled activities to, at least, being indirectly controlled.				
6. Choose the high-priority critical evaluation activities over which you or the CMs do not have control and allocate special time and other resources so that those critical evaluation activities do not consume more time than scheduled.				
7. Reserve sufficient slack time to handle unforeseen problems or constraints throughout the evaluation. For example, when there is no logical sequence among activities, they may be completed at the same time (if resources are available).				

Table A.1 (continued)

8. Agree with the CMs on the specific dates set for each of the evaluation activities and the overall evaluation, to make sure again that all the resources (such as people or materials) will be available at the time they are needed.				
9. Gather feedback on a regular basis using a previously agreed-upon system (for example, meetings, emails, and surveys as feasible). This will help you and the CMs monitor the critical activities and make updates as needed.				
10. Provide each CM and other stakeholders as appropriate with a summary report of this experience (including a report with the schedule of each critical evaluation activity) as lessons learned for future similar situations within collaborative evaluations.				

Table A.2 Clarify the Expectations

Model for Collaborative Evaluations (MCE) Checklist
The checklist includes several checkpoints to be scored as follows:
1 = Addressed, 2 = Partially Addressed, 3 = Not Addressed, and 4 = Not Applicable.

Clarify the Role of the Evaluator	1	2	3	4
1. Ask general questions to the CMs about their expectations of your role. For example, "I am interested in learning about your perceptions of what my role should be within the collaborative evaluation" produces abundant responses.				
2. Listen to the expectations the CMs have of your role (for example, how they expect you to behave and their specific concerns). Always allow room for the CMs to provide their answers at their own pace without being judgmental.				
3. List what you believe are the CMs' expectations of your role as the evaluator. This is a very important step that helps you prepare in advance a thorough and appealing message of what your role will be in the collaborative evaluation.				
4. Present a summary of your qualifications (such as a biographical sketch) and how you can be a valuable asset to the collaborative evaluation. For example, explain your background, your ethical values, and how they link with the evaluation goals.				
5. Inquire about the CMs' emotions (for example, their motivation regarding the evaluation) or how they feel about you and the collaborative evaluation. In this way, you can later address their concerns when you clarify your role as the evaluator.				
6. Present your specific role as the evaluator, mentioning how it relates to the CMs' expectations and the evaluation scope. For example, clarify what you are there to do (and not to do) in order to ensure an effective working relationship.				
7. Request feedback and distinguish real requests or concerns from personally beneficial opportunities. Remember that you are continuously tested for any vulnerable areas throughout the evaluation, so be confident of what you are doing.				
8. Help the CMs look beyond their particular perspectives in order to reach an understanding of your role and its relationship to the evaluation. You might use a responsibility assignment matrix (RAM) to visually document your role and responsibilities.				
9. Gather feedback on a regular basis using a previously agreed-upon system (for example, meetings, emails, and surveys as feasible). This will help you and the CMs monitor the suitability of the evaluator's role and make updates as needed.				
10. Provide each CM and other stakeholders as appropriate with a summary report of this experience (including a formal description of your evaluation role) as lessons learned for future similar situations within collaborative evaluations.				

Table A.2 (continued)

Clarify the Role of the CMs	1	2	3	4
1. Ask each CM about their qualifications and expectations of the potential evaluation role they would play. For example, ask general questions so CMs are able to feel free to choose answers that reflect their priorities or major concerns.				
2. Write down in detail what each of the CMs expects to do within the evaluation, before discussing any particular task. This is not the time to be judgmental; instead, this is the time to generate all the information possible about their expectations.				
3. Identify each CM's needs within the collaborative evaluation to develop a methodical and logical view of how to meet each of them. This needs identification should use unbiased methods and strategies to provide accurate information.				
4. Inquire about how you can address each CM's evaluation needs (carefully distinguish their real requests or concerns from personally motivated inquiries), and assist each CM to provide ideas for making improvements if feasible.				
5. Discuss with each individual CM their qualifications (such as skills, background, or technical knowledge in a particular area) and why you believe they can be a valuable asset to the collaborative evaluation by performing a specific role.				
6. Help each of the CMs look beyond individual expectations to reach an understanding of their role (including what needs to be done) and its relationship to the evaluation. For example, use a RAM for visual documentation.				
7. Agree with each of the CMs on the role that best fits both their expectations and the evaluation goals, and make sure that they feel good about it. For example, allow the CMs to naturally settle into their roles without feeling pushed into them.				
8. Sign with each CM (if needed) a document with the previously agreed-upon information to ensure a commitment to the collaborative evaluation. Among other things, the document may contain the CMs' roles, resources, and reporting responsibilities.				
9. Gather feedback on a regular basis using a previously agreed-upon system (for example, meetings, emails, and surveys as feasible). This will help you and the CMs monitor the suitability of the role of each CM and make updates as needed.				
10. Provide each CM and other stakeholders as appropriate with a summary report of each of their roles, and ensure they understand how each part relates to the evaluation and other CMs' roles (to avoid any confusion in the future).				

Table A.2 (continued)

Clarify the Evaluand Criteria and Standards	1	2	3	4
1. Provide copies of the evaluation questions to the CMs and other stakeholders at the beginning of the meeting. This keeps the focus on the evaluation questions and allows new relevant ideas to be associated with them.				
2. Present the proposed evaluand criteria for each of the evaluation questions and ask for feedback. For example, criteria may be implicit in the evaluation question wording or they may need to be elicited from participants.				
3. Present the proposed evaluand standards and ensure they are clearly understood (they have the same meaning for everyone) and fit particular evaluand requirements. This is done to avoid misunderstandings when later reporting the evaluation results.				
4. Receive feedback about each proposed criterion and consequent standards. For example, is each criterion relevant? Which results for a specific criterion would be acceptable in this collaborative evaluation? Is there prior information?				
5. Look for areas of potential conflict (for example, disagreements on specific levels of performance) that could jeopardize the success of the meeting in order to immediately solve them and maximize the benefit of the collaborative evaluation.				
6. Agree on specific changes of the evaluand criteria and standards (before evaluation data are collected) to reflect the evaluation vision. For example, what changes will be considered as positive (or not) within this evaluation effort?				
7. Ensure that all the needed criteria and standards have been included (by taking a holistic view), and that they are unbiased. Otherwise, a dishonest stakeholder could later wrongfully claim that the evaluation results are exactly as expected.				
8. Present the evaluand standards to be used for each criterion based on the prior feedback received. For example, standards may be absolute (numbers or scales), or they may be relative (better or worse than) to a comparison evaluand.				
9. Gather feedback on a regular basis using a previously agreed-upon system (for example, meetings, emails, and surveys as feasible). This will help you and the CMs monitor the evaluand criteria and standards and make updates as needed.				
10. Provide each CM and other stakeholders as appropriate with a summary report of this experience (including an updated version of the evaluand criteria and standards report) as lessons learned for future similar situations within collaborative evaluations.				

Table A.2 (continued)

Clarify the Evaluation Process	1	2	3	4
1. Provide copies of the preliminary evaluation plan (what needs to be done) to each of the CMs prior to the meeting. In this way, everyone can read it in advance and suggest new ideas to be shared later with other relevant stakeholders.				
2. Hang posters on the wall with information about the evaluation scope, and the criteria and standards for judging the evaluand. By doing this, you and the CMs can refer back and avoid short-term goals taking over the collaborative evaluation.				
3. Review the overall evaluation plan step-by-step and how each important portion was chosen. This includes the evaluation questions, resources (such as people or equipment), activities (for example, data collection), and schedule.				
4. Describe in detail the communication needs of everyone involved (including who has to provide what information and when they should complete each task) and how they are linked to their overall evaluation roles and responsibilities.				
5. Discuss which specific SWOTs are most likely to influence the evaluation process and how they are going to be monitored. This can provide a means for early identification and clarification throughout the collaborative evaluation effort.				
6. Request feedback to adjust the evaluation as necessary (for instance, if a CM finds a particular inconsistency), while ensuring that each of the suggestions provided are specific, relevant, and achievable within time and budget constraints.				
7. Elicit other key stakeholders' feedback on the viability of the overall evaluation process in order to make adjustments in light of the feedback received. This step is fundamental for stakeholders to later use the collaborative evaluation results.				
8. Address concerns and comments to everyone's satisfaction before the end of this clarification period (such as when a particular resource will be available). Remember that unresolved issues will have a negative effect on the evaluation sooner or later.				
9. Ensure that the CMs and key stakeholders have accepted the evaluation (for example, by having them sign a contract or formal agreement) with the understanding that it may be updated in the future if an important or unforeseen need arises.				
10. Gather feedback on a regular basis using a previously agreed-upon system, such as meetings, and summarize it in a written format (including actions implemented and the reasons for them) so it is available to each CM and other stakeholders as appropriate.				

Table A.2 (continued)

Clarify the Evaluation Budget	1	2	3	4
1. Provide a general (or specific, as appropriate) copy of the preliminary evaluation budget to key stakeholders (for example, client, CMs, board members, and funders) that accurately reflects the needs of the collaborative evaluation.				
2. Explain each general item within the evaluation budget to avoid major revisions later. For instance, include the information used to develop the budget (such as bottom-up estimating) and the provisions made to mitigate risks (such as inflation).				
3. Justify the specific figures within the evaluation budget to individual parties (for example, the client, each of the CMs, and other relevant stakeholders) depending on how those figures are associated with their contribution to the collaborative evaluation.				
4. Test the validity of each of the budget figures by requesting individualized feedback (make sure decimal points and commas are accurate, among other things), while ensuring that all the comments are clearly documented and reflect the evaluation scope.				
5. Request feedback on the feasibility (including future costs that may occur) of the evaluation budget in terms of offering a realistic amount (neither too high nor too low) that is based on the resources available during the collaborative effort.				
6. Agree on amendments to the budget, as appropriate, to make sure that all the figures are accurate. For example, ask colleagues with relevant expertise in the area to prioritize which specific changes in the evaluation budget are necessary.				
7. Provide a general (or specific, as appropriate) copy of the updated evaluation budget for approval. In this way, the client, and others as needed, will revise and approve the final budget after clarifying any foreseeable problems.				
8. Allow sufficient time for proper revisions of the evaluation budget to make new updates as required. For example, updates in the budget may need to serve constantly changing or unexpected evaluation needs (such as budget cuts).				
9. Gather feedback on a regular basis using a previously agreed-upon system (for example, evaluation performance versus budget feasibility). This will help you and the CMs monitor the evaluation budget and make any changes as needed.				
10. Provide each CM and other stakeholders as appropriate with a summary report of this evaluation budget experience (including actions implemented and the reasons for them) as lessons learned for future similar situations within collaborative evaluations.				

Table A.3 Establish a Collective Commitment

Model for Collaborative Evaluations (MCE) Checklist
The checklist includes several checkpoints to be scored as follows:
1 = Addressed, 2 = Partially Addressed, 3 = Not Addressed, and 4 = Not Applicable.

Establish a Shared Evaluation Vision	1	2	3	4
1. Agree with the client, and other key stakeholders as appropriate, on the preliminary evaluation vision. This agreement is achieved as soon as the client approves the evaluation (for example, by signing a contract or formal agreement).				
2. Present to CMs the preliminary evaluation vision statement approved by the client (one or two short sentences). The vision should be an ideal yet realistic statement of what will be reached at the end of the collaborative evaluation.				
3. Make sure that CMs really understand the meaning of the vision (with a clear message tailored to them), because this will help relate the present to the desired collaborative evaluation, working back from the future to the present.				
4. Encourage CMs, through an open discussion, to question every aspect of the vision (for example, check that it is truly achievable). This will allow you and the CMs to familiarize yourselves with any concerns and solve them to ensure commitment.				
5. Use the technique of brainwriting to help each CM prepare an improved, easy-to-remember statement of the evaluation vision. Make sure everyone thinks about how the vision may affect the group and not just their individual tasks.				
6. Present the updated vision statement (discussing anything you or the CMs disagree with or potential obstacles observed to achieving it), and make sure to include the client, and key stakeholders as needed, for final agreement.				
7. Write on a poster the attainable evaluation vision and keep it in focus throughout the collaborative evaluation. At the beginning of each meeting, spend the first minutes discussing the agenda and how it can be linked to the vision.				
8. Prepare each of the CMs to achieve the vision while understanding and acting on their evaluation needs (such as communication or training), as feasible. For example, act on the CMs' evaluation needs that affect the vision the most.				
9. Gather feedback on a regular basis using a previously agreed-upon system (for example, meetings, emails, and surveys as feasible). This will help you and the CMs monitor the evaluation vision and make updates as needed.				
10. Provide each CM and other stakeholders as appropriate with a summary report of the shared evaluation vision experience (including actions implemented and the reasons for them) as lessons learned for future similar situations within collaborative evaluations.				

Table A.3 (continued)

Establish Recommendations for Positive Actions	1	2	3	4
1. Hang on a visible wall a poster titled "Recommendations for Positive Actions" and leave it in the same location during every collaborative evaluation meeting (this is for easy reference throughout the evaluation process).				
2. Explain to the CMs that every time they observe a controllable action that needs improvement (for example, you or a CM continuously arrive late to meetings), they should write it down as a positive action (such as "arrive to meetings on time").				
3. Reassure CMs that each of the recommendations for positive actions will be an optimistic response to a particular undesirable action (and not about a specific individual), to avoid making them demoralizing, too rigid, or overly permissive.				
4. Collect all the anonymous recommendation notes (that is, without names or identification numbers so nobody knows who wrote what) at the end of each meeting, taking into consideration that some of those notes may be blank.				
5. Read aloud the new potential recommendations (while you remind the CMs not to pass judgment on any of the ideas generated at this point) and provide time for each CM and yourself to clarify, reflect, prioritize, and agree on the final recommendations.				
6. Write all the new recommendations on the poster, remembering that they should be precise, limited in their number, and impersonal in order to be more effective. The latter is because the worst types of conflicts are the ones that address personal issues.				
7. Agree with the CMs on how the new recommendations for positive actions will be implemented, what type of support or help will be needed, and how those recommendations will be monitored and consistently rewarded throughout the evaluation.				
8. Enforce each recommendation respectfully, equally, and consistently, because it would not be fair to skip one at a particular time and impose it at another time. Otherwise, CMs will assume that the recommendations are meaningless, and you will lose credibility.				
9. Gather feedback on a regular basis using a previously agreed-upon system (for example, meetings, emails, and surveys as feasible). This will help you and the CMs monitor the suitability of these recommendations and make updates as needed.				
10. Provide each CM as appropriate with a summary report of the recommendations for positive actions experience (including actions implemented and the reasons for them) as lessons learned for future similar situations within collaborative evaluations.				

Table A.3 (continued)

Establish Means Toward Conflict Resolution	1	2	3	4
1. Acknowledge the presence of conflict as soon as it appears, and make sure that you (and any affected CMs) are calm and objective in order to be respected. If not, then have a recess to put the conflictive situation into perspective.				
2. Meet with the affected CMs and any other relevant individuals (being respectful and approachable yet firm and concise) to explain your good intention to effectively solve the conflict and the specific rationale of the meeting.				
3. Promote self-awareness by showing appreciation for positive actions, and immediately respond to cues that signal the escalation of negative actions. For example, you may say that any type of power struggle or manipulation is unacceptable.				
4. Encourage the CMs' input by acknowledging their feelings (for instance, look for incongruence between what they say and how they say it) and explain that their input should focus on the behavior or action, their suggested solution, and compromise.				
5. Make sure that you understand every CM's feedback. For example, wait for their response without interrupting, paraphrase their comments (limiting this to only what the CM shared with you), and then wait for their reply on this information.				
6. Keep the focus on one specific conflictive issue at a time and, when it is appropriate, interconnect all the issues (balancing any opposing views) to form the big picture and later arrive at the most convenient solution within the collaborative evaluation.				
7. Analyze the situation against the evaluation expectations and the type of method that can be used for dealing with the conflict, in order to make adjustments to meet the gap (for example, lower the evaluation expectations).				
8. Ask CMs for feedback on your analysis, and value any objections because they can improve the process. If you have doubts on some CMs' honesty, ask for written feedback or a private meeting in order to ensure a true conflict resolution.				
9. Implement appropriate actions to solve the conflict, once it is fully understood. For example, you may choose to work more closely than usual with specific CMs, or you may also reassign those CMs to a less critical evaluation task.				
10. Follow up on the conflict resolution progress (perhaps by obtaining continuous feedback) and summarize it in a written format (including source of conflict, how it is being solved, and its specific consequences) that is available to all the affected CMs.				

Table A.3 (continued)

Establish Decision-Making Procedures	1	2	3	4
1. Acknowledge the existence of a decision that needs to be made (for example, which type of data-collection and analysis methods are to be used), and think of initial ideas on its overall significance to the collaborative evaluation.				
2. Establish priorities through a structured approach that divides the potential decision to be made into smaller and more manageable parts. Those parts could be interconnected at any time throughout the collaborative evaluation.				
3. Select the best style of decision making for the particular situation and choose how outcomes will be measured. For example, use a hierarchical decision-making style when, due to expertise, only you or a few CMs can be involved.				
4. Determine the amount of time that will be taken for making a decision (it varies with each type of decision), and establish backup plans if the deadline is not going to be met (such as to postpone the decision or change the decision-making style).				
5. Meet with all the appropriate CMs for their feedback (understanding everyone's perspective). For example, ask specific questions on potential decisions, expected consequences, and the probability of occurrence (avoid interruptions)				
6. Meet with each of the appropriate CMs, as feasible, in order to share the information collected and use adequate techniques to identify new possibilities. This is because some CMs may find it difficult to publicly express their ideas.				
7. Examine every possibility and then present them to all the appropriate CMs (acknowledging your own opinion and being ready to make any changes as needed) in order to agree on the best decision to be made within the collaborative evaluation.				
8. Implement convenient and concrete decision-related actions in a timely manner (once they have been agreed upon with the appropriate CMs). Also, keep in mind that you may need to update those actions (and the CMs involved in them) as needed.				
9. Use adequate check-out options to know whether or not the CMs feel included in the decision-making procedures and how willing they are to implement the decision. For example, address the issues you or other CMs believe need improvement.				
10. Provide each CM and other stakeholders as appropriate with a summary report of the decision-making experience (including actions implemented and the reasons for them) as lessons learned for future similar situations within collaborative evaluations.				

Table A.3 (continued)

Establish Reward Options	1	2	3	4
1. Ask each of the appropriate CMs for their feedback regarding their evaluation interests and most valued intrinsic or extrinsic rewards. For example, ask how those rewards should be connected to specific levels of evaluation performance.				
2. Match the CMs' interests, whenever possible, with specific evaluation tasks assigned to them. This ensures the work is intrinsically desirable enough for CMs to contribute to the collaborative effort, and elevates the possibility of succeeding.				
3. Meet with all the CMs in order to share, as appropriate, the information collected on rewards and use adequate techniques (such as brainwriting) to identify new possible ideas. For instance, CMs may find it difficult to publicly express or share their ideas.				
4. Examine every reward option's feasibility, and then agree on the best individual and group rewards based on their connection with evaluation achievements. Obviously, those rewards will be expected once they are established.				
5. Develop an objective standardized system (to review the CMs' individual and group contributions) and share it with the CMs for their feedback. This increases awareness about how to improve current and future performance so everyone can be rewarded.				
6. Use the review system to periodically check the CMs' performance within specific evaluation goals. For example, this review could include asking for the feedback of CMs' colleagues in order to have a full understanding of the surrounding environment.				
7. Encourage collaborative work (assessing group and not only individual performance), and as CMs achieve specific milestones, provide immediate and meaningful rewards with available resources (such as a letter of commendation).				
8. Be equitable when recognizing CMs for the success of their efforts to avoid dissatisfaction or competition. For example, a reward highly valued by one CM may differ for another CM because its value is in the eye of the beholder.				
9. Monitor rewards on an ongoing basis to check if they continue to appropriately motivate CMs, and update them as needed. This is because several kinds of circumstances (for example, personal issues) can alter a CM's response to a particular reward.				
10. Provide each CM and other stakeholders as appropriate with a summary report of the rewards experience (including actions implemented and the reasons for them) as lessons learned for future similar situations within collaborative evaluations.				

Table A.4 Ensure Open Communication

Model for Collaborative Evaluations (MCE) Checklist
The checklist includes several checkpoints to be scored as follows:
1 = Addressed, 2 = Partially Addressed, 3 = Not Addressed, and 4 = Not Applicable.

Ensure Active Participation	1	2	3	4
1. Verify that all the CMs understand their roles (without perceptions of rankings) and the reason for their involvement in the evaluation. When CMs understand the implications of their contributions they actively support the evaluation efforts.				
2. Identify CMs who might have developed informal alliances and how those affect, positively and negatively, the integrity of the evaluation process. For example, as opportunities arise, you may consider interacting in those alliances (such as lunch invitations and parties).				
3. Determine the communication needs (for instance, the type of information required or the communication style) of each of the CMs and how they expect those needs to be addressed during the session to facilitate an open discussion.				
4. Distribute a preliminary outline of the agenda at the beginning of each session (this gets CMs into the subject matter of the proposed agenda), and throughout it, encourage CMs to offer their input (for example, suggestions and challenges).				
5. Break the group into subgroups, as appropriate, whenever you encounter CMs who feel too shy to express their opinions to large groups, or who try to monopolize the session. This gives all the CMs an opportunity to have their ideas heard.				
6. Acknowledge and understand everyone's position on the issue discussed in the session. For example, privately ask any CM who appears unhappy whether there is anything you or other CMs may do to gain their support or involvement.				
7. Seek opinions with an open mind by using alternative mechanisms to ensure active participation (such as focus groups, interviews, observations, questionnaires, and records review) that are appropriate to the specific situation.				
8. Test the commitment of each of the CMs, perhaps demonstrated in writing, to ensure they are willing to fully support the outcome of the session (for instance, if you suspect a particular CM does not fully support a decision).				
9. Gather feedback on a regular basis using a previously agreed-upon system (for example, meetings, emails, and surveys as feasible). This will help you and the CMs monitor the participation process and make updates as needed.				
10. Keep a journal with information from the session (such as minutes) to follow up, and circulate it as appropriate so that CMs feel fully involved. As a result, you and the CMs can use the information to bring evaluation improvements.				

Table A.4 (continued)

Ensure Careful Listening	1	2	3	4
1. Use appropriate techniques to ensure complete listening (including mirroring gestures, eye contact, and friendly expression) and wait patiently during pauses, because generally the most important information follows them.				
2. Observe the speaker's nonverbal actions (such as body language or tone of voice) to better understand the message and the speaker's feelings about it. For example, what the CM is saying should be in congruence with how the CM is saying it.				
3. Provide short and encouraging responses or statements to show that you are attentively following the conversation. At this point, you should ask only open-ended questions and avoid giving any unrequested judgments or advice.				
4. Pause for a few seconds after the speaker has finished talking, to reflect on what was said and how it was said before you respond. This shows that you are interested in the issue and considering carefully its meaning and implications.				
5. Summarize the information received without deeper analysis and wait silently for the speaker to validate if your summary was correct. For example, "I believe what you are saying is that you would like to add another evaluation question."				
6. Think carefully and, if needed, use the speaker's responses to ask other specific questions in order to gain further detail from the new information. You may ask the speaker to provide a nontechnical example to illustrate the point being made.				
7. Get the speaker's perspective on the next possible steps and then help in respectfully guiding toward an adequate solution. For example, ask, What do you feel I should do now in order to help you meet the evaluation objectives?				
8. Send a friendly email to the speaker (and other appropriate members) with a summary of the meeting. For example, describe what happened in the meeting, who interacted, the information discussed, and the points agreed upon and not agreed upon.				
9. Gather feedback on a regular basis using a previously agreed-upon system (for example, meetings, emails, phone calls, and surveys as feasible). This will help you and the CMs monitor the listening process and make updates as needed.				
10. Provide each CM and other stakeholders as appropriate with a summary report of this experience (if it is a particularly illustrative experience) as lessons learned for future similar situations within collaborative evaluations.				

Table A.4 (continued)

Ensure the Message Is Clear	1	2	3	4
1. Analyze the message (for example, its meaning and possible interpretations) in a systematic way in order to clearly determine what you want to accomplish by it, and how it reflects on other CMs and the overall collaborative evaluation.				
2. Carefully choose each of the words of the message you want to communicate, while being totally direct and sincere, so your nonverbal gestures will be in complete harmony with your words, helping to clearly convey the message.				
3. Select the most appropriate way to communicate the message (such as verbally) in an understandable and timely way. For example, use appropriate and simple language (avoid technical words), stories, pictures, graphics, or audiovisuals.				
4. Provide the same basic information in several reinforcing ways (including copies of materials) to ensure that the full message is communicated, as thoroughly as possible, even if there are different perceptions between you and the CMs.				
5. Verify that the CMs (or other participants) understand the message communicated and its parts to make sure of its clarity. Have a relaxed atmosphere within the collaborative evaluation so CMs feel free to communicate.				
6. Overcome any potential communication barriers (for instance, written versus oral or formal versus informal) and make adjustments as needed to ensure the message is totally understood by the specific CMs. Where necessary, use additional examples.				
7. Determine the CMs' level of receptiveness of the message (demonstrated by verbal and nonverbal gestures or by signing their approval on formal agreement documents) and the future steps related to it within the collaborative evaluation.				
8. Devote time for communicating regularly with individual CMs in order to determine if everyone is sufficiently informed (such as regarding the latest key issues) and provide a vehicle for learning about their evaluation needs and concerns.				
9. Follow up with CMs on the ongoing communication of the message (for example, agree on deadlines for specific activities) and make updates as needed on the clarity of the message throughout the collaborative evaluation.				
10. Provide each CM and other stakeholders as appropriate with a summary report of this experience (if it is a particularly illustrative experience to share) as lessons learned for future similar situations within collaborative evaluations.				

Table A.4 (continued)

Ensure Immediate Feedback	1	2	3	4
1. Establish a friendly atmosphere in which any feedback (positive or negative) is viewed as a constructive opportunity for improvement so there is no intimidation from undesirable repercussions within the collaborative evaluation.				
2. Agree on a methodology to make sure you and the appropriate CMs, and other stakeholders as needed, are informed of the evaluation and its progress (for example, through meetings, minutes, emails, draft reports, suggestion boxes, videos, and brochures).				
3. Ask periodically for suggestions and ideas regarding the collaborative evaluation (such as about general or specific procedures). In this way, you and the CMs will be encouraged to reflect on your feelings and particular improvement ideas.				
4. Listen carefully, respectfully, and enthusiastically to all the suggestions received. This transmits confidence that each suggestion is being taken seriously and will be followed up as appropriate in the collaborative evaluation.				
5. Give a regular update on the progress of specific evaluation tasks and their relationship to the overall collaborative evaluation. For example, schedule specific evaluation milestone meetings (such as weekly, monthly, or as required).				
6. Be available to meet at nonscheduled times in order to share unexpected issues or concerns that have arisen in the collaborative effort. For example, a CM may need to meet with you to talk briefly and make an evaluation decision.				
7. Take CMs aside (either as individuals or in small groups) and solicit information by asking how they think the collaborative evaluation is doing and how it might be improved. For example, use questionnaires and telephone interviews.				
8. Ask for others' individual comments (for instance, from colleague evaluators or experts) or feedback regarding similar evaluation circumstances to learn from them. For example, what would they do if facing the same situation?				
9. Thank every specific individual with a written note for the help offered through their feedback. For example, you may say that you appreciate their comments on a particular issue, and then explain how you will proceed on them.				
10. Provide each CM and other stakeholders as appropriate with a summary report of this experience (including a report of the feedback and its viability) as lessons learned for future similar situations within collaborative evaluations.				

Table A.4 (continued)

Ensure the Need for Change Is Justified	1	2	3	4
1. Recognize the need for change due to a diagnosis of the evaluation situation and everyone affected by it. For example, after identifying the gap between the present and ideal state, ask the CMs what should be done differently.				
2. Ask for feedback from others in similar evaluation circumstances (including colleague evaluators and experts) in order to accumulate relevant information. For instance, what would they do if facing the same evaluation situation?				
3. Choose the best type of information (such as figures, tables, documents, or reports) that can justify a rational argument for the proposed change. For example, map out the previous relevant processes that led to the need for change.				
4. Anticipate negative responses to or criticism about your argument (which may be completely rational and well founded) by preparing several detailed and well-supported possible alternatives or plans to help explain your argument.				
5. Use a two-way communication to present the suggested step-by-step plan for change (such as showing concrete, attainable goals and results) with clear facts on how the proposed change is linked to the collaborative evaluation vision.				
6. Acknowledge and understand everyone's position, including yours, on the need for change. For example, ask any CMs who appear unhappy with the change how they will be affected by it, and how you (or others) may gain their support.				
7. Seek additional ideas with an open mind (be willing to modify your own ideas) by using alternative mechanisms to ensure participation (such as questionnaires, interviews, or records review), and clear up misunderstandings.				
8. Check the commitment of each of the CMs to ensure they agree (in writing if the changes are significant) to fully support the change. This is especially important if you suspect that a CM who perhaps is silent does not fully support the decision.				
9. Agree with the CMs on the next steps or procedures to follow within the collaborative evaluation (for example, in areas in which more support or training should be offered or other main priorities) as a result of the approved change.				
10. Gather feedback on a regular basis using a previously agreed-upon system, such as meetings, and summarize it in a written format (including specific facts on progress measures) so it is available to each CM and other stakeholders as appropriate.				

Table A.5 Encourage Effective Practices

Model for Collaborative Evaluations (MCE) Checklist
The checklist includes several checkpoints to be scored as follows:
1 = Addressed, 2 = Partially Addressed, 3 = Not Addressed, and 4 = Not Applicable.

Encourage Appreciation for Individual Differences	1	2	3	4
1. Learn as much as you can about each of the CMs' individual characteristics. For example, ask the CMs for a biographical sketch or get information from them on specific issues relevant to the collaborative evaluation.				
2. Create a summary list of the most important features that reflect the individual characteristics among the CMs. With this list in mind, you may be able to fit the CMs' characteristics to the needs of the collaborative evaluation.				
3. Meet with each of the CMs to discuss their (and your) individual characteristics and the relationship of these to the evaluation. Understanding of these characteristics can provide evaluation opportunities that will stimulate you and the CMs.				
4. Seek clarification (with a courteous and positive attitude) about their individual characteristics when meeting with each of the CMs, as convenient. For example, if doubts arise after the meeting, you might follow up to clarify them all.				
5. Listen, rather than just making statements or educating CMs about their individual characteristics. For example, wait silently and patiently during pauses in a conversation, because generally the most important comments come after them.				
6. Request feedback from each of the CMs to add or delete information from the initial individual characteristics list. In other words, identify any contrasting points of view through the generation of alternative ideas or possibilities.				
7. Agree with the CMs, as appropriate, on a final list that clearly describes everyone's (yours and the CMs') individual characteristics (such as how they complement yours or other CMs' and how they could be linked to the evaluation expectations).				
8. Align the CM's main characteristics with the collaborative evaluation expectations. For instance, a CM whose characteristics are "fair" and "skillful in quantitative or qualitative methods" could collaborate with the data-collection design.				
9. Gather feedback on a regular basis using a previously agreed-upon system (for example, meetings, emails, and phone calls as feasible). This will help you and the CMs monitor the appreciation for individual differences and make updates as needed.				
10. Provide each CM and other stakeholders as appropriate with a summary report of this experience (including an updated list with everyone's biographical sketch) so they are able to understand how everyone's differences can be helpful for the evaluation.				

Table A.5 (continued)

Encourage Fairness and Sincerity	1	2	3	4
1. Exhibit fairness and sincerity toward the CMs (and other stakeholders) at all times to encourage them to follow this example as well. For instance, ensure excellent working conditions (such as an open-door policy) for each of the CMs.				
2. Use a clear and rational system to communicate the evaluation information to each of the CMs from the beginning of the collaborative process. Keep in mind that this system has to be congruent with the evaluation vision.				
3. Be consistent in avoiding ambiguity to increase the CMs' sense of knowing what is expected throughout the evaluation. For example, use the same assessment procedures, so the same type of performance earns the same type of outcome.				
4. Ask each of the CMs, as appropriate, general questions that encourage total sincerity on an ongoing basis. For example, give each of the CMs an opportunity to express their true feelings related to the collaborative evaluation process.				
5. Identify, with the CMs' help, the advantages and disadvantages associated with each collaborative evaluation task and any available alternative assumptions in order to select the least biased defensible option(s) for completing the task.				
6. Encourage constructive criticism and act on it. For example, ask the CMs for their opinions on other evaluation tasks, invite them to present divergent perspectives, and ask them to provide suggestions for improvement throughout the evaluation.				
7. Have frequently updated information and resources available while making sure that you and the CMs have the expertise to use them. For example, ensure that the CMs know how to use the technology available (such as the Internet and databases).				
8. Thank each of the CMs, publicly or privately as appropriate, by consistently letting them know that their fairness and sincerity exhibited throughout the collaborative evaluation process is highly appreciated and valued.				
9. Gather feedback on a regular basis using a previously agreed-upon system (for example, meetings, emails, and surveys as feasible). This will help you and the CMs monitor the fairness and sincerity process and make updates as needed.				
10. Provide each CM and other stakeholders, as appropriate, with a summary report of this experience (if this is a particularly illustrative experience of fairness and sincerity) as lessons learned for future similar situations within collaborative evaluations.				

Table A.5 (continued)

Encourage Benchmarking	1	2	3	4
1. Make sure that you and the CMs have a clear understanding about the evaluand and the evaluation before you approach the benchmarking process. In this way, everyone can agree on what is needed and how the information will be used.				
2. Study all the information available on specific benchmarks (such as any area in which their performance is better). Among other things, you may use the Internet or request brochures to identify and review all the perceived benchmarks.				
3. Identify key people (both internal and external to the evaluation) whose input would be important, and periodically update names, addresses, and contact numbers. For instance, you might cross-reference those names if possible.				
4. Contact those specific individuals who may be helpful for the benchmarking and find out the lessons they have learned (such as mistakes and how they solved them). For example, contact people who possess a desired evaluation skill.				
5. Compare the benchmark practices (including products, services, models, and instruments) in order to apply them to concrete action plans. For example, apply the learned information in recommendations of how to reach particular objectives.				
6. Participate in relevant national or international events, such as presentations, seminars, and conferences. These offer a wide range of opportunities to develop particular knowledge for you and the CMs to use in the collaborative evaluation.				
7. Solicit information on similar collaborative evaluation reports from national or international evaluation centers or institutions. This may help you develop local and overseas contacts that can be able to give variety to your benchmark focus.				
8. Present the information collected as a result of this benchmarking process in a formal meeting in order to agree with the CMs on relevant options (such as valuable areas that can be used) to update the collaborative evaluation activities.				
9. Gather feedback on a regular basis using a previously agreed-upon system (for example, meetings, emails, and surveys as feasible). This will help you and the CMs monitor the benchmarking process and make updates as needed.				
10. Provide each CM and other stakeholders, as appropriate, with a summary report of this experience (including actions implemented and the reasons for them) as lessons learned for future similar situations within collaborative evaluations.				

Table A.5 (continued)

Encourage Teaching by Example	1	2	3	4
1. Exemplify general appropriate behavioral characteristics (including enthusiasm, responsibility, sensitivity, and dedication), so others understand what is expected from them as well and relate with one another in a similar manner.				
2. Encourage active learning by consistently opening the opportunity for everyone (such as you and the CMs) to talk about what they are learning, relate it to their past experiences, and apply it to the collaborative evaluation.				
3. Help CMs become more comfortable with their evaluation roles and responsibilities by introducing repetition to the teaching efforts. For example, rely on multiple approaches to provide stimuli and enrich the learning process.				
4. Identify external individuals who are not part of the collaborative evaluation but who could be able to perform a critical role (such as a coach, a mentor, or a model) in order to further specific evaluation knowledge or skills.				
5. Become attuned to learning opportunities, and use them to show your own commitment. For example, improve the CMs' efforts in needed areas by being ready to provide opportunities in training (or development) and implementation.				
6. Promote interaction among key individuals (both inside and outside the evaluation) to facilitate learning in specific areas. This ensures that everyone (such as you and the CMs) is a facilitator rather than just an evaluation spectator.				
7. Assess individual and group performance to monitor continuous learning progress (for example, what you and the CMs should have learned) and change the teaching methods to reflect the feedback concerning what everyone still needs to learn.				
8. Organize a reading library that helps you and the CMs, as feasible, to be in touch with contemporary evaluation writings (for instance, evaluation journals). This is an excellent way of acquiring new evaluation skills and enhancing competencies.				
9. Gather feedback on a regular basis using a previously agreed-upon system (for example, meetings, emails, and surveys as feasible). This will help you and the CMs monitor the teaching-by-example process and make updates as needed.				
10. Provide each CM and other stakeholders as appropriate with a summary report of this experience (including actions implemented and the reasons for them) as lessons learned for a better or more innovative way of improving the teaching-by-example process.				

Table A.5 (continued)

Encourage Flexibility and Creativity	1	2	3	4
1. Facilitate an evaluation environment in which you and the CMs feel welcome to apply your expertise in other areas outside specific responsibilities. For example, continuously look for opportunities to invite others' expertise as needed.				
2. Encourage proactivity among you and the CMs by searching on an ongoing basis for new alternatives in the collaborative evaluation. For example, look at the upcoming evaluation tasks from a different and original perspective.				
3. Avoid criticizing new ideas or assumptions ("Yes, but . . . ") before they, or any other alternative, have been fully described. For example, consideration of ideas should be done afterward, when all the options have been discussed.				
4. Clarify any doubt (with respect and sensitivity) in order to ensure that every idea is designed to meet the needs of the collaborative evaluation. For example, prepare answers to common objections (such as, Why should we follow this idea?).				
5. Reframe a seemingly meaningless idea by looking at the situation from another perspective and encouraging fresh thinking (using the appropriate flexibility and creativity technique) to understand how the idea relates to specific priorities.				
6. Assess each of the proposed ideas in order to summarize the most important options. For example, avoid rushing into any negative decision until understanding if some minor adjustments can make a positive difference.				
7. Agree on an initial tryout or pilot of strong ideas and how they should be implemented (for example, how the new ideas can address current evaluation problems). This is done to make a clear balance between imagination and logic.				
8. Adjust for external factors that affect the collaborative evaluation to apply updated information as feasible. Although you and the CMs have your own ideas, you should remain open to other new ones and be willing to adapt to change.				
9. Conduct periodic meetings with the CMs to communicate advances in the latest evaluation implementations and to obtain ongoing feedback on other ideas (one idea at a time to avoid confusion) in order to make updates as needed.				
10. Provide each CM and other stakeholders as appropriate with a summary report of this experience (if it is a particularly illustrative experience) as lessons learned from success and failures for future similar situations within collaborative evaluations.				

Table A.6 Follow Specific Guidelines

Model for Collaborative Evaluations (MCE) Checklist
The checklist includes several checkpoints to be scored as follows:
1 = Addressed, 2 = Partially Addressed, 3 = Not Addressed, and 4 = Not Applicable.

Follow Guiding Principles for Evaluators	1	2	3	4
1. Provide a copy of the American Evaluation Association's (AEA's) guiding principles for evaluators to the CMs and other relevant stakeholders, as appropriate. (A full description of these principles is available on the AEA's website at http://www.eval.org).				
2. Discuss with all the CMs each of the AEA's guiding principles for evaluators, to make sure there is a clear understanding of their meaning and implications (or make any clarifications as feasible) within the collaborative evaluation.				
3. Use check-out procedures on each of these guiding principles for evaluators. As an example, a full description of the guiding principles checklist for evaluating evaluations is available at http://www.wmich.edu/evalctr/.				
4. Follow the AEA's guiding principle for evaluators, systematic inquiry. It is when evaluators (such as you) conduct a systematic, data-based inquiry of the evaluand, adhering to the highest technical standards for an accurate and credible outcome.				
5. Follow the AEA's guiding principle for evaluators, competence. It is when evaluators (such as you) provide effective performance to stakeholders due to their background (for instance, appropriate education or abilities) regarding the evaluation tasks.				
6. Follow the AEA's guiding principle for evaluators, integrity and honesty. It is when evaluators (such as you) attempt to ensure honesty and integrity in their own behavior and the entire evaluation process, for example, in areas related to tasks undertaken.				
7. Follow the AEA's guiding principle for evaluators, respect for people. It is when evaluators (such as you) respect the security, dignity, and self-worth of the respondents, clients, and other stakeholders with whom you interact during the evaluation.				
8. Follow the AEA's guiding principle for evaluators, responsibilities for general and public welfare. It is when evaluators (such as you) consider the different interests and values that may be related to the general and public welfare.				
9. Gather feedback on a regular basis using a previously agreed-upon system (for example, meetings, emails, and surveys as feasible). This will help you and the CMs monitor each of these guiding principles and make updates as needed.				
10. Provide each CM and other stakeholders as appropriate with a summary report of this experience (including how these guiding principles for evaluators were applied to specific issues) as lessons learned for future similar situations within collaborative evaluations.				

Table A.6 (continued)

Follow Evaluation Standards	1	2	3	4
1. Provide a copy of the evaluation standards (such as the program evaluation standards) to the CMs and other relevant stakeholders, as appropriate. (A full description of these standards is available on the JCSEE's website at http://www.jcsee.org/).				
2. Discuss with all the CMs each of the evaluation standards, to make sure there is a clear understanding of their meaning and implications. Keep in mind that the program evaluation standards also includes the attribute evaluation accountability.				
3. Provide a copy of the metaevaluation (evaluation of an evaluation) checklists to the CMs and other stakeholders, as appropriate. (A full description of these checklists is available on the Evaluation Center's website at http://www.wmich.edu/evalctr/).				
4. Discuss with all the CMs and other relevant stakeholders each of the metaevaluation checklists to make sure there is a clear understanding of their meaning, application, and implications within the collaborative evaluation (or make clarifications as needed).				
5. Follow the evaluation standards grouped under the attribute, utility. They are intended to ensure that the evaluation will be useful (that is, informative, timely, and influential), when stakeholders find evaluation processes and products valuable in meeting their needs.				
6. Follow the evaluation standards grouped under the attribute, feasibility. They are intended to ensure that the evaluation is practical, diplomatic, adequately supported, efficient in the use of resources, and can be implemented as planned.				
7. Follow the evaluation standards grouped under the attribute, propriety. They are intended to ensure that the evaluation will be conducted legally, ethically, and with due regard for the welfare of those involved in it, or affected by its results.				
8. Follow the evaluation standards grouped under the attribute, accuracy. They are intended to ensure that the evaluation will produce technically sound, accurate, and credible information (such as valid interpretations or conclusions linked logically to the data).				
9. Gather feedback on a regular basis using a previously agreed-upon system (for example, meetings, emails, and surveys as feasible). This will help you and the CMs monitor the suitability of the evaluation standards and make updates as needed.				
10. Provide each CM and other stakeholders as appropriate with a summary report of this experience (including how these evaluation standards were applied to specific issues) as lessons learned for future similar situations within collaborative evaluations.				

Table A.6 (continued)

Follow the Collaboration Guiding Principles	1	2	3	4
1. Provide a copy of the collaboration guiding principles to the CMs and other relevant stakeholders if appropriate. (A full description of these collaboration guiding principles is also available on our website at http://www.collabeval.com).				
2. Discuss with all the CMs each of the collaboration guiding principles, to make sure there is a clear understanding of their meaning, application, and implications (or make clarifications as needed) among everyone involved in the collaborative effort.				
3. Follow the collaboration guiding principle, development. It is when you and the CMs use training (such as workshops or seminars) or any other mechanism (for example, coaching or mentoring) to enhance learning and self-improvement.				
4. Follow the collaboration guiding principle, empathy. It is when you and the CMs show sensitivity, understanding, and a thoughtful response toward the feelings or emotions of others, therefore better managing a positive reaction to your collaborative environment.				
5. Follow the collaboration guiding principle, empowerment. It is when you and the CMs develop a sense of self-efficacy by delegating authority and removing any possible obstacles (such as negative feelings) that might limit the attainment of established goals.				
6. Follow the collaboration guiding principle, involvement. It is when you and the CMs constructively combine forces (complementing each other's strengths and weaknesses) throughout the collaboration in a way that is feasible and meaningful for everyone.				
7. Follow the collaboration guiding principle, qualification. It is when you and the CMs have a high level of knowledge and skills needed to achieve an effective collaboration. For example, be prepared for dealing with issues directly affected by your background.				
8. Follow the collaboration guiding principle, social support. It is when you and the CMs manage relationships with others (such as productive networks) in order to establish a sense of belonging and a meaningful and holistic view of social-related issues.				
9. Follow the collaboration guiding principle, trust. It is when you and the CMs have a firm confidence in or reliance on the sincerity, credibility, and reliability of everyone involved in the collaboration evaluation (trust takes time to build and can be eliminated easily).				
10. Gather feedback on a regular basis using a previously agreed-upon system, such as meetings, and summarize it in a written format (including the current use of each principle) so it is available to each CM and other stakeholders as appropriate.				

Glossary

Acceptance is when you (and the CMs) know the risk exists and prefer to accept its consequences if it occurs. If necessary, you may do the minimum planning to overcome it.

Accuracy Standards are intended to ensure that the evaluation will produce technically sound, accurate, and credible information (for example, valid interpretations or conclusions linked logically to the data) about the features that determine the evaluand value (Joint Committee on Standards for Educational Evaluation, 2003, 2009, 2011).

Action can be anything that a person does (such as thinking, talking, walking, and reading) resulting from an attitude.

Active Participation is when individuals (such as you and the CMs) take part and contribute with reciprocal input in the collaborative evaluation process to enhance it.

Activity is what an initiative offers or does with the inputs in order to lead to specific outputs.

AEA is the American Evaluation Association (a full description of this association is available on the AEA's website at http://www.eval.org).

AEA's Guiding Principles for Evaluators were developed to guide the professional practice of evaluators and to inform evaluation clients and the general public about the principles they can expect from professional evaluators.

Anger is a normal, natural emotion that, if communicated constructively, alerts others to your needs, thereby creating an opportunity for reconciliation and support (Hankins & Hankins, 2000).

Arrow Diagram Method (ADM) is a method of constructing a network diagram using arrows to represent the activities and connecting them at nodes (for example, circles) to show the dependencies (PMI Standards Committee, 2008).

Attitude is a positive or negative feeling or mental state of readiness that exerts specific influence on a person's response (such as to people, objects, and situations).

Audience is a person, or group of persons, who receives the evaluation results (for example, a written or an oral evaluation report).

Authority is a specific form of power that is officially recognized or accepted by others as the legitimate or formal way to exercise control.

Avoidance is when you (and the CMs) do not accept the risk option because of the potentially unfavorable results. Hence, you try to eliminate a specific risk event by eliminating its cause.

Benchmarking is the process of determining an outstanding point of reference or benchmark that serves as a standard for comparison or judgment.

Brainstorming is an idea-generation technique that promotes the spontaneous sharing of collaborative evaluation ideas through nonjudgmental discussion between you and the CMs (or other stakeholders).

Brainwriting is an idea-generation technique that promotes the spontaneous sharing of evaluation ideas in writing, when little verbal communication is allowed (also called nominal group technique).

Careful Listening is when individuals (such as you and the CMs) pay full attention and show a desire to understand what others have to say (letting go of personal ownership of ideas).

Change is a process for substituting current patterns of behavior or actions for new ones in the hope of benefiting the collaborative evaluation.

Charismatic Power is the ability of an individual to gain support because of personality or style of behavior (that is, personal charisma). This individual has ideas and beliefs so admired that others want to become more like him or her.

Chart is an outline that shows evaluation information in the form of a graph, diagram, or map.

Clear Message implies providing information that everyone accurately understands as intended.

Coaching is the individualized tutoring that makes it easier for individuals (such as you and the CMs) to learn by creating purposeful relationships that lead to growth and support within the collaborative evaluation.

Coercive Power, also called penalty power, is the ability to (directly or indirectly) punish noncompliance, or control potentially punishing resources that will induce others to avoid them.

Collaboration is a process in which two or more people actively work together in a mutually beneficial and well-defined relationship in order to achieve a vision not likely to occur in isolation.

Collaboration Guiding Principles are established tenets that guide the professional practice of collaborators. These principles are development, empathy, empowerment, involvement, qualification, social support, and trust.

Collaboration Members (CMs) are specific stakeholders (possessing unique characteristics) who work jointly with the evaluator(s) to help with particular tasks in order to achieve the collaborative evaluation vision.

Collaborative Evaluation is an evaluation in which there is a substantial degree of collaboration between evaluators and stakeholders in the evaluation process, to the extent that they are willing and capable of being involved (see, for example, Cousins, Donohue, & Bloom, 1996; Rodríguez-Campos, 2005, 2012b).

Collaborative Evaluators are in charge of the evaluation, but they create an ongoing engagement between evaluators and stakeholders, contributing to stronger evaluation designs, enhanced data collection and analysis, and results that stakeholders understand and use (Rodríguez-Campos & O'Sullivan, 2010).

Collective Commitment is a compromise to jointly meet the evaluation obligations without continuous external authority or supervision.

Communication is a process of social interaction (such as speaking, listening, or writing) used to convey information and exchange ideas in order to influence specific actions within the collaborative evaluation.

Competence is when evaluators (such as you) provide effective performance to stakeholders due to their background (for example, appropriate education or abilities) regarding the evaluation tasks.

Conflict is an antagonism or a contest of opposing forces within the collaborative evaluation and evidence of a gap between the vision and the current reality.

Contingency Plan represents predefined action steps you and the CMs should take if a risk occurs. It helps to prepare for a potential crisis and to do what is necessary to fix it (such as know whom to notify).

Creativity is the quality of being able to produce original ideas and fruitful collaborative evaluation work.

Criteria are points of reference used for judging the value (such as merit or worth) of the evaluand.

Critical Evaluation Activities are high-priority actions that directly determine the completion of the collaborative evaluation on time, so they must be carefully managed.

Critical Path is the longest road or evaluation duration in the network. Hence, it shows the shortest possible time when the overall collaborative evaluation can finish.

Data Collection and Analysis is the systematic compilation and examination of information from which evaluation conclusions may be drawn.

Decision is a choice or judgment made from among several alternatives as a reaction to a specific problem within the collaborative evaluation.

Decision Making is the process by which the best possible evaluation decision is determined, when you or the CMs, as appropriate, have the opportunity and right to influence such a decision.

Delphi Technique is an idea-generation technique used to gather ongoing written feed-back from anonymous individuals (such as you and the CMs) through question-naires (mailed, online, and so on) until a reasonable consensus is reached.

Development is when you and the CMs use training (such as workshops or semi-nars) or any other mechanism (for example, mentorship) to enhance learning and self-improvement.

Direct Cost is equivalent to the evaluation expenses, and may include the sum of resources such as (a) the evaluators, the CMs, and other staff salaries (for privacy purposes you may choose to share this information only with your client and key parties); (b) travel expenses (including airfare, ground transportation, and car mileage); (c) facilities and equipment (including property assets, environment requirements, and computers); (d) communications (including mail, telephone, and an Internet monthly bill); (e) services (including computer data entry, data analysis, printing, and copying); and (f) others (including lodging, meals, and training support).

Diversity is the variety existent among individuals (such as you and the CMs) on par-ticular dimensions that clearly differ from our own.

Earliest Finish Time (EFT) is the earliest time when each evaluation activity can finish, based on the network logic and any schedule constraints.

Earliest Start Time (EST) is the earliest time when each evaluation activity can start, based on the network logic and any schedule constraints.

Effective Practices are sound established procedures or systems for producing a desired effect within the collaborative evaluation.

Effectiveness is a relationship of impact. This measurement is marked by the capacity of exerting positive influence on what an individual perceives regarding the evaluand.

Efficacy is a relationship of achievement or capacity of producing an intended result (such as meeting a target).

Efficiency is a relationship of costs. In other words, it is the capacity to accomplish a job with a minimum expenditure of assigned resources (including money, time, and materials).

Empathy is when you and the CMs show sensitivity, understanding, and a thoughtful response toward the feelings or emotions of others.

Empowerment is when you and the CMs develop a sense of self-efficacy by delegating authority and removing any possible obstacles (such as negative feelings) that might limit the attainment of established goals.

Empowerment Evaluators view stakeholder participants as in control of the evalua-tion—empowerment evaluators are critical friends providing advice and guidance to maintain rigor and keep the evaluation on target (Fetterman & Wandersman, 2010).

Evaluand is anything evaluated, such as a system, organization, program, project, or personnel (also called evaluee).

Evaluation is a systematic study designed and implemented to determine the value (such as merit or worth) of an evaluand, providing a basis for guiding the decision-making process.

Evaluation Accountability Standards refer to the responsible use of resources to produce value (Joint Committee on Standards for Educational Evaluation, 2011).

Evaluation Budget is an estimate of expenditures for the collaborative evaluation over a given period of time. It is a statement of financial or monetary plans for the evaluation activities.

Evaluation Execution is the phase when the activities of an evaluation plan are implemented. It results in the completion of an evaluation that will meet the specific deliverable requirements of the client.

Evaluation Plan is an arrangement of the flow of work that shows in advance what will happen throughout the implementation of the collaborative evaluation.

Evaluation Planning is the phase when an evaluation plan is developed in order to establish standard procedures for achieving a shared vision.

Evaluation Process is a structured set of activities (with a clear beginning and end) designed to generate an evaluation product, such as an evaluation report for a specific client. It can be deconstructed into several subprocesses or phases, including planning, executing, and reporting.

Evaluation Question is an inquiry that provides focus for the collaborative evaluation, because it establishes what specific answers the evaluation is expected to provide.

Evaluation Report is a document or presentation that provides useful evaluation information in a formal and specialized way. A report can be written, oral, or both and presented to a small or large audience with the specific intention of relaying evaluation information.

Evaluation Reporting is the phase when data are extracted from one or more sources and converted into an evaluation report format.

Evaluation Scope is the area covered by the collaborative evaluation itself or the range of work to be accomplished. It provides clear information about what the evaluation will and will not focus on, depending on the boundaries set.

Evaluation Standards are the commonly agreed-upon principles of professional practice in the conduct and use of evaluation, that when implemented will lead to greater evaluation quality.

Evaluator is the individual (such as you) who accepts responsibility for the overall evaluation and its results, employing defensible criteria to judge the evaluand value.

Expectation is the anticipation that good (or bad) may come out of the collaborative evaluation. It is the assumption, belief, or idea we have about the evaluation and the people involved.

Expert Power is the ability of an individual to gain support on the basis of special expertise or knowledge. Others want that expertise so much for themselves that they will be induced to comply in order to benefit from it.

External Evaluation is an evaluation conducted by independent evaluators who are not employees of the organization where the evaluation is done.

Fairness means that individuals (such as you and the CMs) are trustworthy, just, credible, and equitable. There is neither prejudice nor favoritism toward particular individuals and tasks.

Feasibility Standards are intended to ensure that the evaluation can be implemented as planned (Joint Committee on Standards for Educational Evaluation, 2003, 2009, 2011).

Feedback is the response to an inquiry that, if done well, ensures a high level of sharing and understanding for a meaningful communication within the collaborative evaluation.

Flexibility is the capacity to willingly consider new options for accomplishing the collaborative evaluation tasks, even though those options might differ from one's own views or evaluation style.

Float is the amount of available time an activity has without delaying the final evaluation deadline (also called *slack*).

Flowchart is a diagram that provides the specific steps, critical procedures, or actions to follow in a crisis (for example, emergency response operations) through a logic structure.

Formal Agreement is a negotiated arrangement, typically a written document, that is accepted by all parties involved and contains important evaluation information (for example, evaluation plan and role of the CMs).

Formative Evaluation is conducted when the evaluand is in its developmental stages in order to make decisions for improving and strengthening it during those stages.

Gantt Chart is a bar chart that visually indicates how long an evaluation activity will take to be completed. It includes a time scale on the horizontal axis and the evaluation activities on the vertical axis.

Guidelines are principles that direct the design, use, and assessment of the collaborative evaluations, their evaluators (such as you), and their CMs.

Indirect Cost, sometimes known as shared cost, overhead, or general and administrative cost, is generally a prescribed percentage of the direct cost.

Individual Differences refers to the mixture of characteristics among individuals (such as you and the CMs) within the collaborative evaluation that account for variation on how they react to the same experiences.

Input includes all the resources invested and used by an initiative in order to achieve its activities, outputs, and outcomes.

Integrity and Honesty is when evaluators (such as you) attempt to ensure honesty and integrity in their own behavior and the entire evaluation process.

Internal Evaluation is an evaluation conducted by evaluators who are employees of the organization where the evaluation is done.

Involvement is when you and the CMs constructively combine forces throughout the collaboration in a way that is feasible and meaningful for everyone.

Latest Finish Time (LFT) is the latest time when each evaluation activity can finish, based on the network logic and any schedule constraints. In the critical path method, it is the latest possible point in time that an evaluation activity may be completed without delaying a specified deadline (such as the evaluation finish date).

Latest Start Time (LST) is the latest time when each evaluation activity can start, based on the network logic and any schedule constraints. In the critical path method, it is the latest possible point in time that an activity may begin without delaying a specified deadline (for example, the evaluation finish date).

Leader is an individual (such as you) with the ability to encourage and influence a particular behavior in other individuals to voluntarily attain a mutual goal.

Legitimate Power, also called formal power, is the ability to gain support because of an individual's position. It is the authority conferred by holding a position in an organization recognized as having a legitimate right to obedience.

Logic Model is a tool that visually shows, through a graphic illustration or picture, how a particular initiative (such as an evaluand or evaluation) is intended or perceived to occur through logical relationships.

Management Map is a picture that combines in only one graphic several tools (for example, a WBS, a Gantt chart, and network diagrams), including important information needed for developing the evaluation plan.

Manager is an individual (such as you) in charge of establishing strategies; balancing demands; and making decisions through the planning, control, and direction of resources.

Mentoring is the individualized overall guidance by a knowledgeable and trusted advisor (such as you) that has an ongoing impact on the individual's development of new collaborative evaluation knowledge, skills, and abilities.

Milestone is a special achievement (such as a particular deliverable or evaluation report), an important activity, or an event (for example, an activity start or finish date) that marks a major progress in the evaluation.

Milestone Chart is a scheduling tool that divides the evaluation into logical, measurable milestones allowing you and CMs to verify if it is on track.

Mitigation is when you (and the CMs) take preventive measures or make contingency plans to reduce the risk cause or its impact (that is, reducing its probability of occurrence, its monetary value, or both).

Model is a term loosely used to refer to a conception or approach or even a method of doing evaluation (Scriven, 1991). It is "[a] thing or person to be imitated or patterned after; that which is taken as a pattern or an example" (*Webster's Dictionary & Thesaurus*, 2000, p. 629).

Model for Collaborative Evaluations (MCE) is a framework for guiding collaborative evaluations in a precise, realistic, and useful manner. This model revolves around a set of six interactive components specific to conducting a collaborative evaluation. It has a systematic structure that provides a basis for decision making through the development of collaborative evaluations.

Modeling is the process of teaching others through showing the correct or appropriate behavior, with the goal of having the learner observe and imitate these actions.

Motivation is a force that affects individuals' actions (such as yours and the CMs') and explains why people behave in a particular way within the collaborative evaluation.

Need is a deficiency or something wanted at a point in time that acts as a motivator to generate a particular action or behavior.

Network Diagram is a step-by-step display of the activities and their relationships used to determine how much time is needed to complete the collaborative evaluation.

Neuro-Linguistic Programming (NLP) is a model of the neurological processes used to create the maps of how individuals (such as you and the CMs) experience and communicate their environment.

Opportunities are ideal outcomes within the evaluand context that are uncontrollable and could be observed in the future. Their occurrence would facilitate the achievement of the evaluand vision.

Outcome is the effect or change that an initiative makes on stakeholders (individuals, groups, or communities) as a consequence of its outputs.

Output is the direct result of the activities, and it is related to the number of products or services delivered by an initiative in measurable terms.

Participatory Evaluators view control of the evaluation as jointly shared by evaluators and program staff—participants are involved in defining the evaluation, developing instruments, collecting and analyzing data, and reporting and disseminating results (Shulha, 2010).

Perception is the act by which individuals (such as you and the CMs) give meaning to, experience, or interpret stimuli from the collaborative evaluation environment or context.

Personality is the combination of distinctive behavioral, cognitive, and emotional characteristics that shape each person (such as you and the CMs) as a unique being within the collaborative evaluation.

Personnel Evaluation Standards are a set of twenty-seven standards for designing, conducting, and judging personnel evaluations and personnel systems (Joint Committee on Standards for Educational Evaluation, 2009).

PERT Chart or program evaluation and review technique is a specific type of project network diagram that is seldom used today (PMI Standards Committee, 2008).

Power is the force or capacity you and the CMs have to affect others' behavior in the way in which you want and would otherwise not get.

Precedence Diagram Method (PDM) is a method of constructing a network diagram using nodes (for example, boxes) to represent the activities and connecting them with arrows in order to show the dependencies (PMI Standards Committee, 2008).

Program Evaluation Standards are a set of thirty standards, and their goal is to ensure useful, feasible, ethical, accountable, and sound evaluation of programs, projects, and materials (Joint Committee on Standards for Educational Evaluation, 2011).

Propriety Standards are intended to ensure that the evaluation will be conducted legally, ethically, and with due regard for the welfare of those involved in it, or affected by its results (Joint Committee on Standards for Educational Evaluation, 2003, 2009, 2011).

Qualification is when you and the CMs have a high level of knowledge and skills needed to achieve an effective collaboration. It means that you and the CMs are prepared for dealing with relevant performance issues that are directly affected by the individual's background.

Qualitative Methods use rich descriptions, inductive logic, and flexible designs to collect and analyze information with minimal concern for quantities (Creswell, 2009; McMillan, 2012; Yin, 2011).

Quantitative Methods emphasize numbers, measurements, deductive logic, and control to collect and analyze information with a focus on establishing quantities (Creswell, 2009; McMillan, 2012).

Q-sort is an idea-generation technique used for the purpose of obtaining ratings in which the individuals (such as you and the CMs) have to prioritize or rank, by a series of sorting procedures, a list of cards with descriptive statements.

Recommendations for Positive Actions are a set of formal suggestions (established by you and the CMs) that facilitate specific change toward more effective actions and social harmony.

Respect for People is when evaluators (such as you) respect the security, dignity, and self-worth of the respondents, clients, and other stakeholders with whom you interact during the evaluation.

Responsibilities for General and Public Welfare is when evaluators (such as you) consider the different interests and values that may be related to the general and public welfare.

Responsibility Assignment Matrix (RAM) identifies which resources (such as people or materials) are going to be available for each of the evaluation activities.

Reward Options are important ways to recognize and reinforce the ability of individuals (such as CMs) to build upon short- or long-term goals in order to achieve the collaborative evaluation vision.

Reward Power is the ability of an individual to control others' rewards, inducing others to comply with this individual's wishes (for example, regarding salary, promotion, bonuses, future work assignments, and other privileges).

Risk is a measure of uncertainty that involves the probability of attaining (or not) a specific evaluation achievement. Also, it is the possibility that something (such as political instability) could interfere with the completion of the evaluation.

Risk Analysis provides early recognition or warning signs of potential risks (what can go wrong and what is most probable).

Role of the CMs is a description of the set of actions expected from each of the CMs in terms of what needs to be done in the collaborative evaluation (for example, what each CM is there to do, or what potential effects they have on the collaborative effort).

Role of the Evaluator is a description of the set of actions expected from the evaluator in terms of what needs to be done in the collaborative evaluation (for example, what you are there to do, or what potential effects you have on the collaborative evaluation).

Schedule is the planned dates and times for performing the evaluation activities.

Sincerity means that individuals (such as you and the CMs) are genuine, straightforward, honest, and candid when communicating with each other.

Situation is a combination of formal and informal circumstances determined by the relationships that surround and sustain the collaborative evaluation.

Slack is the amount of available time an activity has without delaying the final evaluation deadline (also called *float*).

Social Support is when you and the CMs manage relationships with others in order to establish a sense of belonging and a meaningful and holistic view of social-related issues.

Stakeholder is a person who is interested in the collaborative evaluation because he or she may be directly or indirectly affected by its results.

Standards are commonly agreed-upon guidelines that provide information to distinguish how well the evaluand is doing or performing on specific criteria.

Strengths are current characteristics of the evaluand that contribute to the achievement of its vision.

Student Evaluation Standards are a set of twenty-eight standards for use in a variety of educational institutions (Joint Committee on Standards for Educational Evaluation, 2003).

Summative Evaluation is conducted once an evaluand is stabilized in order to judge its final value (such as merit or worth) or aid in a decision about its future; for example, prolonging, expanding, or terminating the evaluand.

SWOTs are the evaluand Strengths, Weaknesses, Opportunities, and Threats that affect the collaborative evaluation process.

System is a group of interdependent elements organized to form a whole with a clear and unique purpose, in which the particular way that elements are organized affects the performance of the whole.

Systematic Inquiry is when evaluators (such as you) conduct a systematic, data-based inquiry (quantitative, qualitative, or both) of the evaluand, adhering to the highest technical standards for an accurate and credible outcome.

Tabletop Exercise is used to discuss, rehearse, and solidify the response to a potential crisis.

Teaching by Example is when an individual (such as you or the CMs) illustrates and fosters learning through knowledgeable modeling, guidance, and support.

Threats are negative outcomes within the evaluand context that are uncontrollable and could be observed in the future. They are obstacles that would impede (or interfere with) the achievement of the evaluand vision.

Total Cost or actual cost is the sum of the direct cost and the indirect cost.

Training is a systematic instruction in which activities are designed and facilitated by an expert (inside or outside the collaborative evaluation) with the purpose of enhancing specific skills and knowledge.

Transfer is when you (and the CMs) deflect the risk, share it with others, or even transfer the entire risk to them (for example, through insurance). Thus you try to convert the risk into an opportunity.

Triangulation is the corroboration of data by comparing the results collected from different methods or sources.

Trust is when you and the CMs have a firm confidence in or reliance on the sincerity, credibility, and reliability of everyone involved in the collaboration.

Utility Standards are intended to ensure that the evaluation will be useful (for example, informative, timely, and influential) (Joint Committee on Standards for Educational Evaluation, 2003, 2009, 2011).

Values are the beliefs, convictions, and ways of thinking considered important or right that guide your (and the CMs') actions regarding particular choices within the collaborative evaluation.

Vision is the ability to anticipate in a credible and realistic way the ideal state or big picture to be reached or accomplished at the end of the collaborative evaluation.

Weaknesses are current characteristics of the evaluand that constitute an obstacle for the achievement of its vision.

Work Breakdown Structure (WBS) is a method of dividing the major work components in the collaborative evaluation (such as the evaluation questions) into smaller, more manageable units in order to improve the accuracy of the evaluation plan.

References

Alderfer, C. P. (1969). An empirical test of a need theory of human needs. *Organizational Behavior and Human Performance, 4*(2), 142–175.

Alkin, M. (2004). *Evaluation roots: Tracing theorists' views and influences.* Thousand Oaks, CA: Sage.

American Evaluation Association. (2004). *American Evaluation Association guiding principles for evaluators.* Retrieved from http://www.eval.org/GPTraining/GP%20Training%20Final/gp.principles.pdf

Austin, J. E. (2000). *The collaboration challenge: How nonprofits and business succeed through strategic alliances.* San Francisco: Jossey-Bass.

Avison, D., & Torkzadeh, G. (2009). *Information systems project management.* Thousand Oaks, CA: Sage.

Bartz, C. (2004, January). Leading by feel: Keep it honest. *Harvard Business Review, 82*(1), 36.

Bastoe, O. (1999). Linking evaluation with strategic planning, budgeting, monitoring, and auditing. In R. Boyle & D. Lemaire (Eds.), *Building effective evaluation capacity: Lessons from practice.* Piscataway, NJ: Transaction.

Bell, J. B. (2010). Managing evaluation projects. In J. S. Wholey, K. E. Newcomer, & H. P. Hatry (Eds.), *Handbook of practical program evaluation* (3rd ed.). San Francisco: Jossey-Bass.

Bellinger, G. (2011). *Systemic perspective: Vol I Foundations* (2nd ed.). [Kindle Edition].

Bennis, W. (2004). The seven ages of the leader. *Harvard Business Review, 82*(1), 46–53.

Bennis, W., & Nanus, B. (2003). *Leaders: Strategies for taking charge* (2nd ed.). New York: Harper Paperbacks.

Berkun, S. (2008). *Making things happen: Mastering project management (theory and practice).* Sebastopol, CA: O'Reilly Media.

Best, J. W., & Kahn, J. V. (2005). *Research in education* (10th ed.). Boston: Pearson Education.

Block, P. (1993). *Stewardship: Choosing service over self-interest.* San Francisco: Berrett-Koehler.

Boardman, J., & Sauser, B. (2008). *Systems thinking: Coping with 21st century problems.* Boca Raton, FL: CRC Press.

Boeije, H. R. (2010). *Analysis in qualitative research.* Thousand Oaks, CA: Sage.

Burns, J. (2010). *Leadership.* New York: HarperPerennial.

Carter, L., & Minirth, F. (1993). *The anger workbook: A 13-step interactive plan to help you.* Nashville: Thomas Nelson.

Cousins, J. B., Donohue, J. J., & Bloom, G. A. (1996). Collaborative evaluation in North America: Evaluators' self-reported opinions, practices, and consequences. *Evaluation Practice, 17*(3), 207–226.

Coutu, D. L. (2004, January). Putting leaders on the couch: A conversation with Manfred F. R. Kets de Vries. *Harvard Business Review, 82*(1), 65–71.

Creswell, J. W. (2009). *Research design: Qualitative, quantitative, and mixed methods approaches* (3rd ed.). Thousand Oaks, CA: Sage.

Creswell, J. W., & Plano Clark, V. L. (2011) *Designing and conducting mixed methods research* (2nd ed.). Thousand Oaks, CA: Sage.

Cronbach, L. J. (1982). *Designing evaluations of educational and social programs.* San Francisco: Jossey-Bass.

Crowe, A. (2006). *Alpha project managers: What the top 2% know that everyone else does not.* Kennesaw, GA: Velociteach.

Daniels, A. C. (2000). *Bringing out the best in people: How to apply the astonishing power of positive reinforcement.* New York: McGraw-Hill.

Denzin, N. K., & Lincoln, Y. S. (2005). *The Sage handbook of qualitative research* (3rd ed.). Thousand Oaks, CA: Sage.

Dilts, R. (1983). *Applications of neuro-linguistic programming.* Cupertino, CA: Meta Publications.

El Ansari, W., & Phillips, C. J. (2001). Interprofessional collaboration: A stakeholder approach to evaluation of voluntary participation in community partnerships. *Journal of Interprofessional Care, 15*(4), 351–368.

Ellinger, A. D. (2003). Antecedents and consequences of coaching behavior. *Performance Improvement Quarterly, 16*(1), 5–28.

Englund, R. L., & Bucero, A. (2006). *Project sponsorship: Achieving management commitment for project success.* San Francisco: Jossey-Bass.

Fabac, J. (2006). Project management for systematic training. *Advances in developing human resources, 8,* 540–547.

Fetterman, D., & Wandersman, A. (2010, November). *Empowerment evaluation essentials: Highlighting the essential features of empowerment evaluation.* Paper presented at the American Evaluation Association Conference, San Antonio, Texas.

Fiedler, F. E. (1967). *A theory of leadership effectiveness.* New York: McGraw-Hill.

Fink, A. (2003). *How to design survey studies* (2nd ed.). Thousand Oaks, CA: Sage.

Fink, A. (2005). *Evaluation fundamentals: Insights into the outcomes, effectiveness, and quality of health programs* (2nd ed.). Thousand Oaks, CA: Sage.

Fitzpatrick, J., Sanders, J., & Worthen, B. (2011). *Program evaluation: Alternative approaches and practical guidelines* (4th ed.). Upper Saddle River, NJ: Prentice-Hall.

Friedman, H. S., & Schustack, M. W. (2010). *Personality: Classic theories and modern research* (5th ed.). Upper Saddle River, NJ: Prentice-Hall.

Garaway, G. B. (1995). Participatory evaluation. *Studies in Educational Evaluation, 21,* 85–102.

George, W. (2004, January). Leading by feel: Find your voice. *Harvard Business Review, 82*(1), 35.

Gibson, J. L., Ivancevich, J. M., & Donnelly, J. H. (2008). *Organizations: Behavior, structure, processes* (13th ed.). Burr Ridge, IL: McGraw-Hill.

Goleman, D. (2004, January). What makes a leader? *Harvard Business Review, 82*(1), 82–91.

Gray, A., Jenkins, B., & Segsworth, B. (2001). *Budgeting, auditing and evaluation: Functions and integration in seven governments.* New Brunswick, NJ: Transaction.

Guba, E. G., & Lincoln, Y. S. (1992). *Effective evaluation: Improving the usefulness of evaluation results through responsive and naturalistic approaches.* San Francisco: Jossey-Bass.

Hankins, G., & Hankins C. (2000). *Prescription for anger: Coping with angry feelings and angry people.* Newberg, OR: Barclay Press.

Harris, C. (2003). *NLP made easy.* Bel Air, CA: Elements Books.

Heifetz, R. (2004, January). Leading by feel: Question authority. *Harvard Business Review, 82*(1), 37.

Heldman, K. (2009). *PMP Project management professional study guide* (5th ed.). Indianapolis: John Wiley & Sons.

Herzberg, F., Mausner, B., & Snyderman, B. (1993). *The motivation to work.* New Brunswick, NJ: Transaction.

House, E. R., & Howe, K. R. (2000). Deliberative democratic evaluation. *New Directions for Evaluation, 85*, 3–12.

House, R. J. (1971). A path goal theory of leader effectiveness. *Administrative Science Quarterly, 16*(3), 321–338.

Irlenbusch, B., & Ruchala, G. K. (2008). Relative rewards within team-based compensation. *Labour Economics, 15*, 141–167.

Ivancevich, J. M., Konopaske, R., & Matteson, M. T. (2010). *Organizational behavior and management* (9th ed.). Boston: McGraw-Hill.

Joint Committee on Standards for Educational Evaluation. (2003). *The student evaluation standards: How to improve the evaluation of students.* Thousand Oaks, CA: Sage.

Joint Committee on Standards for Educational Evaluation. (2009). *The personnel evaluation standards: How to assess systems for evaluating evaluators.* Thousand Oaks, CA: Corwin Press.

Joint Committee on Standards for Educational Evaluation. (2011). *The program evaluation standards: A guide for evaluators and evaluation users.* Thousand Oaks, CA: Sage.

Kelley, H. H. (1971). *Attribution in social interaction.* New York: General Learning Press.

Kelley, R. (1992). *The power of followership.* New York: Currency and Doubleday.

Kendrick, T. (2004). *The project management tool kit: 100 tips and techniques for getting the job done right.* Saranac Lake, NY: Amacom.

Kerzner, H. (2009a). *Advanced project management: Best practices on implementation.* Hoboken, NJ: John Wiley & Sons.

Kerzner, H. (2009b). *Project management: A systems approach to planning, scheduling, and controlling* (10th ed.). Hoboken, NJ: John Wiley & Sons.

Kerzner, H., & Saladis, F. (2009). *Value-driven project management.* New York: ILL Publishing.

King, B. M., Rosopa, P. J., & Minium, E. W. (2011). *Statistical reasoning in the behavioral sciences* (6th ed.). Hoboken, NJ: John Wiley & Sons.

Kouzes, J. M., & Posner, B. Z. (1995). *The leadership challenge: How to keep getting extraordinary things done in organizations.* San Francisco: Jossey-Bass.

Kreitner, R. (2009). *Management* (11th ed.). Boston: Houghton Mifflin.

Krueger, R. A., & Casey, M. (2008). *Focus groups: A practical guide for applied research* (4th ed.). Thousand Oaks, CA: Sage.

Ladika, S. (2008). *Project management: A systems approach to planning, scheduling, and controlling* (10th ed.). Hoboken, NJ: John Wiley & Sons.

Lewis, D. (1995). *The secret language of success: Using body language to get what you want.* New York: Galahad Books.

Lewis, J. P. (1999). *The project manager's desk reference. Comprehensive guide to project planning, scheduling, evaluation, and systems.* New York: McGraw-Hill.

Lewis, J. P. (2010). *Project planning, scheduling, and control: A hands-on guide to bringing projects in on time and on budget* (5th ed.). New York: McGraw-Hill.

Maccoby, M. (2004, January). Narcissistic leaders: The incredible pros, the inevitable cons. *Harvard Business Review, 82*(1), 92–101.

MacMaster, G. (2000). Can we learn from project histories? *PM Network, 14*(7), 66–67.

Maslow, A. H. (1991, March). Critique of self-actualization theory. *Journal of Humanistic Education and Development,* 103–108.

McClelland, D. C. (1962, July-August). Business drive and national achievement. *Harvard Business Review, 40*(4) 99–112.

McMillan, J. H. (2012). *Educational research: Fundamentals for the consumer* (6th ed.). Boston: Allyn & Bacon.

Meadows, D. H. (2009). *Thinking in systems.* London: Earthscan.

Meredith, J., & Mantel, S. J. (2011). *Project management: A managerial approach* (8th ed.). Hoboken, NJ: John Wiley & Sons.

Morgan, S. E., Reichert, T., & Harrison, T. R. (2002). *From numbers to words: Reporting statistical results for the social sciences.* Boston: Allyn & Bacon.

O'Connor, J., & Seymour, J. (2011). *Introducing NLP: Psychological skills for understanding and influencing people.* Berkeley, CA: Conari Press.

Offermann, L. R. (2004, January). When followers become toxic. *Harvard Business Review, 82*(1), 54–60.

O'Sullivan, R. G., & D'Agostino, A. (2002). Promoting evaluation through collaboration: Findings from community-based programs for young children and their families. *Evaluation: The International Journal of Theory, Research and Practice 8*(3), 372–387.

Owens, R., & Valesky, T. (2010). *Organizational behavior in education: Leadership and school reform* (10th ed.). Upper Saddle River, NJ: Prentice-Hall.

Patton, M. Q. (2008). *Utilization-focused evaluation* (4th ed.). Beverly Hills, CA: Sage.

Pawson, R., & Tilley, N. (1997). *Realistic evaluation.* Thousand Oaks, CA: Sage.

Pinto, J. K., & Trailer, J. W. (1999). *Essentials of project control.* Silva, NC: The Project Management Institute.

PMI Standards Committee. (2008). *A guide to the project management body of knowledge: PMBOK guide* (4th ed.). Newtown Square, PA: Project Management Institute.

Pondy, L. R. (1967). Organizational conflict: Concepts and models. *Administrative Science Quarterly, 12,* 296–320.

Porter, L. W., & Lawler, E. E. (1968). *Managerial attitudes and performance.* Homewood, IL: Richard D. Irwin.

Prentice, W. C. (2004, January). Understanding leadership. *Harvard Business Review, 82*(1), 102–109.

Rincones-Gómez, R. (2009). Evaluating student success interventions: Principles and practices of student success. *Achieving the Dream: Community Colleges Count.* Retrieved from http://www.achievingthedream.org/resource/evaluating_student_success_interventions_principles_and_practices_student_success

Rincones-Gómez, R., & Rodríguez-Campos, L. (2003). Leadership approaches: Reflections from experienced and novice leaders [Monograph]. *International Journal of Learning, 9,* 3–14.

Rodríguez-Campos, L. (2005). *Collaborative evaluations: A step-by-step model for the evaluator.* Tamarac, FL: Llumina Press.

Rodríguez-Campos, L. (2012a). Stakeholder involvement in evaluation: Three decades of the *American Journal of Evaluation. Journal of MultiDisciplinary Evaluation 8*(17), 57–79.

Rodríguez-Campos, L. (2012b). Advances in collaborative evaluation. *Evaluation and Program Planning.* doi: 10.1016/1.evalprogplan.2011.12.006

Rodríguez-Campos, L., & O'Sullivan, R. (2010, November). *Collaborative evaluation essentials: Highlighting the essential features of collaborative evaluation.* Paper presented at the American Evaluation Association Conference, San Antonio, Texas.

Rodríguez-Campos, L., & Rincones-Gómez, R. (2001). Involving the community in education initiatives: An evaluation of a neighborhood-based business training program. *Common Ground Publishing, 8,* 3–22.

Rodríguez-Campos, L., & Rincones-Gómez, R. (2003). Defining and measuring leadership: Structural equation modeling in practice [Monograph]. *International Journal of Learning, 9,* 5–19.

Rothgeb, C. L. (2003). *Abstracts of the standard edition of the complete psychological works of Sigmund Freud.* New York: Jason Aronson.

Royse, D. D. (2010). *Program evaluation: An introduction.* Belmont, CA: Wadsworth.

Sandler, J., Spector, P., & Fonagy, P. (1991). *On narcissism--An introduction.* International Psychoanalytical Association. New Haven, CT: Yale University Press.

Sawle, W. S. (1991) Concerns of project managers: Crisis project management. *PM Network 5*(1), 25–29.

Schmidt, T. (2009). *Strategic project management made simple: Practical tools for leaders and teams.* Hoboken, NJ: John Wiley & Sons.

Scriven, M. (1991). *Evaluation thesaurus* (4th ed.). Newbury Park, CA: Sage.

Scriven, M. (1993). Hard-won lessons in program evaluation. *New Directions for Program Evaluation, 58,* 1–107.

Scriven, M. (2005). Checklists. In S. Mathison (Ed.), *Encyclopedia of evaluation.* Thousand Oaks, CA: Sage.

Sergiovanni, T. J. (2004). *The lifeworld of leadership: Creating culture, community, and personal meaning in our schools.* San Francisco: Jossey-Bass.

Sergiovanni, T. J., & Starratt, R. J. (2006). *Supervision: A redefinition* (8th ed.). Boston: McGraw-Hill.

Shadish, W. R. (1995). Philosophy of science and the quantitative-qualitative debate. *Evaluation and Program Planning, 18,* 63–75.

Shulha, L. (2010, November). *Participatory evaluation essentials: Highlighting the essential features of participatory evaluation.* Paper presented at the American Evaluation Association Conference, San Antonio, Texas.

Stackpole, C. (2009). *A project manager's book of forms.* Hoboken, NJ: John Wiley & Sons.

Stake, R. E. (1980). Program evaluation, particularly responsive evaluation. In W. B. Dockrell & D. Hamilton (Eds.), *Rethinking educational research.* London: Hodeder & Stoughton.

Stufflebeam, D. L., Madaus, G., & Kellaghan, T. (2000). *Evaluation models.* Boston: Kluwer Academic.

Takeuchi, H. (2004, January). Leading by feel: Go for the gemba. *Harvard Business Review, 82*(1), 36.

Tashakkori, A., & Teddlie, C. (2010). *Handbook of mixed methods in social and behavioral research* (2nd ed.). Thousand Oaks, CA: Sage.

Thamhain, H. J., & Wilemon, D. L. (1996). Criteria for controlling projects according to plan. *Project Management Journal,* 75–81.

Thomas, R. M. (2003). *Blending qualitative and quantitative research methods in theses and dissertations.* Thousand Oaks, CA: Corwin Press.

Thomas, W. H. (2012). *The basics of project evaluation and lessons learned.* Boca Raton, FL: CRC Press.

Weiss, A. (2009). *Getting started in consulting* (3rd ed.). Hoboken, NJ: John Wiley & Sons.

Weiss, C. H. (1998). *Evaluation: Methods for studying programs and policies.* Upper Saddle River, NJ: Prentice-Hall.

Weissman, J. (2009). *Presenting to win: The art of telling your story.* Upper Saddle River, NJ: Prentice-Hall.

Wigfield, A., & Eccles, J. (2002). *Development of achievement motivation.* San Diego, CA: Academic Press.

Wilson, B. (2000, September). The lone ranger is dead—Success today demands collaboration. *College and Resource Libraries News, 61*(8), 698–701.

Winer, M., & Ray, K. (2002). *Collaboration handbook: Creating, sustaining, and enjoying the journey* (6th ed.). St. Paul, MN: Amherst H. Wilder Foundation.

Wysocki, R. (2011). *Effective project management: Traditional, agile, extreme.* Indianapolis: John Wiley & Sons.

Yin, R. K. (2011). *Qualitative research from start to finish.* New York: Guilford Press.

Yong, L. M. (1994). Managing creative people. *Journal of Creative Behavior, 28*(1), 16–20.

Yukl, G. A. (2009). *Leadership in organizations* (7th ed.). Upper Saddle River, NJ: Prentice-Hall.

Zaleznik, A. (2004, January). Managers and leaders: Are they different? *Harvard Business Review, 82*(1), 74–81.

Zimmerman, M. A. (1995). Psychological empowerment: Issues and illustrations. *American Journal of Community Psychology, 23*, 581–599.

Index

About the Authors

Dr. Liliana Rodríguez-Campos earned her Ph.D. degree in evaluation, measurement, and research design. For this degree, she received a Provost's Special Recognition and an Outstanding Dissertation Award by Phi Delta Kappa Honor Society. Also, as part of her educational background, she earned her bachelor's degree in systems engineering with honorific mention, and her specialist and master's degrees in project management in engineering with summa cum laude honors. Furthermore, she received a President's Special Recognition for her second master's degree in educational leadership with a concentration in evaluation, measurement, and research design.

Dr. Rodríguez-Campos is nationally and internationally recognized for her collaborative approach to evaluation. She has been awarded with several honors and educational scholarships, including the American Evaluation Association's Marcia Guttentag Award (http://youtube.com/watch?v=r9d-LVmrTJo), a Faculty Fellowship from the American Association of Hispanics in Higher Education (AAHHE), the Golden Apple Award for her educational excellence and commitment, and the University of South Florida's Hispanic Heritage Faculty Award. Her peers have acknowledged her professional qualifications through invitations to her to make presentations and serve in national and international leadership roles in evaluation. She has been a planning and control manager, and a consultant in the business, nonprofit, and education sectors. Her work history includes evaluations, metaevaluations, and capacity-building projects in Latin America, the Philippines, and the United States.

Dr. Rodríguez-Campos has collaborated with colleagues on several projects, serving, for example, as the co-principal investigator and director of evaluation for a $2.3 million U.S. Department of Education grant. She has designed and delivered numerous workshops and courses at the university level in evaluation, metaevaluation, research, informatics, consulting, project planning, and control management. She has written a variety of publications in Spanish,

English, and Chinese on leadership, organizational engineering, and evaluation approaches that bring stakeholder groups together. In addition, she has presented her work at national and international conferences in countries including Australia, Brazil, Canada, China, Cuba, England, Greece, Holland, Hong Kong, India, Italy, Jamaica, Latvia, Malaysia, Mauritius, Puerto Rico, Singapore, South Africa, Spain, the United States, and Venezuela.

Dr. Rodríguez-Campos is associate professor and director of the Center for Research, Evaluation, Assessment and Measurement at the University of South Florida. During five years, she served as a co-chair of the Professional Development Committee and as a board member at the Michigan Association for Evaluation. Currently, she serves in the board of directors at the Evaluation Capacity Development Group and as the program chair of the Collaboration, Participatory, and Empowerment Evaluation Topical Interest Group of the American Evaluation Association. Dr. Rodríguez-Campos's expertise with leadership, metaevaluation, multicultural and collaborative evaluation capacity building, project management, organizational engineering, and training are her strongest professional contributions.

Dr. Rigoberto Rincones-Gómez is the associate vice president for institutional research, planning and effectiveness at Broward College. He oversees the institution's research, planning, and effectiveness processes to help improve student access, engagement, retention, and completion while helping to address the factors that have an impact on student success and designing specific interventions and policy to assist the college's students.

Dr. Rincones-Gómez came to Broward College from Achieving the Dream, Inc. (ATD), where he served as the national director of data coaching for more than five years and was responsible for directing all aspects of ATD's data coaching, including recruiting, training, and mentoring a team of more than thirty senior data coaches. He authored ATD's guide on logic models and evaluation, which is used by more than 150 community colleges and universities across the country. He has more than seventeen years of national and international leadership experience working with student success, assessment, strategic planning, and evaluation-related projects from the business, nonprofit, and education sectors.

Dr. Rincones-Gómez is a published author and speaker on a variety of higher education topics. His writings include publications in Spanish, English, and Chinese on leadership, organizational engineering, and evaluation approaches that bring stakeholder groups together. He has been awarded with several honors and educational scholarships at the national and international levels. In addition, he has substantial teaching experience at the developmental, undergraduate, and graduate levels. He conducts training on logic models and evaluation, as well as indicators of institutional effectiveness.

He earned his Ph.D. degree in evaluation, measurement, and research design, receiving a Provost's Special Recognition and an Outstanding Dissertation Award from the Phi Delta Kappa Honor Society. Also, as part of his educational background, he earned his bachelor's degree in mechanical engineering and his specialist and master's degrees in project management in engineering with summa cum laude honors. Furthermore, he received a President's Special Recognition for his second master's degree in educational leadership with a concentration in evaluation, measurement, and research design.